FROM ARAFAT TO EVEREST

Nick,

A book to feed
your adventurousness.

Farah
xo

20.11.15

Published by Brolga Publishing Pty Ltd
ABN 46 063 962 443
PO Box 12544, A'Beckett St, VIC, 8006, Australia
email: markzocchi@brolgapublishing.com.au

National Library of Australia Cataloguing-in-Publication entry

Squirrell, Mark.
From Arafat to Everest : how surviving war zones inspired a
climb to the top of the world
9781921596476 (pbk.)
Soldiers–Australia–Biography.
Motivational speakers–Australia–Biography.
355.0092

Printed in Hong Kong
Cover by David Khan
Cover photograph: Squiz on the summit of Mount Everest
Typeset by Imogen Stubbs

FROM
ARAFAT
TO
EVEREST

MARK SQUIRRELL

To those who search daily for their next meal,
I truly hope your fortunes change.

TABLE OF CONTENTS
(AND LOCATIONS)

PROLOGUE
EXCERPT FROM "THE FINAL ASSAULT"

As the oncoming traffic loomed closer, I noticed some of them were from our expedition. They did not deliver good news. Mount Everest's summit was still many hours away and I was currently climbing towards the South Summit: the false peak before the Hillary Step. After a two minute interlude I again found myself trudging along with Dorge (my Sherpa) in tow. To my right was a bird's eye view of the contentious lands of Tibet, the flat brown lands stretched for hundreds of kilometres to the horizon. In contrast, the landscape to the left was awash with white snow and jagged peaks. Ama Dablam, with its sharp and pointed summit, was far below and no longer looked impressive … from this angle it looked like a five storey building nestled between sky scrapers. I pulled out my camera and took a few quick snaps. I doubted it would get any better than this … I already felt like I was on top of the world.

The climb to the South Summit, a false peak short of the actual summit, seemed never-ending. Without any rocks along the way or anything visible above the peak, perspective on the distance was almost impossible to determine. One thing was for sure though, with more groups overtaking us I was moving well below the average speed for this part of the mountain. My assessment was confirmed when Henry came on the radio, wanting to speak directly to me.

Digging my heels into the snow I sat back against the slope.

"Squiz, this is Henry. Come in. Over."

"Henry, this is Squiz. I'm here. Over."

"Squiz, I've just spoken with some of the other guys and they tell me you are still well below the South Summit. How are you feeling? Over."

"Henry, I'm still feeling like crap. I just can't seem to move without nearly huffing my guts up. Over."

"Squiz, this is Henry. It's nearly four hours since we last spoke. I needed you to make it at least to the South Summit in that time. I'm afraid you'll never make the summit and get back to Camp Four before the afternoon winds at the rate you're going. Over."

My heart sank.

"Henry, I'm actually not all that far from the South Summit. And I still feel as if I've got a bit of juice left in me. Over."

"Squiz, the bigger problem is your oxygen. Your oxygen bottle will soon be running low. I've left it until the last moment to contact you. You'll have to turn around now or you won't have enough oxygen to get back down. I've got a Sherpa coming off the Hillary Step at the moment who will catch up with you shortly and hand over the oxygen I organised for you earlier. You'll need it to get back down to Camp Four. Squiz, I know this is not what you want to hear, but I have no choice. Over."

I was devastated. Sitting only hours away from the summit, after six weeks of hard work and tens of thousands of dollars invested, I was being told to turn around. But there was more to it than just that. Little did I know at the time, I had been building up to this very moment for the last eight years. This was my very own opportunity to help make a difference, to make a unique contribution to those who struggled to survive on a daily basis. During my time as an aid worker in some of the world's most brutal war zones I had been conditioned and inspired by those whom I had come to help. I was now climbing on their behalf, carrying with me the flag of the United Nations World Food Programme. I had to continue if I was to help raise awareness for the 840 million people that roamed the world looking, with desperation and fear, for their very next meal.

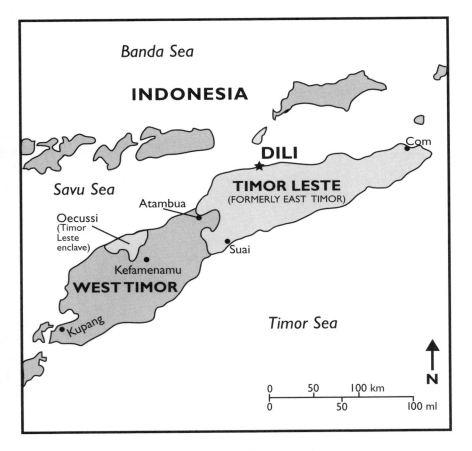

Map of Timor

ONE
AID WORK 101

EAST TIMOR SNAPSHOT

1702: *Portuguese colonial rule begins.*

1942-1945: *Australian soldiers fight alongside the Timorese in an attempt to repel the Japanese advance through SE Asia. 60,000 Timorese lives (13% of population) are lost whilst supporting Australian troops.*

1950: *West Timor (previously governed by the Dutch East Indies) becomes one of the thousands of islands that now make the Republic of Indonesia.*

1974: *The Portuguese Government announce their plans to depart and begin to prepare East Timor for self rule, allowing political parties to fill the leadership void.*

28 November 1975: *FRETILIN (leading political party) declares independence from Portugal.*

7 December 1975: *The Indonesian military/authorities enter East Timor and occupy its lands with brutal force.*

1998: *Suharto (President of Indonesia) steps down and international pressure* is ramped up for a United Nations-sponsored referendum on independence for East Timor.

30 August 1999: 78.5% of the population vote for independence, sparking a violent backlash from pro-Indonesian supporters.

22 October 1999: Squiz arrives in Dili.

My heart began pumping hard as I peered outside the window of the small United Nations Dash-7 airplane, trying to see what a war zone looked like. Below, white sands, turquoise water and a green forest canopy in bright morning sunlight painted a perfect picture of a lush tropical island. How could the ravages of war – carnage, poverty and mayhem – be camouflaged within this apparently serene setting?

The plane banked sharply and all I could see was blue sky and distant ocean. We'd turned ninety degrees and were now travelling parallel to the coast, the tops of palm trees suddenly within arms reach as the plane dived to make the landing strip. The usual roar of the engines followed the screeching tyres hitting the tarmac; it was a smooth landing.

"Welcome to the Comoro International Airport, Dili, East Timor," a tinny voice said over the speaker.

Australian soldiers in camouflage fatigues with weapons slung over their shoulders directed the plane to its parking spot. One of the pilots crawled out from the cockpit and opened the door, and hot and humid air engulfed the cabin. I foraged around in my day pack for my sunglasses as I moved with the other passengers to the exit door.

"Ladies and Gentlemen … move immediately away from the aircraft towards the white building," barked a soldier standing at the base of the steps.

We moved in single file across the tarmac. More soldiers were standing nearby to ensure we didn't step out of line. A passenger ahead of me, an overweight man with a large camera slung over his shoulder, stepped to one side and pulled a packet of cigarettes from the blue fishing vest he wore over his white shirt. I judged him to be a seasoned photo-journalist from his demeanour and attire. Before he had a chance to take a cigarette from the packet I noticed one of the soldiers moving quickly towards us.

"Sir! Put those cigarettes away and follow the instructions," yelled the twenty-something soldier.

The Australian troops in charge of the airport were running the show with a very tight rein, so much so that it felt like we were a group of adolescent army recruits coming off a bus and about to face boot camp. They seemed to be in charge of immigration and customs as well – we didn't see any Timorese nationals until we moved out past the final barricade into a small tiled foyer where drivers and colleagues were patiently waiting for incoming passengers. In the few short months since the referendum and subsequent deployment of the Australian-led International Stabilisation Force, it appeared that order had been returned to this part of the country.

I glanced around the unimposing mob, secretly pleased that the military had vetted-out the normal crowd of dubious individuals who loiter around airport terminals waiting to pounce on unsuspecting foreigners. I read my name on a placard and looked up and smiled at the thirty-something woman with dark hair who was holding it. She returned the smile and began walking my way.

"Hi there, you must be Squiz," she said with a gentle English accent.

"I am. And you?" I replied.

"My name is Lisa. I'm the Emergency Response Team Leader … sounds impressive, hey?" she replied, conspiratorially.

"Certainly does, especially considering the size of the emergency."

"Well … the truth is, there are only three others in the team at the moment and you make the fourth so it's not like I'm in charge of a huge team. Mighty glad you are here though as we have a heap to do."

I followed Lisa towards a shiny white Toyota Hilux without registration plates that was parked in a nearby car park. It looked to have just rolled off the production line and even had a strong 'new car' smell when I opened the door. We shut our doors in unison as Lisa started the car and turned the air conditioner to its maximum setting. It was all beginning to feel surreal. I still hadn't seen any signs of warfare, had breezed through the 'Australian' immigration check, and was being shielded from all the dilemmas that a developing country's airport normally offers. But the bubble of protection was burst the very second we drove past the Aussie troops that manned the exit to the airport.

The emptiness of the road ahead was eerie. We turned left at a roundabout with rubble and rocks scattered across the middle of the turning circle, following a rusty sign to 'Dili Centre'.

A group of young teenage boys loitered in the centre of the road. They looked towards us as we approached but chose not to move off the single lane carriage way. We veered around them as they eyeballed our vehicle. Two camouflaged Army Land Rovers sped towards us. I tried to see if I recognised any of the passengers as they went past but they were driving too quickly for me to notice. I was on high alert, not wanting to miss any of the new sights and sounds. I felt energised by the new and unfamiliar surroundings, unlike that fat journalist who appeared blasé about arriving in Dili. I was pumped up and excited about my new employment opportunity, and anxious to explore the place that was making front page headlines back home.

On either side of the road were the remains of houses and shops. The 'scorched earth' policy of the pro-Indonesian militia that I'd heard about in the media was now up close and personal. Twisted sheets of corrugated iron lay amongst the charred remains of the buildings, discernable only by the blackened walls that remained standing. Here and there I noticed men and women foraging through the blackened shells that once were homes or shops ... and I assumed they were only foraging in dwellings that once belonged to them. Seeing the images first-hand rather than on a TV screen magnified my feeling of sadness, the melancholy coming from knowing that the destruction had been caused by mankind rather than by an uncontrollable natural force. As we neared the centre of Dili the level of destruction appeared more widespread. There were far more people in the streets, wandering aimlessly across the road or along the dirt paths that made the sidewalks. They looked to be lost and, like me, were wide-eyed, taking in the new look of their capital city.

A rusty old fence surrounded what appeared to be the port. Coils of fresh concertina wire had been placed on the top and the entrance was heavily manned by Aussie troops. We turned right and began heading inland on another narrow road with the odd scattering of rocks from recent days of disturbance. Four hundred metres from the port was a checkpoint to prevent non-United Nations, Aid Agency or military vehicles from entering the military zone that housed the Peacekeepers' HQs. We had the right coloured skin and were immediately waved forward.

I noticed a group of soldiers wearing dark green camouflage uniforms. They were Indonesian troops. I was surprised to see them only fifteen metres from the Australian-run checkpoint, lurking around in front of what was apparently their barracks. Most of them wore their shirts undone and were more interested in watching a game of cards between their comrades than what was going on in the nearby streets.

We drove on. Military personnel on foot zigzagged from one fortified compound to another for the next three hundred metres to the next checkpoint, the exit from the military zone. A speed bump at the checkpoint slowed us down and the soldier on the inside of his sandbag barrier looked intently at our vehicle. The road soon turned sharply to the left – ahead was a large set of blue gates protecting the driveway to the UN compound. We rounded the bend and slowed once more to take the next driveway after the UN on the same side of the road.

Un-armed civilian guards – three Timorese men in their forties – controlled a makeshift barrier on the dirt track that led to a school. They immediately let our vehicle pass. The school comprised of a central quadrangle, surrounded on all four sides by two-storey buildings. We pulled up before entering the quadrangle as the area looked congested. Portable toilets, large green tents and generators were getting in the way of dozens of international faces as they darted from one classroom to another.

"Okay, Squiz, so this is it. Welcome to our home and office in East Timor," said Lisa as she turned off the engine.

Lisa pointed to the second floor of the building we had just pulled up alongside. I looked at the pale yellow concrete structure; the windows were devoid of any glass and paint peeled from the external walls. We walked towards an opening in the centre of the building – the doors had been removed from the double door entry. As we began to climb the dusty stairwell I smelled the unmistakable dank aroma of stale urine.

"It's not the cleanest of places," Lisa commented seemingly unperturbed. "We have a chronic shortage of space, but it's relatively safe because of the UN next door. We have to be out of here in a month though, as the UN wants to reopen the school. We're really hoping that you will be able to find us an alternate option in the coming weeks."

At the top of the stairs we turned right and walked to the end of a corridor, made narrow by an accumulation of boxes. Lisa pushed aside a lightweight curtain in the door well and gestured for me to enter. I entered and found myself taking a deep breath – the room in front of me was a shambles. Trestle tables lined the walls but were barely visible for the boxes of food, paper, computer equipment, first aid stores and bottled water that were piled underneath and on top of them. A few gaps between boxes allowed room for the odd laptop, washing bucket, or chopping board. The remainder of the room was covered with mosquito domes, sleeping mats and open bags of personal clothing.

"Welcome to the life of an aid worker in an emergency," Lisa quipped.

"Thanks … it looks kind of cosy … I suppose."

"You got that right. There are already seven of us eating, sleeping and working from this room. You will make the eighth. We are sharing it with CESVI, the Italian-based Aid Agency. They aren't too bad but their Emergency Coordinator, Marco, snores louder than a freight train."

"Hmmmm, that doesn't sound like much fun."

"It certainly isn't, but at least we have a roof over our heads. That puts us streets ahead of most of the Timorese. In fact, we do alright. See those tents out there?"

I looked into the quadrangle.

"Every second day we are allowed to have a bucket bath. Men showered this morning so you will have to wait until Monday for your first go. They only bring in a small tanker of water so make sure you're there by at least seven in the morning, 'cause there's probably over a hundred men in this camp now."

That afternoon Lisa placed me on a chair amongst the congestion and had me read through a few documents to help with my orientation. I'd spent the last few years in the recruitment industry in Melbourne, while serving part time in the Australian Army, so I was completely unfamiliar with the jargon and acronyms in the reports. Lisa, a veteran aid worker, helped patiently to fill in the details.

The International Rescue Committee (IRC), a Non Government Organisation (NGO) or aid agency, had sent an emergency response team to East Timor to assess and assist with the needs of the people following the Timor Crisis of mid-1999. The team consisted of four experienced aid workers with extensive knowledge of emergency shelter, water and sanitation, public health and refugee tracking. The plan was for the team to conduct a rapid assessment of the situation, prepare programme proposals for donor organisations such as the Australian Agency for International Development (AusAID) or the UK's Department for International Development (DFID), and should a grant be received, set up the framework for a larger team to implement the assistance.

▲ ▲ ▲

I had been itching to be deployed to East Timor ever since the crisis had hit the media headlines in early 1999, but when Australian troops were called up my unit wasn't among them. I knew it was going to be a long time before I would be given my opportunity and so I began looking for alternative means to get amongst the action. IRC was the vehicle that allowed me to get on the ground.

I didn't leave Australia with a goal to save mankind or to build a career within the aid industry. At the time I was solely focused on completing my one-month contract so that I could return to my cushy lifestyle in Melbourne, with perhaps a few tales to tell the grandkids in the years to come. But I was ready and willing to put in one hundred percent to help IRC with its mission during the short period of time that I was to be in Dili.

▲ ▲ ▲

It was my job to provide security support to the emergency team and to prepare for the future operations. Like all NGOs, IRC did not allow its staff to carry firearms and so my support came in the form of liaison with the military forces, analysis of the situation on the ground and setting up standard operating procedures to deal with injury, conflict flare up and the retrieval of incoming aid. Over the next week I trawled through the streets of Dili to get an understanding of its layout, visiting the critical infrastructure such as hospitals, hotels and airports, and I gradually began to make contact with other NGO security personnel and military liaison officers.

Within the space of just seven days the number of people on the streets appeared to double. The last of the Indonesian soldiers quietly left the country, but word soon got round, encouraging more people to return to Dili from the interior of the country and from West Timor. It was obvious a housing crisis was imminent. It was already not uncommon to hear of three or four families, with an average of six children in each, bunkering together in a one or two bedroom house. The shortage caused a frantic scramble by the NGOs to locate buildings that could be used for housing, accommodation or both. At every opportunity I'd pull over on the side of the road and make enquiries about the status of any building that looked to be in a decent state. Anything even half respectable was already accounted for. I began to consider sites that had been previously set on fire, thinking we could refurbish them and then lock in a long term rental agreement.

Five hundred metres up the road from the NGO schoolyard I found a building that was burnt out but structurally still solid. The small house next door was rundown but had not been torched. With freshly washed clothes draped across the bushes in the front garden, I assumed that there were occupants who might be able to help me locate the owner. The tree-lined canopy over the narrow driveway gave me welcome protection from the blistering sun, but prevented a visual line of sight to the back garden.

Sitting on the side veranda was an old man with grey hair. He had a piece from an engine, maybe a carburettor, in his greasy hands and a pile of tools beneath his seat.

"Excuse me, sir," I said politely.

He looked up, surprised to hear an English voice.

"Do you speak English?" I asked.

"Yes ... welcome."

"I was wondering if you knew who owned the place next door and how I could get in contact with them."

"It's owned by Alexio Da Cruz, but I don't know where he is. I have heard that he was forced onto a truck and then taken to West Timor. But I don't know for certain as I'd already left for the hills."

"Oh," I answered, a little despondent. "I'm sorry to hear that. I'm from an aid agency and we might be interested in renting his block to set up an office."

"Well if he comes back I can let him know. Would you be interested to look at another place in the mean time, a house that has not been burnt down?"

"Definitely!" I couldn't reply quickly enough.

The old man placed the carburettor on the ground and stood up.

"Just wait a minute; I need to get the keys."

I waited anxiously as he wiped his dirty hands with an old rag and walked slowly inside, steadying himself with a wooden walking stick. I began wondering how far away the building was and whether I would have to break one of IRC's ground rules: no non-employees were allowed in the IRC vehicles.

He returned and asked me to follow him as he moved towards the back of the house. Slowly he ambled past an old 1970s Series III Land Rover with the bonnet propped open. The driveway beyond the vehicle was covered in leaves and lined by more bushy trees but just twenty metres past the old man's house was a white pebbly car park, in front of a large white building with a tiled roof and black tinted windows. The front door was tight and took all his persuasion to open. When the double doors finally swung apart I felt like I'd won the lottery.

Marble floors, clean white walls and tasteful oriental furniture filled the spacious four bedroom home. I looked through the house, impressed that it was already kitted out with air conditioning units, a water well and generator. In the lounge room I noticed a ceramic dish propped up amongst other trophies for badminton and soccer. A red military beret and the words 'Kopassus 1995' were written on the plate.

The old man could see I was fascinated by this object. The Kopassus were the Indonesian Army's Special Forces unit and sensing that I was concerned about the history of the building, the old man began telling me that the house had belonged to a senior Army officer from the Indonesian military. The old man's wife used to be the cleaner and so was left with a set of keys when the Army officer was posted off the island a few months before. He wasn't coming back and had entrusted the house to the old man.

The house, not visible from the street, had been missed by the probing eyes of all the other NGOs. Locals were not interested in renting the house because they all knew that it was owned by a member of the Indonesian military. I asked him to provide us with official documentation to prove ownership of the building, as well as the delegation of ownership to the old man. All of this was duly forthcoming and within a week, IRC officially opened its first office and accommodation building in Dili. The IRC team was relieved, to say the least, to vacate the schoolyard and the old man's wife was thrilled to come on board as our office cleaner. The old man himself, whom I soon discovered was called Alfredo, went about his normal routine, unperturbed by IRC's busy rigmarole. He spent most of his day tinkering with his much-loved Land Rover and pottering around the garden. In the evenings he could always be found relaxing on the veranda where I had first met him. I often joined him and shared a cold drink as dusk settled on the landscape, intrigued to hear his first-hand insights into the events of just a few months before that eventually led to the deployment of an Australian-led international stabilization force.

Alfredo anticipated that the referendum would not favour the Indonesian supporters and therefore would trigger an ugly backlash. Within 24 hours of the results being announced he had packed up his family, locked the house and headed for the hills in his trusty Land Rover. He told me that as he left Dili, the small minority of Indonesian supporters went on a nationwide killing, looting and burning spree that continued until the Australian-led forces arrived. The Indonesian troops didn't do anything to control the carnage but instead forced people onto trucks that were bound for West Timor.

Often, as we sat enjoying the slightly cooler temperature brought on by nightfall, a friend, neighbour or relative of Alfredo's would saunter down the driveway. Joyful hollers and tears followed as families reunited and retraced their hellish experiences. Alfredo calmly took the time to translate their often sobbing words.

"Squiz, this is my wife's cousin. His name is Arlindo. I haven't seen him since the referendum and wasn't sure if he was alive. He is a poor man and was forced to stay in his home when the violence erupted after the referendum. He stayed there for three days with his wife but then the militia came to his street and began systematically burning down the houses." Alfredo informed.

I looked at the old man as Alfredo talked. His frail sixty-something body was skinny and motionless. He was quiet and looked to be in deep reflection.

"He was forced to flee into the streets with his wife and head for the inland hills that lie to the south of Dili. He clambered up the hill with his decrepit wife in search of safety. For two weeks he lived with hundreds of others in a small monastery, living off food that was collected from the jungle."

I sat their listening to the tales in complete disbelief. My privileged upbringing had sheltered me from understanding what real hardship was all about. I had previously thought that hardship was endured if the house was temporarily flooded out or if a person lost their job and had to rely on social welfare.

It couldn't have been a more poignant reminder of the importance of our work at IRC. In just a few short weeks IRC's emergency proposals had met with success and our team of colleagues began to quickly grow ... as did our emergency projects. IRC set up a network in West Timor to begin reuniting and repatriating families. Bed nets and cooking pots were distributed and emergency shelters provided. I tried desperately to help in any way that I could to ensure that our assistance was delivered. Although it went against the grain, on occasion I pulled out my Army ID card to help move our goods through the airport and port facility. I was caught up in the emotional wave of the moment, not used to dealing with such high-need circumstances. My hard work paid off and Lisa asked if I could extend my one month contract. It didn't feel right to knock back the request so I settled in for another two months.

▲   ▲   ▲

My naïvety and overly passionate attitude was unmistakable to those more accustomed to suffering, chaos and insecurity. Amadeo, one of our drivers, was among those who registered my obvious vulnerability. He approached me early one morning, before the official opening hours of the office, with a stern face.

"Squiz, my friend, I have a favour to ask."

"Yes mate, of course."

"My life savings are in Bank Indonesia. They have closed their branch here in Dili. I cannot get my money. Can you help?"

I looked at Amadeo; a terribly skinny man with only two teeth left on his upper jaw. I knew that he had ten children and had recently lost his house, but what could I do? I rubbed my forehead thoughtfully.

"Mate, I'd love to help but I don't have any special way to get your money out," I answered with a furrowed brow.

"What about if you go to Kupang in West Timor? You can pull out the money from the bank there," he suggested.

His quick reply indicated that he had thought it through before approaching me.

"Amadeo, I'm Australian. It's not a good time for me to visit West Timor at the moment."

"I can organise people on the ground to help, and even get you a car," he replied hopefully.

"Okay, look, let me think about it for a while. I have a feeling it won't be that easy."

That night I was unable to get Amadeo and his predicament out of my mind. I really wanted to help him get his money back. Christmas was only two weeks away and so I asked Lisa if she would let me visit Kupang around that time. We were expecting to have a few days of downtime so I knew it wouldn't be too disruptive to my work schedule. She thought it was a great idea as I could get a better appreciation for the repatriation programme that we were running at the same time. Our staff in West Timor had very few visits from those working in East Timor, and hence felt very isolated from the rest of the team.

My heart felt light as I was able to tell Amadeo to give me all the ID that he owned as I prepared a delegation of authority letter for him to sign. He was ecstatic. It was good to be able to give him a glimmer of hope, especially this close to Christmas, even though I did suspect the hope would sour into disappointment. I confess I was excited merely at the prospect of visiting West Timor, but not at all confident I would succeed in retrieving his money. Nonetheless, Amadeo told me that he had lined up a vehicle and gave me the address of where I could find it. It belonged to his cousin and had been driven to West Timor six months before to avoid the ensuing carnage. His cousin, now back in East Timor, didn't have the time or money to bring it back; he was too busy rebuilding his house. Amadeo assured me that I would be welcome to drive it back, should I find the opportunity.

On 24th December '99 I headed to the airport with a bag of clothes, some paperwork and my wallet; minus my Australian Army ID card.

TWO
BEHIND ENEMY LINES

In the darkness I saw a man with a clipboard. Quickening my pace, I walked across the runway towards him, still surprised that the airport authorities were allowing me to wander around aimlessly on the tarmac.

"Excuse me mate, are you with IOM?" I yelled.

"Yes, I am." He replied with a strong Irish accent.

"Great. I just got off the plane from Dili and the pilots mentioned that I'll need to book my return flight well in advance. Are you the man I need to see?"

"Well, yes, I am responsible for the manifest, but I can't guarantee a seat on any of our flights back to Dili. You are aware that we are running the flights to help return refugees and so they are given first priority?"

"Yeah, no worries mate," I drawled in my best Australian accent. "I understand."

Thinking ahead I wrote down the name and work details of Bob, the Operations Coordinator for International Organisation for Migration (IOM), just on the off chance that I would need his help. The IOM were helping to return refugees via air, land and sea. With any luck everything would go well with Amedeo's cousin's vehicle and I wouldn't need IOM's services to hitch a ride back to East Timor ... but one never knows.

It was not long after 6:30pm and the IOM flight to the capital of West Timor, Kupang [that I had just disembarked] was the last for the day. The terminal was closing down by the time I had made my way through the relatively simple immigration procedure and so airport security guards locked the sliding doors behind me. The only lights that remained on were those above my head, lighting the pickup point in front of the terminal. I stood alone under the light as though I had been left on stage, unsure as to who was left in the audience (or in this case, the car park). It wasn't a comfortable feeling; it was unnerving enough just having an Aussie passport in my back pocket.

A man in a small white car pulled up alongside the curb with his passenger side window down.

"You won taxi sir?"

"No thanks, mate," I shot back.

"No more taxi, sir. Me last one ... very cheap," he urged.

"I'm okay, thanks."

He drove on, a plume of black smoke bellowing from his tiny exhaust pipe. I began wondering if I should have let him go. I was supposed to be picked up at the airport by a guy called Budi, one of the IRC staff working in the refugee camps. Ten minutes passed and I was still standing anxiously in the same spot. Then a welcome muffled noise could be heard in the darkness. It was a motorbike, sounding as though the driver needed to drop it down a few gears. Peering into the night I could make out the rider – a thick set young man with a cigarette hanging out of his mouth. Behind him was a skinnier lad; neither were wearing helmets.

They pulled up in the same spot where the taxi had previously parked.

"Harro, you must be Mr Squiz," said the skinny guy.

"Yes, mate. And you are Budi?"

"Certainly am, and this is Guntur, who also works for IRC."

I stepped forward to shake their hands. Guntur didn't say anything, opting instead to take in another drag of his cigarette. He didn't look like someone you'd want to get on the wrong side of with his menacing square jaw and short cropped haircut.

"Just hang here and we will go and pick a taxi from down the road," I was told.

They returned five minutes later with the same taxi that I had let go previously. I threw my backpack on the rear seat and followed it in. Budi exchanged a few words with the taxi driver and we moved off, following the motorbike. Half an hour later I found myself outside a small house etched into the side of a steep hill.

Warm beers and lots of smoking seemed to be the order of the night. I enjoyed getting to know the lads before retreating to a rickety single bed on the second level of this modest dwelling. I fell asleep quickly, feeling completely at ease with the West Timorese people.

▲ ▲ ▲

It wasn't until Boxing Day that I could begin to look for the vehicle that Amadeo had promised. With a hand written letter of introduction and sketched map of the house location, I headed off on the back of Budi's motorbike. Like Guntur's, it was slow and laboured heavily when climbing hills; and the fact that Budi tended to stay in the high gears regardless of the speed or incline of the road didn't help matters much. After ambling aimlessly around the outskirts of Kupang, an area without clearly marked street signs or house numbers, we were forced to take directions from locals.

Eventually we arrived at a little shack with a tin roof and chicken coop propped up against the side wall. Initially the occupants seemed a little confused to receive not only an unknown face in Budi, but also a pale-skinned foreigner. Thankfully their caution rapidly turned to joy when they realised that indirectly we were acquainted with Amadeo's cousin. It took around ten minutes of dialogue in Bahasa between Budi and the family before Budi turned to me.

"Well, the good news is that the car is out the back and they don't have any worries with us taking it, but the bad news is that there are a few problems with it."

"Such as?" I asked, knowing I wasn't going to want to know the answer.

"They recently tried to start the vehicle but couldn't get it going. They think, though, that the problem might be just a flat battery. The vehicle is now out of registration, but they reckon we can get a temporary permit from the police station."

"Okay. Can we have a look at it?" I replied, thinking that didn't sound too bad.

Budi translated the question and we were duly led around to the back of the house where two young boys were flapping around with the corners of a blue tarp. As they untied the veil and lifted it back from the vehicle I couldn't believe the vision before me. Car? This was a green mini bus with tinted windows. The side door was the type that slid to one side and folded up in the process, with access to the rear compartment. One of the boys opened the door to retrieve a spare tyre as the wheel on the back axle was both bald and flat. What a jalopy!

An old man meandered out of the house and handed Budi a set of keys. My new friend looked blankly at me, explaining he only had a licence for a motorbike. After seeing how he'd driven the motorbike I was only too glad to take the keys off him and with minor repairs completed, such as changing the tyre, I jumped in behind the steering wheel of my new chariot. The floor was rusty and the velour seats felt sticky from lack of use and prolonged exposure to heat. Except for a thin strip running lengthwise across the centre, the entire windscreen had been heavily tinted. As I adjusted the rear vision mirror a team gathered at the front, poised to push the vehicle onto the road. I looked for the handbrake and found it resting on the front passengers seat ... broken.

"Ready, Squiz?" Budi yelled.

"Yeah, mate. Let's go!"

Removing a block of wood from the front tyre, the makeshift motor team proceeded to push the bus, coaxing it to move backwards. I steered onto the dirt road, pumped the brakes, and turned the wheel downhill. Releasing the brakes I began rolling forward as the vehicle picked up speed and I double checked that the ignition was on and the gear stick was in second gear. I let the clutch out. Coughing and spluttering, the green beast came to life with a high pitched buzz from the two-stroke engine. The team was overjoyed, hollering their success as they journeyed back up the road.

The next day I drove Budi to three police stations in an attempt to acquire a temporary registration for the vehicle and permission to cross the border. This proved to be my initiation to the anarchical and ramshackle excuse for "due process" in a developing country. Only the innocence of inexperience could have led me to believe things could possibly have been any other way. It took hours of questions and numerous false leads before we gave up trying to do the right thing, accepting we would have to bribe our way out of any complications. The next step was obvious … a quick trip to the main branch of Bank Indonesia.

The bank occupied the first two levels of an imposing glass-walled tower. With experience mushrooming exponentially in my Western psyche as each hour passed, good sense told me to enter the domain of bureaucracy alone; after all there was no point in Budi becoming embroiled in the expected complications. The first pleasant surprise was that the lady behind the counter spoke English. Producing Amadeo's ID and my letter of authority I began to explain my intention to withdraw his money and close the account. The woman asked me to wait and walked off to speak with her manager. Anxious sweat beads formed in my palms as I considered a myriad of possible outcomes, and how I might talk my way out of each of them.

The bank teller returned.

"That is fine, sir. You will need to fill out these forms and then the cashier on the second level will be able to pay the amount owed."

What an anticlimax!

"Thank you so much," I said, keeping it simple to disguise my obvious relief.

Once the stash was safely in my clammy hands I quickly stuffed the wads of Rupiah into my daypack, hoping no one else caught a glimpse of the substantial haul. Amazingly, the entire exercise had only taken twenty minutes.

"Budi, success!" I cheered. "I'm ready to head for the border."

"Okay," he answered. "I've spoken to my friends. We will leave early tomorrow morning. They will meet us at Guntur's house."

"How many friends are coming along?" I asked, trying to sound as though the number of passengers didn't matter to me.

"Just two. They want to visit the border as well, and see the Australian soldiers."

"And how will you all return when I head across the border?"

"We can get public mini-busses back to Kupang."

It seemed okay to me. If they wanted to see the border and meet a few Aussies it seemed a small price to pay for the invaluable assistance I'd received.

▲　▲　▲

I pumped on the brakes of the mini-bus just after 7am to pull up alongside Guntur's house. Budi, sitting in the front seat, jumped over into the back compartment and lifted up a large block of wood that jammed the side door shut. Without it, the door swung open whenever the vehicle made a left hand turn. He jumped out and rushed to place the chock behind a wheel so as I could take my foot off the brake pedal.

Looking ready for anything, Guntur and two friends came out from the house. Like Budi, none of them had a licence to drive a car or bus so I took the driver's seat and began following instructions to exit the streets of Kupang. Labouring across the landscape it seemed wiser to drive slowly as I was both unfamiliar with the road rules and also cautious of the erratic behaviour of other road users. I'd quickly become accustomed to the fact that public buses and mini-vans manoeuvred through the streets without any regard whatsoever for other traffic. It reminded me a little of playing a video game back home, only this time all too frighteningly real.

"Squiz, that school over there is a refugee camp," Budi called.

I pulled over, eager to see what had attracted his attention.

"What? The whole school has been turned into a refugee camp?" I gasped.

"Yep, but this one is only temporary. Most of the people here want to return back to East Timor. We've already helped quite a lot of the families move back."

Trying to absorb everything before me, I was initially reminded of the school that IRC lived and worked from when I first arrived in Dili, but I soon realised that this place was far worse. Here, women were cooking from open-air fireplaces as their children rolled about in the nearby muddy fields. Tarps and old pieces of plastic sheeting were hanging from the walls to give additional living space for the hundreds of residents. I couldn't see any generators, showers or portable toilets. The images of this refugee camp remain firmly etched in my mind to this day and I recall feeling, well, a little precious. I couldn't believe I'd felt uncomfortable about the tight living arrangements in our shared NGO facility only a few months before. What I was seeing now was real hardship.

I was also annoyed with myself for getting so frustrated that Budi and I were unable to walk into a police station and get a permit, issued on the spot, to cross the border. That whole exercise was trivial in the extreme compared to the anguish these refugees were enduring. Many of them had been brought to West Timor forcefully and had no idea whether they should return, let alone how they would get back. It was also likely they'd face fierce resentment from those who stayed in East Timor if they returned to their homes. Conversely, they faced a grim future in West Timor should they attempt to rebuild their life in a place where they would never be able to gain citizenship. These refugees were in a no-win situation.

The single-lane road leading west of Kupang was narrow but in good condition, meandering through lush green valleys with jungle foliage and paddy fields that seemed as though they had been there forever. Although the traffic thinned out, the road became no less congested as we pressed on and the number of dogs, humans and goats increased. Not only did I have to remain acutely focused so as to avoid an actual accident, I also had to remember that an accident would spell trouble with the authorities.

We buzzed along at a steady pace until Budi mentioned that another refugee camp was coming up on the left hand side of the road. This time I was instructed to keep moving at all costs. The camp had been constructed many years before and was in an isolated area. It housed the families of those who had relatives in the anti-separatist militia and provided a safe haven for the militia themselves. It was common knowledge amongst refugee workers such as Budi and Guntur that these residents had no intention of returning to East Timor.

A sudden rush of adrenaline sped through my body – it occurred to me that this would be a particularly bad place to get a flat tyre or have a mechanical breakdown. And that thought was no sooner through my brain than the car in front began to slow down. I edged across to the centre of the road to see what was happening in the distance. Two cars and a truck were stopped on the road and a few young men were speaking with the drivers.

"What's happening up ahead?" I asked

"Looks like the militia are out on the road," Budi answered solemnly.

"Don't stop, don't stop!" yelled Guntur.

I pulled out again to see if there was any oncoming traffic. There wasn't. The car in front, only fifty metres from the stopped vehicles, was being waved to slow down by one of the young men.

"You want me to go around them?" I asked.

"Yes, yes! You cannot stop here," Guntur urged.

I continued to hover behind the vehicle in front until it slowed to 20 km/h. The road ahead was still clear so I swung the bus into the other lane and pressed down hard on the accelerator pedal, quietly praying there was enough power in this old jalopy to do the trick. I sat up high in the seat to shield my white skinned face with the upper section of the tinted window screen, suddenly glad to have the protection of that blacked out windshield.

It looked as though most of the militia were preoccupied with the vehicles they had already lured into their net until, almost inevitably, one of them turned abruptly to eyeball our speeding vehicle. I grimaced determinedly and floored it. Yes! There was nothing left for it; all the militia could do was eat the dust of the green machine as it sailed past unhindered into the distance.

"So, what were those guys up to?" I asked, once I felt relatively safe.

"They were probably looking for a lift to the border or demanding money to help with their situation. They get little support from aid agencies," Budi explained.

"Very bad for us to stop … lots of bad guys in that camp," added Guntur.

I couldn't argue with good logic like that.

▲　▲　▲

Apart from needing to lie to my new friends when they enquired as to whether my short hair cut meant that I was a member of the Australian Army (not quite the language they used), the journey continued over the next two days relatively uneventfully until we drove through to the other side of the border town, Atambua.

On the north side was another police checkpoint. This one was stopping all unnecessary movement to the nearby border and I didn't feel we were in a strong position to argue with the authorities. In this case discretion was definitely the better part of valour so I opted to turn back, not wanting the police to discover either the expired registration or the large sum of Rupiah in my backpack.

I found a public phone in Atambua and called Bob at the IOM office in Kupang. He still couldn't guarantee a seat on their flight in two days time but promised he'd put me down as first reserve. I desperately needed to get on the flight because the following two days, either side of the New Year, had no scheduled flights at all and I didn't want to be stuck on the wrong side of the border for the dawn of the new millennium.

▲　▲　▲

On our way back to Kefamenamu, a central town with roads to Kupang, Atambua and Oecussi, Guntur asked if we could go across to Oecussi so as he could see the Australian soldiers. Oecussi was a small enclave situated inside West Timor belonging to East Timor and also protected by Australian soldiers. It would take several more hours to reach Oecussi from Kefamenamu, but Guntur was desperate to make the detour. Inflated media reports and hot gossip had given him an almost child-like fascination about the Rambo-like image of Australian soldiers. I wished at this point that I hadn't used my lack of height (180 cm) as an excuse earlier as to why I couldn't possibly be a member of the Australian Army. I didn't want to let him down so opted to drive north.

A few hours later the bitumen road turned to dirt. As we came around a sharp corner I saw a small wooden hut with a thatched roof shading ten Indonesian soldiers who appeared so casual I could have been fooled into thinking this was just a group of mates gathered for a barbie. A metal boom gate stretched across the road in front of us. We had reached the border.

Guntur jumped from the bus and chocked the wheel before we walked towards the hut as a group. Some of the soldiers were holding their weapons, but most had them hanging from a rafter in the hut – I even noticed a guitar draped amongst the firearms. These soldiers did not seem to be on high alert!

I let the lads greet the soldiers first before I politely tried out my few words of Bahasa. Guntur diplomatically offered them all a cigarette.

"Squiz, the commander says the border is only open for foot traffic and for a few hours a day. It is closed for the rest of today but we can walk across to the Australian side if we want to," Budi translated.

"Are you kidding me?" I tried not to sound quite as surprised as I was.

"No kidding. They say it is fine if we walk across but we will have to leave the car here and return in an hour."

"I'm not sure if that is such a good idea. If the border is closed I'd say the Aussie soldiers won't be too happy to see us approaching from this side."

Guntur, who had been listening intently to our conversation, said firmly, "It is no problem for me. I want to see Australian army man."

"Rightio," I said slowly, not too sure it was okay at all. "Can you just confirm where the Australian soldiers are located, so we don't accidentally startle them?"

"They told us that the road is clear, and as long as we follow it we won't get into trouble. The Australians are on the right hand side of the road just past a barricade."

Guntur started walking down the track. Reluctantly I joined the other boys as they followed after him. The dirt trail was dusty from previous foot traffic and descended sharply before hooking left and flattening out for about 150 metres. At the other end of the flat section was a series of concrete blocks, too big to be moved without machinery. They were blocking the road for vehicular traffic and must have been the barricades that the Indonesian soldiers had referred to. As we moved closer I spotted some rope passageways, probably set up to help coordinate the border crossings. We had reached East Timorese soil. I was certain the Australian soldiers were nearby and would most definitely have a sentry looking out for people who tried to cross outside of the opening hours. I began to feel anxious, not wanting to surprise those I served alongside back in Australia. Even more concerning was the thought that a fellow countrymen could have been looking at me through the sights of his weapon as I walked through the barricades.

Conscious of the potential danger we were walking into I kept talking, so as to give warning of our approach. Nobody stopped us and I couldn't see anyone in the bushes to the right. After three minutes I saw a well-worn track leading off to the right; it had the boot prints with the distinctive 'Y' mould, like those issued to Australian soldiers. I told the lads to wait while I checked out the path. It didn't take long for me to spot a hootchie, an army lean-to used for shelter, painted with the Australian camouflage pattern. The hootchie was set up to block out the unforgiving rays of the blistering afternoon sun. Sitting underneath it were two young soldiers in their early twenties, one cleaning his weapon and the other cooking a meal.

"G'day guys," I said in my broadest Australian accent.

They looked up.

"G'day," said the guy doing the cooking.

"Mate, I'm an Aussie doing some aid work in West Timor. I've just quickly ducked across the border, but will have to go back shortly. Is your boss around?"

"Yep … standby, we'll get him for you."

The guy cleaning his weapon quickly reassembled it and trotted further down the track as I returned to escort my Indonesian colleagues, hoping the person we were about to meet was a big burly bloke who would uphold the I'm-too-short-for-the-Australian-army line I'd fed my travelling companions earlier. No chance. A curious looking soldier was walking towards us, wearing two chevrons on his arm indicating he was a Corporal. He was barely bigger than my Indonesian colleagues, no taller than 165 centimetres. Of all the men in the Australian Army, we had to be met by one of the shortest. I tried not to show my disappointment as I introduced myself and explained who we were. The Corporal was clearly not at all impressed to hear that the Indonesian Forces had allowed us to wander across the border. I sensed that he was also a little disappointed that we had walked right into his outpost without being detected in advance. He did, however, maintain a dignified composure and, much to the enjoyment of Guntur, allowed me to take a photo of him and the 'Indonesian infiltrators'.

As we returned across no-mans-land to our vehicle, Guntur said, "The Aussie soldier is not so big."

I laughed. "Most of them are bigger than that guy."

▲   ▲   ▲

Eventually I made it back to Bob's office and, with a huge degree of relief, heard the welcome news that Bob had reserved me a seat. I would be flying to Dili at midday the next day. The manifest had been signed off, so my seat was now locked in. Apart from the pilots and crew, I would be the only non-refugee on board and there was no doubt in my mind that Bob had done me a huge favour. After dropping off the green machine with Budi and hitching a ride to the airport on the back of his motorbike we said our good-byes as Guntur arrived with another cigarette hanging from his mouth. He threw me a smile and I headed on board. I was at high altitude on a C-130 Hercules plane before I finally crossed the East Timor border for good, an experience shared with about one hundred East Timorese refugees. I glanced around the few pitiful possessions they clung to, vowing never again to take for granted the unhindered mobility that my Australian passport afforded me.

▲ ▲ ▲

That evening I visited Amadeo's house. He and his family were living in a tiny room that used to be the shop he ran from his front yard. It was the only room left on his property that had a roof – a grenade had exploded in the main room destroying the interior and collapsing his house roof. All ten of his kids hovered around as I sat on the veranda, knowing Amadeo wanted me to get straight to the point. Tears welled in his dark eyes as I emptied wads of cash onto the concrete floor in front of him, the equivalent of eight and a half thousand US dollars. He had given up hope of ever seeing the money again. This stash meant the difference between sending his children out to work so he could fix his old house, or sending them to school.

Two days later I was standing in the centre of Dili celebrating the birth of a new millennium with thousands of Timorese who had finally found their freedom after a twenty-four year occupation. The experience was not only humbling but it began fuelling a growing passion to somehow continue my employment within the aid industry. I also had the opportunity that evening to meet briefly with the commander of the Australian-led peacekeeping force, General Cosgrove. He had led an extremely successful mission to Timor, laying the foundations for a prosperous future. Poverty, poor education and weak infrastructure would challenge the country for years to come but their sovereignty had now been returned.

▲ ▲ ▲

Two weeks after the New Year celebrations my contract expired and I returned to Australia to fulfil some military commitments. I felt like I had done my bit during the first phase of operations, but I was far from ready to close the door on aid work. IRC's programmes and systems were up and running and they would touch the lives of thousands of people. But knowing that wasn't enough. I would only be back in Australia for a few months before I felt the urge to get amongst the action again. Having had the experience in East Timor, I could see that I was able to have a greater impact in war zones if I went without a weapon or military uniform. I handed in my army gear, split up with my girlfriend, and got back in contact with IRC.

Map of Albania

THREE
MAFIA AND MEN WITH BALACLAVAS

ALBANIA SNAPSHOT

WW2: *occupied by allied forces.*

1944–1990: *Albania is tightly controlled by Communist leaders. Trade ties are built and subsequently lost with Yugoslavia, the USSR and China. After falling out with the Chinese in the '70s and, with no other communist partner to side with, Albania undergoes a period of complete isolation. Borders are closed and movement of people and goods is stopped.*

1991: *Albanians violently rise up against the ever weakening communist party. One third of the three million population head overseas (mainly to Europe). Gangs roam the streets committing crime with virtual impunity as the police are overwhelmed by the anarchy.*

1990s: *Albanians spread their tentacles across Europe and begin building a powerful mafia network. The Croatian and Bosnian wars with Serbia cause instability to the north of Albania and put a block on a lucrative passageway for illegal activities between Europe and the Middle East/Central Asia. The* now open borders of Albania provide a new and more direct route between the two markets.

1999: NATO conducts a seventy-two day offensive to stabilize the region after intense fighting between the Kosovo Liberation Army and Serbia in the neighbouring Kosovo. Four hundred and forty thousand Kosovo Albanian's desperately move across to Albania to avoid the fighting.

May 2000: Squiz arrives in Albania.

"What the hell is a blood feud?" I demanded to know.

"A damn good reason not to stuff these guys around," answered Bill gruffly.

It was my first night in the Balkans and Bill, my new boss, was giving me a few pointers on how to survive the lawless and mafia riddled country of Albania.

"Well, I certainly don't have any intention of doing that. Does drinking beer set them off?" I quipped.

"No, mate. Do you want another one though?"

He was moving towards the fridge, anticipating my answer. Studying the weather-worn lines etched into his face, I listened intently as Bill went on to explain the unwritten law that had evolved over the years, colloquially referred to as a 'blood feud'. In simplistic terms it meant that if an individual was killed, either by mistake or with intent, their family had the right to kill the person who was responsible for the death. There were no exceptions for foreigners. If IRC staff were caught up in a car accident the standard procedure was to get straight to the nearest airport and fly out of the country.

As I sipped on my second beer on Bill's rooftop balcony, I noticed the neighbours lock down their window shutters and secure their metal security doors. The sun had dropped in the dusk sky, and although it was a warm summer night, the fast approaching darkness was the trigger for the locals to retreat for the evening.

"The bad guys come out at night," Bill said simply.

"So should we go inside as well?" I asked.

"No, mate. There's nothing to worry about. The locals are all paranoid. They reckon that the ones who have committed a murder take advantage of the darkness to move about."

"Well, that seems like a good enough reason to go inside," I reasoned.

"Nah, it's all bloody bullshit," he drawled with the hint of a laugh in his voice. "I thought I'd see for myself when I first got here. There wasn't anyone in the streets after dark, other than police. In fact, it's probably the safest time to move about; at least there aren't any of the lunatic drivers on the streets."

I began to understand what Bill was referring to the next day. We were picked up in the morning by an IRC driver in a green Mercedes Benz. I confess to thinking it was a little odd to be getting into a luxury European built car when heading off to work with an aid agency, but we weren't the only Mercedes on the road. As we drove on the narrow streets to a larger recently sealed road, it seemed as though we were sailing on a black sea awash with dozens of both old and late model Mercedes. This, apparently, was the car of choice for Albanians.

Our local driver didn't stop to give way to traffic from either direction. He hardly even looked one way or the other as our vehicle began to blend into the chaos. Gazing out the window, intent on soaking in my new surroundings, the grime and poverty of a developing country was self-evident. Every road junction had a designated place for the locals to dump their domestic rubbish, uncontained and vulnerable to the slightest of breezes. The electricity lines sagged, congested by multiple lines leading directly to the haphazardly built shops and houses below. Ahead, a policeman in the middle of the road waved a plastic lollypop-shaped sign in a fruitless attempt to have the vehicles move to the correct side of the road. I couldn't help but feel sorry for him. A few of the drivers obeyed his directions; most did not.

"So Bill, what's the go with all of the Mercedes, mate?" I asked. "I mean the country looks like it's in a mighty desperate state but still there are Mercs all over the place."

"It's all a product of the mafia's work," he replied. "They are stolen from Europe and allowed to be imported into the country by the government. Even the official government cars have been stolen from Europe. You can pick up a late model Mercedes for only a few grand at one of the markets. So it's only the poor farmers who still have to use the traditional Albanian transport from the communist days."

"Oh yeah, what type of car is that?" I asked.

"Horse and cart."

▲　▲　▲

Now that I was deployed on my second mission as an aid worker I began looking more purposefully at the professional opportunities within the aid industry. Within IRC's operations in the Balkans alone there seemed to be a constant evolution in work opportunities that moved parallel to the ever changing and developing situation on the ground. Already working in Kosovo the IRC had deployed a team to Albania, similar to the one I had been a part of in East Timor and immediately after the NATO-led offensive. The team kicked off operations to help with the influx of refugees in the border town of Kukes, the northern city of Skhodra and the capital city of Tirane. Because of the close ethnic ties between the refugees and Albanians, this was one cross-border influx that didn't turn into a complete catastrophe. Instead of gathering in overflowing and under resourced camps, the majority of refugees were able to be cared for by relatives, or were accepted into the homes of generous Albanians. The IRC was able to quickly transition its assistance from humanitarian relief to development projects, the latter designed to bolster the government infrastructure and community living standards for future difficulties or emergencies. By the time I arrived in May 2000, IRC's office in Skhodra was helping to refurbish the train station, local schools and the homes of the families that had temporarily taken in refugees. Bill and I were working on a programme designed to increase the capacity of the National Fire Brigade. We did this by conducting two-week training sessions that skilled the firemen in medical response, cliff rescue, four wheel driving and crisis management. Initially we focused our attention on the villages that lay in the north of the country, as these were the most vulnerable and poorly equipped. Before coming to Albania I had expected that all emergency response organisations, worldwide, would have some basic levels of competence, training and trust within the community. Not an unreasonable thought, but it turns out I was naïve. It certainly wasn't the case in Albania. The Albanian Fire Brigade was a boys' club, stifled by a communist work ethic of 'do no work, do no harm, still get paid'. After a few months of training an organisation that I had quickly earmarked as unprofessional, I found that I too, in this instance, was lacking a solid work ethic.

▲　▲　▲

Luke 'Goz' Gosling, a good friend of mine from Australia, joined us to help expand the crisis management module within the training schedule. On the first Saturday Goz hit town he was initiated … by fire. I recognised the look of astonishment on his face as we traversed streets awash with water from overflowing drains that had been blocked for hours by the mass of rubbish picked up by the mid-afternoon thunderstorms. Being an old hand at this, I swerved around large pools of water with some confidence, heading across to the southern neighbourhoods of Tirane, an area I didn't know so well. The earlier rains had made the road slippery. If I was driving back in Australia I would have slowed, being more cautious in the potentially dangerous circumstances. But we weren't in Kansas any more, Toto. It was kind of liberating to know I could test the vehicle's limits without a thought as to the consequences.

I ploughed through swollen puddles, increasing speed and quietly thinking I was probably impressing my friend, until just fifty metres before the end of the road. I slammed the breaks on, sliding the locked wheels all the way to the intersection. Our heads jolted back in unison, hitting the headrests as the car jerked to a halt. I let the clutch out and slammed my foot down on the accelerator. The tyres spun furiously, unable to get complete traction on the wet road as we headed out of the intersection.

Somehow I kept a semblance of control, putting the high beams on in an attempt to identify the small side street we were headed to. The big fences, piles of rubbish and muddy laneways all looked the same in this land of endless garbage.

"Flamin' hell, man. I'm not recognizing any of this," I finally admitted.

"I thought you said you'd been to this house before," Goz queried.

"I have, but it wasn't at night. Maybe we should have turned left at the train station. Hold on!"

Goz leant forward and picked up a bottle of Vodka from the floor to stop it from rolling around and tucked it between his legs as I reached for the handbrake and simultaneously pulled back hard whilst turning the steering wheel. The rear end of the car swung around, screeching as though it was in agonising pain. We'd turned 180 degrees in two seconds. Once more I accelerated hard as we began heading back towards the train station.

"Whoo hoo! Drive it like you stole it, mate!" Goz cheered, like a kid at his first Crusty Demons of Dirt Derby, turning up the volume on the radio.

My trusty mate had brought some good old Aussie music with him, and I must admit it did feel oddly comforting to hear the familiar strains of Midnight Oil blaring out of the speakers. The road on the other side of the train station didn't reveal any familiar sights either. I rang Bledhar, the host of the party we were heading for, who told us to return to the train station so he could direct us in person to the house. I was just about to pull up at the station when a blue van came speeding out of the darkness in front of us. My immediate reaction was to brake, skidding our car to a rather undignified halt. The van mimicked our manoeuvre but had been moving at a much higher speed. Its tyres locked in a direct collision course with us, coming to rest just two metres from the front of our car, at which point I let out the breath I had been unaware I was holding.

Goz and I sat there motionless, eyes wide open, with the music still blaring at a high volume. It was as though we'd just walked into a really bad B-grade movie. I watched in utter disbelief as the side door of the van abruptly yanked open and two men pointing AK-47s directly at our vehicle jumped out. This was no accident. They were both wearing black balaclavas with two eye holes and a slot for their mouth. They took a few hurried steps to position themselves either side of the front end of our vehicle and I felt a rush of adrenaline surge through my body. I sat paralysed by the sight of their pointed barrels, unwilling to move in case any action from me triggered a reaction from one of them.

Just as I was beginning to think, "There are only two of them," two more, clones of the first pair, leapt from the back of the van with weapons raised for action. I could see their mouths opening and closing, and knew they were yelling out commands, but our blaring music drowned out their words. These guys were pros. They moved quickly and in sequence; this was obviously a well rehearsed drill. Although the second pair to exit the van were moving faster than the first, everything suddenly seemed to be unfolding in slow motion. My brain was on high alert, completely focused on the 3-D video game-esque performance being played out before me.

One of the masked men reached Goz's door and wrenched it open. Out of the corner of my eye I could see him being pulled out of the car by his shirt; then a moment later the same was happening to me. I raised my arms as I was yanked from the car to let it be known that I had no weapon and wasn't intending to resist the aggression. I knew these guys were trying to communicate with us, screaming words of Albanian in my ear, but I couldn't understand a word. My comprehension of the language seemed to matter little when the fist that had grabbed my collar was shoved into my neck as my feet hit the ground. I lunged forward, bracing myself against the side of my vehicle. A sharp point was thrust into the centre of my back. I knew it was the barrel of the gun but it felt as sharp as a knife. The insides of my ankles were kicked hard to widen my legs and put me off balance. It worked – I felt helpless. Fleetingly I considered that the man thought I was ignoring him because of my lack of verbal replies to his shouting so I attempted to open dialogue.

"We don't speak Albanian. English only. No Albanian," I yelled.

"Shut up," snapped the man behind me.

I looked through the window to the other side of the car, realising that Goz was propped up against the car in the same position as I was. Another man came from the van and walked towards the open door that I had just been pulled from as the man behind me searched my upper body, roughly, starting with my arms. I took a deep breath wondering what on earth they wanted from us. At least we were both still alive … for now. I consoled myself with the thought that if these guys wanted to kill us, they would have done it by now.

"Who are you? Why are you here?" barked the man who was walking towards my open door.

"We are two Australians, working in Albania with an aid agency," I explained, trying to sound convincing.

"This is bullshit. Why you drive like this?" he yelled.

There was no immediately plausible explanation for that. As though it was his God given right the man searched me, pulling my mobile phone and wallet from my pockets and flinging them on the front seat. Against any shred of logic that was left in the moment I hoped this was all they were after. Of course that was ridiculous. They had us right where they wanted us. What possible motive could they have for stopping there? Sure enough the man who had just asked me questions started rummaging through the centre console before leaning across and grabbing the bottle of Vodka that Goz had left on the passenger's seat. He stood back.

"You are drunk!"

"No!" I insisted. "I haven't had anything to drink. That is for later."

"Where is passport?"

"In my bag."

The man behind me grabbed my right hand and pulled down on my arm. He did the same with my left. Cold handcuffs wrapped around my wrists, squeezing painfully into my flesh, and clinked shut.

"Where is passport?" he yelled again.

"It's in my bag … on the backseat." I replied, obediently.

Our eyes connected. It didn't take a degree in psychology to see he was angrier than the fires of a volcano, and I suspected he didn't understand what I was saying. Another loud voice, screaming Albanian words, suddenly sounded behind me. It distracted the men in balaclavas. I wanted to turn and look but wasn't sure how the masked men would react if I twisted my body. The man who had been questioning me in broken English suddenly began screaming a response to the other voice in Albanian. All I could do in the confusion was pray this was not complicating an already highly-charged situation.

Time seemed to stand still. I knew only seconds and minutes were passing yet those seconds and minutes dragged on eternally as if unwilling to release us. If only I understood Albanian, perhaps then at least I'd know how to respond to the voices arguing behind me.

The cold steel cutting into my flesh was suddenly loosened. The handcuffs had been released! Deeming it safe to move I turned around and saw Bledhar. True to his word he'd arrived to meet us at the train station. He did not look happy as he continued to speak with a raised voice to the men with guns.

"Check your wallet. Make sure everything is there," he growled.

My wallet lay unopened alongside my mobile phone on the seat. I checked it. Everything was there. Goz did the same with his and we hopped inside the car.

"They are untouched, Bledhar," I assured him.

"Good. Follow me," he ordered.

Slowly I reversed away from the men. They had lowered their weapons but were still glaring at us with murderous intent. Bledhar ran back to his car and drove down the road in the direction that the van had come from. Without need for further instructions I followed him.

"Welcome to Albania, Goz," I quipped, trying to sound light-hearted.

"What the hell was that all about?"

"I think they were the Special Police, but I'm not sure."

Goz didn't answer but I could almost sense him wondering what exactly "special" meant.

Bledhar continued for a hundred metres past the last working lamppost before pulling over in the darkness to the side of the road and gesturing for me to come alongside him. Goz rolled down his window.

"Man, you guys are so lucky," Bledhar said as he looked up at our vehicle.

"Who were those guys?" Goz wanted to know.

"Man, they're the Special Police. They were going to lock you guys up and throw away the key. They said they thought you were getting ready to do a drug deal. They watched you go back and forth a few times and thought you were clearing the road to make sure there weren't any police in the area."

"So how did you get us out of that one?"

"Didn't you hear me go off when I first arrived? I was screaming at them for arresting two high ranking diplomats from the Australian Embassy. I said that if they went any further it would turn into a diplomatic incident and they would have hell to pay."

I don't think I'd ever been more grateful to, or impressed by, anyone. Clearly a person needed to be part guerrilla, part psychologist and part actor to survive in this harsh foreign land. Bledhar, an Albanian who worked with us at IRC, informed us later that the Special Police are constantly on the look out for the mafia gangs involved in drugs. It sounded quite noble until he explained that the real motive for seeking out these criminals is that they're in a position to pay the healthiest bribes when caught red handed. And because the Special Police are dealing with the most dangerous of criminals, they are forced to hide their identities to prevent assassination attempts when off duty. That explained why they were wearing balaclavas. The whole incident was a sharp reminder that I was a long way from being prepared for the trials ahead. I was naïve and immature, and I'd been sucked into a false sense of security believing that I was immune from the dangers of the land. From that moment on I never forgot that I was vulnerable. I could have ended up in jail and dragged the IRC name down with my own reputation. I vowed to always uphold good standards of behaviour, and to certainly curb my passion for driving erratically, now that I had made a commitment to make a go of the aid industry.

▲　▲　▲

Eight highly educational months later, the issues in Kosovo that brought me to Albania were no longer placing a direct threat there. Consequently the eyes of those responsible for allocating funds to development programmes such as the fire brigade training were soon distracted by other, more alarming, issues. In the short period I'd been in Albania we'd managed to train hundreds of firemen and certainly contributed to their emergency response capabilities. Although my time was up in the Balkans, my passion to work in the aid industry was beginning to burn like a wildfire in the wind. I let IRC know that I was ready and able to go wherever they had a shortfall. The idea of going back to Australia no longer sounded appealing.

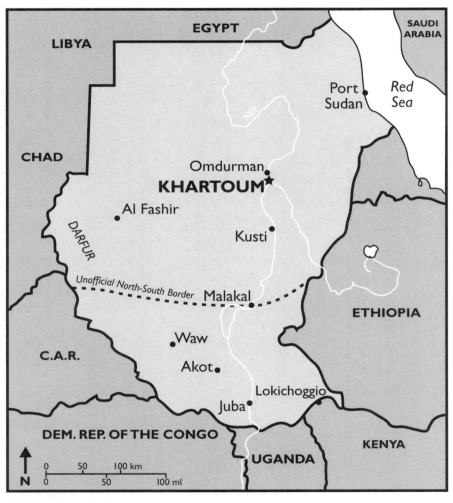

Map of Sudan

FOUR
INSPIRED BY IMPOVERISHED BOYS

SUDAN SNAPSHOT

6th Century: *Christianity floods into the southern regions of Sudan whilst Arab crusaders spread Islam through the north.*

1821: *The Egyptians, with the help of the Ottoman Empire, occupy and annex the area recognised today as Sudan. Tensions between the various religious and ethnic groups grow as they compete for the wide-ranging and abundant resources (slaves, wood, water and exotic animals) found throughout the country.*

1885: *The northerners rise up against the Ottoman-Egyptian rule and take control of Khartoum. The whole of Sudan is declared an Islamic State.*

1889: *With the help of Egypt, the British begin to administer the country. Christian missionaries are allowed to again operate in the south.*

1943–1953: *The British establish the North Sudan Advisory Council and withdraw. Only four out of the eight hundred new governmental positions are given to the south.*

1955 – 1972: *Civil war sparked by biased governance.*

1972: *Addis Ababa Agreement allows for self rule in the south.*

1978: *Oil is discovered in southern Sudan.*

1983: *Civil war erupts again between the north and south, this time over religion and oil rights issues.*

1990s: *Civil war intensifies after a coup in Khartoum and severe drought causes widespread famine. The UN responds by setting up 'Operation Lifeline Sudan' (OLS); a collective international relief effort supported by NGO's and UN humanitarian agencies. Lokichoggio, on the border of Sudan and Kenya, is selected as the logistics base for all humanitarian cargo entering southern Sudan.*

March 2001: *Squiz heads for Lokichoggio.*

I could have been flying over the remote deserts of central Australia. For several hours I'd been scanning the endless plain of withered creek beds and rocky outcrops that looked to offer little life support for humans, beasts or vegetation alike. Then finally a sign of civilisation: a one hundred metre strip of black tarmac. The plane made a sudden nose dive in preparation for a landing.

Alighting from the aircraft there could be little doubt I was in the heart of the African continent. Tall, lean airport staff wearing blue overcoats raced to remove luggage from the undercarriage, undeterred by the blistering surge of heat bouncing off the tarmac below. A man with the darkest skin I'd ever seen stood at the base of a narrow ladder leading to the door of the plane, directing passengers in a deep voice to the shiny tin shed that doubled as an arrivals and departures terminal. The perimeter fence was awash with blue and white – thousands of plastic bags had been pinned to the barbs after being tossed around in the whisking wind. The tin shed itself provided little sanctuary from the unforgiving heat, and the air was heavy with the body odour of those who delivered the baggage.

A middle aged man wearing an IRC t-shirt was waiting anxiously at the baggage collection counter, his new boss among the ten arrivals. I smiled at him and nodded. "Hello, Mr. Mark?"

"Jambo!" I replied.

He laughed, revealing a large set of white teeth.

"You speak Swahili, sir?"

"Unfortunately only one word at the moment," I grinned.

I followed as Lameck led the way across a dirt car park to a white four wheel drive. A gust of hot dry air swirled across the car park, picking up red dust. I dived into the vehicle for sanctuary.

Lameck drove us along the dusty road of Lokichoggio village towards the Operation Lifeline Sudan camp passing tall thin men wearing nothing more than sheets wrapped around their groins as they cruised barefoot along the dirt paths beside the road. Some carried small wooden hand-carved seats and traditional walking sticks while others grasped hunting spears. Every woman of child bearing age had either a baby strapped to her back or was pregnant. Those with newborns were not using fancy baby holders or pushing prams; instead a simple piece of cloth, knotted at the front, secured the newborns to their backs. Children were running in between their towering parents, oblivious to everything but their games; the older ones chasing a rolling tyre or pushing improvised toys made from anything circular.

After a kilometre the street narrowed and Lameck began to slow down. Flimsy stalls and small shops made from wonky wood and corrugated iron lined the street on either side of us. People were gathered in small groups of five to seven, watching the foot traffic and talking. I locked eyes with nearly everyone I saw. They stared back with the same intensity, surprised to see the face of a white man.

Turning into a street on the left I noticed a group of five women talking, each wearing a mass of colourful beaded necklaces from their chins to the tops of their breasts. Were it not for their shaved Mohawks I would have stared with astonishment at their bare breasts. Lameck sensed my surprise and began to tell me about OLS and Lokichoggio. I blushed, embarrassed that I'd been caught out.

"So the OLS camp was established to provide aid to those across the border in southern Sudan, it wasn't mandated to assist the people here in Lokichoggio or the nearby villages. In fact some of the locals have probably suffered as a result of the camp," Lameck explained.

"Really … why is that?" I asked.

"Well, before the OLS camp was built, Lokichoggio was just the junction of two dried up creek beds. As soon as the runway and camp were built, thousands of people flocked to the area in search of handouts and jobs. It's meant that a lot of nomadic tribe's people have left the traditional life to now live in squalor around the camp. They all live in these humpies, hoping that one day things will get better," Lameck said as he pointed to the side of the road.

Well-trodden dirt paths meandered in between single-roomed structures that stood no taller than five foot high and ten foot in diameter. Walls were made from mud and tree branches whilst the roofs were covered in a multitude of plastic bags, and the remains of tarpaulins or straw thatching.

As we slowed to enter the gates of OLS, I spotted a child sitting beside a humpy playing with a plastic bag, some rocks, and a few sticks. He was building a miniature humpy: a sad and poignant reflection of how he saw the world around him.

"Bloody hell mate, looks like we are entering Fort Knox!" I exclaimed.

Big blue and white gates prevented us from driving any further down the track. On either side of the gate was a ten foot tall cyclone fence with razor wire hanging in coils off the top.

"It has to be like this. We have food, electricity from generators and water on the inside, not to mention all of the aid that is going to Sudan. There is no other way to keep everyone out."

A security guard in an ill-fitting uniform came out from a side gate and approached our vehicle.

"This is my new boss, he doesn't have any ID yet … it's his first day," said Lameck as he held up his own ID card.

The gate opened and we drove through. I immediately sensed order and energy. To the right were dozens of warehouse-sized tents, with trucks being unloaded and loaded by teams of fit-looking men in tattered clothing. They were moving supplies of bagged wheat flour, tins of cooking oil and medical supplies. In front of us were permanent buildings, painted white and covered by corrugated roofing. Dozens of people, who looked to be from all over the globe, moved between the buildings, or stood in pairs puffing on cigarettes.

Lameck parked in front of the white buildings and gave me a tour of the compound. Accommodation ranged from dormitory-style rooms with fans, to self-contained units fitted with private bathrooms and air conditioning. The senior UN staff had the better options, whilst the most junior NGO workers shared the more modest abodes. I was given a room to myself with a ceiling fan and refrigerator: 'middle class' in the camp hierarchy.

There was a common catering company serving the residents of the OLS camp, and the community all ate and drank together according to a timetable: 08:00–09:00, 12:00–13:00, and 19:00–20:00. A guard force of around sixty men had been employed to survey the perimeter and control the access points to the compound; recruited locally, they represented the handful of people who had benefited from the OLS compound being established in Lokichoggio.

The shared toilet and showering facilities looked primitive. It was hot all year round so cold water was all that was available. The shower block had individual, but roofless, cubicles. Alongside the shower block were the toilets – and these were roofed. The cubicles consisted of a wooden box with a hole cut into the top, placed over a large open hole.

"Be careful if you go to use these during the day … there are so many flies that you can get knocked off your feet!" Lameck joked.

▲　▲　▲

I'd arrived in Lokichoggio during May 2001 to head the five-person team handling the logistics and administration for IRC's operations in southern Sudan. The team, including Lameck, supported dozens of medical training facilities and primary health care centres across the breadth of the southern Sudan area. Being on my third humanitarian mission I found it much easier to get on top of my duties in the office and also connect socially to those with whom I shared the camp facilities. I was slowly feeling like I was part of the aid industry and that I might even know a thing or two about life in a conflict zone. But that was only when I was on the inside of the camp; I was yet to find out that this was not a reflection of reality in a developing country or war zone. I still had a lot more learning to do. But now that I had made a one hundred percent commitment to the aid industry, I began to wonder about making a personal contribution outside of the workplace to help those in need. A series of interactions and conversations with impoverished children would inadvertently trigger a desire to do more.

▲   ▲   ▲

In order to better understand the needs of our operations I regularly visited our medical facilities in Sudan. On one occasion a man in his mid-twenties called John had been allocated as my driver because he spoke excellent English. John was a resident of Akot, a remote place in the centre or southern Sudan where IRC had a field office. We set out to travel by road early in the morning to visit a primary health care centre that was operating fifty kilometres from the IRC field office. I'd been informed the round trip would take all day because of poor road conditions. As we slowly negotiated the pothole riddled road I struck up a conversation with John to help break the ice.

"So how long have you been with the IRC?" I asked.

"I started working four years ago," John told me.

"And all that time you have been working as a driver?"

"Oh, I started initially as a security guard but was then moved to this driving position."

"Rightio, so you're a local lad from Akot?"

"Yep."

"And what were you doing before you joined the IRC?"

"I was in the army, as a fighter."

"How long did you serve with them?"

"Ten years," he replied, after a moment to think about it.

I tried to do the sums. How could he have done four years with the IRC and ten years with the army if he only looked 25 years old? I didn't want to be rude by digging deeper, but couldn't help but satisfy my curiosity. "So, if you don't mind, can I ask how old you are?"

"I am twenty-four years old."

I frowned.

"You are twenty-four years old and have done ten years with the army and four years with the IRC. How old were you when you joined the army?"

"Ten," he answered as though it was obvious, or I was dumb.

My eyes opened wide. "Can you tell me a bit more about your time in the army?" I queried.

"I joined when I was young because I wanted to be with my older brothers. They had been called up by the SPLA a few years before. The SPLA, yeah … the Sudanese People's Liberation Army that is fighting the North?"

"Yep, go on," I said.

"I had four older brothers and we all wanted to fight because my father had died during combat when I was just three. When I first started, I was just moving ammunition and other supplies to the fighters on the front line. But as I got older, I was allowed to start fighting. Eventually I had to leave as all my brothers were killed in action."

"All four of your brothers?" I asked, horrified.

"Yep. There is a rule that each family is entitled to have at least one male back at home. I was the last one left and had to return to support my mother and sisters. That's when I went back to Akot and started working for the IRC."

I stared out through the window thinking about the fact that I was being driven through Sudan by a former child soldier who had lost his father and brothers to the war and who was now responsible for feeding an extensive family. Quietly I hoped he didn't ask me questions about my upbringing in Australia, something I was beginning to understand was quite privileged. Thankfully our conversation stalled.

Later in the day John and I came across a herd of big-horned cattle that were resting on the side of the road. There were about sixty big beasts being held in a small area by their owners.

"Hey John, can we stop? I want to ask these guys some questions and maybe grab a photo," I said.

"No worries," he replied as he slowed the vehicle to a halt.

We both hopped out of the car and walked to a group of old men sitting under the shade of a tree.

"John, can you ask these guys where they are headed?"

"They are moving south-west towards Uganda, that's about 250 kilometres away," John translated.

"Bloody hell, what are they going all that way for?"

"To sell the cattle, they get a much better price down there."

The majority of beasts had impressive horns sprouting upwards for close to a metre in length. I wanted to get a photo and so scanned the herd for the biggest set of horns. Towards the rear I noticed a little boy, not older than twelve, walking amongst the cows and picking up the fresh, steamy cow dung with his bare hands. He tossed it high in the air, hurling it as far into the bush as he could manage.

"Hey John? What's up with this little guy out the back?"

"Well, his job is to hurl dung to prevent a build up of manure that would otherwise contaminate the area."

The old men in charge laughed out loud when I innocently asked to take a picture of the boy, but said it was okay. When the boy realised what I was doing he made a bee-line for the nearest bull. Squatting by its side, he tickled the beast's belly. To my utter astonishment the child washed manure from his hands with the bull's urine. It was the nearest tap and he didn't want to be seen in the picture with poo on his hands!

▲　▲　▲

Reality checks were evident even in the immediate surrounds of the OLS camp. Outside the front gate of Lokichoggio lay an improvised football field. It was a small dusty bit of turf, just slightly larger than a tennis court, the boundaries visibly marked by the UN's fence on one side and a row of thorny shrubs on the other. A group of ten or so boys, aged between eight and fourteen, gathered there most afternoons to play around with whatever they could find. Undeterred by the sweltering afternoon heat, the kids chased after each other, kicking around an old coke can or trying to fly kites made from fishing line and old plastic bags. They didn't have any fancy play equipment or bicycles to keep them entertained, rather they had each other and their childish spirit … and in that they were rich beyond measure.

Whilst in Nairobi on a short break from work I walked past a sports shop and noticed a soccer ball hanging in the front window. I turned and walked inside to enquire about the cost. It was less than ten Aussie dollars and looked to be of reasonable quality. This seemed a small price to pay considering the joy I knew it would bring to those kids. I understood it couldn't solve the issues that surrounded the OLS camp, but I was certain a simple soccer ball would bring a smile to those who were used to playing with improvised toys on the barren playing field.

On the afternoon that I arrived back at the gates of OLS the young boys were gathered as usual, chasing after each other without a care in the world. I asked to be let out of the vehicle before we entered the gates and dived into my bag to locate the shiny black and white ball. As I pulled it out from amongst my clothes I could smell the new leather. Walking onto the dusty field I watched as the boys continued to play, too enthralled by their game to notice my presence. I kicked the ball high up into the air above where they were playing. They stopped, looked up, and watched as the ball went over their heads to the other end of the field. Two of them ran after it but the rest stood still, gazing at me with bemusement. I moved towards them with a big smile on my face.

"Jambo!" I yelled.

"Hello, mista. Jambo, sir."

The two who had chased after the ball raced back towards us, the taller of the two holding the new ball tightly against his torn red t-shirt.

"So, boys, I want to give you this ball so you can play soccer. I am giving it to all of you, not just one or two of you. Do you understand that?"

A couple of them nodded, indicating they understood. I studied the boy holding the ball in his raggedy t-shirt, dirty shorts and bare feet.

"I want you to take the ball home at the end of each night. That doesn't mean you own the ball, and you must make sure that the others can use it if they want to. Is that okay?" I asked.

"Yes, sir," the boy replied.

I looked around at the other boys, at their worn clothing and their snotty noses. Each of them was motionless, as though they had never received a gift before. I glanced back at the boy with the ball, who looked to be one of the older boys and a natural leader of the group.

"You can play football now," I explained simply.

The ball was thrown onto the ground, causing an immediate reaction. The boys had come alive. They all chased after the black and white leather, yelling and screaming with delight whilst jostling for position. As the cloud of dust being kicked up by their frenzy thickened I turned my back and walked towards the OLS gates feeling satisfied that I had done my small bit to help those who endured such harsh and challenging lifestyles.

The next day I took a break in the afternoon, hoping to see the boys kicking up a sizeable cloud of dust around my gift of the day before. To my surprise, the field was empty and the group of boys were sitting under one of the bushes on the outskirts. As I approached I could sense they were not happy.

My first question regarded the whereabouts of the ball. Apparently the kid I had put in charge had taken it to the local market and sold it. I was furious. How could that little brat take something that I had given to the group and sell it? I demanded that they take me immediately to his home. The boys were more than happy to lead me through the humpies to the dwelling of the boy who had been wearing the red raggedy t-shirt. He appeared from the opposite direction as I arrived. Still wearing the same raggedy shirt, worn shorts and bare feet as the day before, he approached us with his head down, not his normal vibrant self at all. I asked to speak with him separately.

"Hey, mate. How are you?" I asked.

"Good," he whimpered, his head still bowed.

"So, what happened to the ball?"

"I had to sell it," he snivelled.

"But, I bought the ball for everyone to use."

"I know, but my mum told me I had to sell it 'cause she needed the money for food."

How blind I had been. My anger turned to a hollow pit of sadness.

Looking around I could see nothing but poverty and despair. Human faeces littered the ground, rubbish was blowing in the wind, and the humpies weren't suitable living quarters for an animal, let alone the family itself.

"I'm really sorry mate. I shouldn't have given you that responsibility." I said.

I had inadvertently caused a rift in the group and felt awful for doing so. Returning to the other group of boys I asked them to accept that their friend had had no choice other than to sell the ball. I think they understood … better than I did, in fact.

A few days later I saw the boys running around after a coke can again. Life, for them, had returned to normal. Although it was pitiful, I felt relieved to see that the group dynamics had recovered so quickly.

▲ ▲ ▲

Joseph claimed to be fourteen. He looked more like ten or eleven to me. He had a noticeable scar running from his forehead to the ridge of his nose. Most afternoons, he ran alongside me as I went for a run along the dried up creek bed on the outside of the camp.

"So mate, how did you get that scar on your face?" I asked, once I felt comfortable that I knew him well enough to enquire.

"My dad threw a rock at me," he replied.

"You're kidding … why did he do that?"

"I'd lost three goats from the family herd. He thought that I'd fallen asleep when I supposed to be looking after them."

"Had you?"

"No, they just got away and I couldn't catch them."

I looked down at my running partner. He wasn't wearing any footwear and so was focused on every foot placement to ensure he avoided the painful rocks and thorns. His little lungs were pumping hard but he barely had a drop of sweat on his brow, he was running well within his limits.

"I'm sorry to hear that mate. So Joseph, the guards at the gate told me that you were waiting around to go for a run with me for most of the day. Don't you have to go to school?" I asked.

"Not really."

"Don't your parents want you to go to school?"

"I don't have any parents," he replied blankly.

Glancing quickly at his huge dark eyes I decided further prying was inappropriate for the moment. Instead I made a point of getting to know him better during the coming weeks, gradually discovering he had run away from his family two years early. After his father had thrown the rock at him, he had panicked and run for three days, arriving in Lokichoggio an exhausted and helpless mess. He was spotted by a man who worked on the inside of the camp but lived on the outside, who was in a position to unofficially adopt the wounded child. He sometimes attended school but as there was little parental supervision or encouragement from the school, he only turned up when he felt like it. The more I learned the more it concerned me that my running routine was distracting him from attending school. Not really knowing the best way to broach the subject, I did my best to prepare for a meaningful chat with the lad.

Food was always a great motivator so after meeting him at the front gate of OLS I took him to the canteen and paid for the smorgasbord. He was overwhelmed by the concept of being able to eat as much as possible, his tiny stomach only able to consume three quarters of the bounty he piled on his plate. During the meal I gently raised my concerns about his lack of attendance at school. To encourage him, I offered to buy a pair of running shoes if he promised to attend school. He agreed.

After lunch we headed off to a stall in the main street that sold second hand footwear. Like the rest of the stalls it was a small tin shed similar in size and composition to a suburban garden shed. Shoes, flip flops, boots and runners hung from the walls and lay in heaps on the ground. Joseph quietly sorted through the piles for a pair he liked. Due to a lifetime spent running around barefooted, or at most wearing flip flops, his feet were wide and hardened, meaning no standard size was going to properly accommodate the abnormal dimensions of his young feet. The pair he settled on was three sizes too long but a snug fit across the top of his foot. At least he was happy.

"Would you like some socks as well?" I asked.

"Some what?" he wanted to know.

"Socks … to wear with your running shoes," I explained.

"Okay," he said, sounding a little unsure.

I took down a pair of white socks wrapped in clear plastic from the wall and handed them to Joseph. He looked at them long and hard, clearly confused. This boy had never worn socks before.

The next day I exited the gate and spotted Joseph on the side of the track waiting patiently for me. No running shoes and no white socks.

"Joseph? Where are your running shoes?"

"At home," he answered simply.

"Why aren't your wearing them for the run?"

"I am saving them for special occasions," he replied proudly.

Map of Aghanistan

FIVE
AID AT ITS WORST

AFGHANISTAN SNAPSHOT

1800s: *The Great Game unfolds; a fight for control over the subcontinent between Britain and Russia. Afghanistan's geographic location puts it on centre stage.*

1919: *Full sovereignty is given back to Afghanistan.*

1970s: *Islamic fundamentalists and pro-western liberals jostle for control of the country.*

1979-1989: *Russian troops occupy Afghanistan. The Mujahadeen, a local militia supplemented with foreign fighters, fight a bloody and heavily destructive war against the Russian occupation. Russian troops withdraw in 1989.*

Early '90s: *The Mujahadeen fail to maintain national control and regional war lords take charge by force. The country is fractionalised and in a state of anarchy. Kidnappings, drug trade, extortion and assassinations are commonplace.*

1994: *A small group of strict Islamic fundamentalists overrun an outpost* *near to Kandahar in the south and kill the garrison commander for raping a young girl. The group call themselves the Taliban and are initially supported by the community to eliminate the lawless behaviour of the warlords.*

September 1996: *The Taliban has rapidly taken over 90% of Afghanistan and Sharia Law (combined with ancient Pashtun tribal codes) is implemented across the country.*

September 2001: *Osama Bin Laden orchestrates the 9/11 attacks against the USA from his camps inside Afghanistan.*

March 2002: *Squiz arrives in Pakistan in preparation for Afghanistan.*

In the first seventy-eight days of operations, from 7 October until 23 December 2002, the USA flew just under 6500 aerial strike missions over the rugged lands of Afghanistan. In total 17,500 deadly payloads fell from the sky seeking to obliterate Osama Bin Laden's terrorist camps and those that harboured his network; the Taliban regime.

One of the most devastatingly effective munitions used was the American-made cluster bomb. Although cluster bombs have come in many shapes and forms over the years, they are all designed around the same concept: a large 'mother' bomb opens up at a pre-programmed altitude to disperse hundreds of little bombs designed to strike a large area on the ground. The bombs used in Afghanistan contained 202 little 'bomblets' and had a failure rate of 5%; which meant that around ten bomblets remained live after hitting the ground. This was considered an acceptable failure rate and sought after by the military tacticians as it actually prevented the enemy from moving within that area for fear of triggering the remaining live munitions.

Hearing of these 'fine' results, one bright spark back in Washington devised a 'hearts and minds' campaign or good will gesture. The operation was designed to ease the suffering and discomfort inflicted on innocent civilians by the cluster bombs that fell near to urban areas. Without much thought, the decision was made to drop processed food rations from the sky, meaning large quantities of food could be quickly dispersed across the country with minimal risk to American soldiers on the ground.

The food parcels were deliberately wrapped in yellow plastic envelopes to help with identification. Word soon spread that rations were being dropped from the sky, prompting kids to rush into the fields in search of the golden parcels. Many food parcels landed in areas where cluster bombs had been previously dropped, and where 5% of bombs were still live. To make things worse, the cluster bomblets being used in Afghanistan at the time were also made from a hardened yellow plastic housing. Hundreds of children made the devastating or fatal error of picking up an unexploded bomb.

▲　▲　▲

I began my journey into Afghanistan from the northern Pakistan city of Peshawar. The IRC had been in Pakistan for many years assisting the needs of the two million or so Afghani refugees who had fled the decades of relentless fighting. Donor money came in thick and fast in an attempt to alleviate the inevitable suffering of those returning to the collapsed war-torn state. IRC was not shy in putting up its hand to get a slice of the action. As the aid money started to flow, IRC scrambled to set up. By the end of February 2002, not long after I arrived in Kabul, IRC was using the easy money to prepare for the arrival of dozens of humanitarian experts. Our programme strategy and depth was weak. I noticed for the first time a blatant over-commitment that was driven by the desire to appear bigger and more influential than other NGOs. It was as though we were a private firm in a market economy, striving for maximum market share. I began to question the purity of our work, something I hadn't considered previously as a novice aid worker.

But regardless of my questions, I got on with what I'd been employed to do. As in East Timor, I was focusing on how best to keep staff and operations alive amid the ongoing conflict. In this instance I partnered up with a super bright individual from the States called 'Long' John Moore, a.k.a. LJ. LJ and I based ourselves out of Kabul and took turns to visit our regional offices, helping them set up security protocols for the offices and operations. My first trip was to the western city of Herat.

All I could see whilst heading in for the landing at Herat was a large dust plateau, barely vegetated – only a few thorny bushes. There was no perimeter fence around the airport, just lumps of twisted metal lining the runway; the remnants of cargo hulls and war machinery. Awaiting our arrival were twenty men wearing the traditional Salwar Kameez, a knee-length over shirt that draped over baggy pyjama-style pants. The men were standing in front of a derelict building, riddled with bullet holes and in need of a coat of paint. It was the airport terminal, no longer serviced with electricity or running water.

I linked up with the IRC driver and we drove ten kilometres along a dry, rocky road to reach the outskirts of Herat. The desert plateau quickly turned into a green haven, with tall trees and the odd patch of grass. Two-metre mud walls lined with shards of broken glass stretched alongside the road, providing a shield for the households within, similar to the visual protection that a burkha provided for the women walking in the streets. Looking ahead, the walls gave the road a corridor-like appearance.

It wasn't until we reached a blue gate on the right that I had my first look at the inside of a compound. The gate swung open as we arrived, the guards attentive to the traffic. A large two storey concrete building was surrounded by a lavish green garden and gravel car park. This was the IRC office in Herat. It could have been a palace were it not for the fact that it was in Afghanistan. Electricity was sporadic and supplement-ed by a noisy generator. The water mains had not worked since the Rus-sian era and so supply was now dependant on deliveries from a donkey and cart. The interior was grimy and stunk of body odour, a reflection of many years of poor cleaning and poor hygiene standards. The atmo-sphere was hierarchical and male orientated, an unavoidable result of only having male employees, all of whom were desperate to keep control of their employment.

Of the twenty men working at the office I thought that Roohullah, our Administration Officer, appeared to be one of the more forward and liberal thinkers.

"My wife has gone back to university now that the Taliban have left," he boasted. I was eager to meet a modern day Afghani household so when he invited me over to his home for a meal I readily accepted.

Another colleague from IRC's Herat office, Syed, joined me for the occasion. We met Roohullah at his gate and were shown to the front living room. Covering the entire floor was a brightly coloured Afghan carpet with matching pillows of dark red and blue hues. In the centre of the room was a tray set with glasses and a bottle of coke.

"Please Squiz, have a seat," Roohullah said.

Syed followed me as I sat cross-legged and leant against a pillow. After Roohullah poured us both a drink I asked if we were expecting anyone else.

"No, just the three of us today," said Roohullah.

"Okay, your wife couldn't make it, Syed?" I enquired.

"She is at home. She is not allowed to attend these gatherings. Roohullah and I are not family so she must not meet him." he informed me.

I looked at Roohullah, in search of clarification.

"He is right Squiz. My wife also is not allowed to meet anyone outside of our immediate family."

"What about her old school friends?"

"Not anymore, she has a family to look after and raise," said Roohullah.

"But what happens if she sees a friend she knows in the street? Are you saying she can't go up and say hello?" I asked courteously.

"Both of our wives must wear the burkha when in public. They are not allowed to talk to anyone."

I sat back and thought how tough it must be in the families where the husbands aren't as "liberal" as Roohullah.

Roohullah stood up and left the room. A silence hung in the air until he popped his head through the door and said simply, "Come."

Syed and I obediently stood up and walked across the hallway to another room just like the one we had left. Lying flat on the ground was a plastic table cloth covered with a spread of food. We sat around the outside of the plastic sheet eying the barbecued mutton, chicken on skewers, grilled onions and tomatoes, cucumbers, carrots, yoghurt and naan bread in front of us. It should have been a feast for the whole family but with male guests in the house it would only be men eating on this occasion.

Roohullah had two daughters, a wife, and he cared for his mother. The only family members that we were allowed to have contact with was the youngest daughter, because she was only five years old. As we ate, we could hear the others moving about the house, shuffling between rooms like servants. Roohullah's wife had cooked our meal and prepared the room whilst we socialised over the cool coke. Once we'd eaten it was her job to clean up after us – after we'd vacated the room.

"In Australia, it is traditional that a guest thanks the host for preparing a meal," I said boldly. "Could I just quickly say hello to your wife to show my appreciation?"

"I am sorry, Squiz. I cannot allow that," Roohullah answered coldly.

"Yeah, but come on mate, surely it wouldn't hurt if I just quickly said 'hi and thanks'."

"No, she cannot meet with you," he said stonily.

A few minutes later a young face appeared in front of the window. Roohullah yelled out immediately in what sounded like stern words, prompting the face to disappear in an instant.

"I am sorry Squiz for raising my voice. That was my other daughter, she was trying to have a look at you as she hasn't seen an Australian before," Roohullah said.

"Rightio … how old is she?" I asked.

"Nine years old," he said.

▲ ▲ ▲

Over the next five months as I moved around Afghanistan I spoke with only four Afghan women. All of them worked for IRC and I was only permitted to speak with them about work issues. I was informed it would be offensive to strike up a social conversation in the hallway. If it were not for the female aid workers and journalists, I could have altogether forgotten what a female face looked like. LJ summed it up after a few months when we were driving to the office one morning.

"Woowhoo … Squizza!" yelled LJ.

Three women, clad in blue burkhas, were walking along the sidewalk.

"Check out the ankles on those chicks!" said LJ.

Sadly I had to agree, they looked pretty good.

Although LJ and I both laughed about the changes we had made to our fetishes on this occasion, seeing the burkha on a daily basis pushed me to think of how I could help generate awareness of the garment on behalf of those who were forced to wear it. I had learnt the hard way in Sudan through the soccer ball and running shoes that trying to fix a problem at the frontline without a strategic plan can sometimes be mis-guided and counterproductive. I bought a burkha from the local market and packed it away for another day. This time I would take the issue out of the country to try and help raise awareness on a larger scale and gen-erate some interest in the situation that Afghani women face.

Just before leaving the country I was ecstatic to hear of a story that helped erode the image that women in Afghanistan were suppressed and powerless. A small article had been written by a foreign journalist on gender roles in Afghanistan. Interestingly, she had begun her survey in Kabul during the height of the Taliban's reign in the late 90s. In those days women customarily walked five paces behind their spouse as a sign of submission to the superiority of the husband.

The journalist returned after the fall of the Taliban and noticed that women were still walking behind their husbands, in fact they were walking even further behind the men and appeared much happier about the custom. When the journalist approached one of the Afghani women and asked, "With the removal of the Taliban, and the new government recognising the equality of women, why do you now seem happy with the old custom that you used to try and change?"

The woman replied simply: "Landmines".

SIX
BURKHA MAN RUNS MARATHON

Squirrell nuts about running

FINALLY, we can put a name to the face of VB Man, the bloke who ran the Melbourne Marathon with a VB carton on his back and a green can in his hand to go with his green singlet.

The runner was Mark Squirrell, who clocked 3hr 37min for the 42.2km from Frankston to Melbourne. That might be a reasonable time for some and a slow time for others, but Mark does have a reason.

"I did it as a bit of joke, as I've just come back from Afghanistan after five very 'dry' months, and so I have been living it up over the last few weeks," he said.

"I had very little time to train. I literally entered three weeks before the event as I only arrived in Australia a few days before that."

For those of you wondering what he was doing in Afghanistan, Mark works for the International Rescue

Committee, which operates in more than 30 developing countries.

This story ran in three newspapers and a glossy sports magazine. The collective attention was sufficient to secure me an appointment at Australia's biggest brewery. The stunt had inadvertently drawn the attention of the media, much to the delight of the work unit responsible for promoting Victoria Bitter (VB). I rang my old friend Goz [who was also in Melbourne at the time] to tell him I'd managed to organise a meeting with the sponsorship managers for VB as he was in the process of organising a concert to raise funds and awareness for the people of East Timor. We both attended the meeting to see if the brewery could make a donation. Two months later, as Goz was standing outside the Collingwood Town Hall on the afternoon of his fundraising event, a huge truck branded with 'VB' pulled up alongside the footpath.

"Hey, mate," called Goz. "I'm Luke Gosling. Are you here to drop off some beers?"

"Yeah, I've got a bit of stuff for you. Let's have a look."

The driver pulled out a running sheet from his back pocket. "We're looking at around seventy boxes of VB, thirty boxes of light beer and forty boxes of soft drinks."

The overwhelmingly generous consignment was duly unloaded, contributing significantly to the monies raised later that evening. Once the donation was in hand a very happy Goz flew out to Darwin to kick off the awareness aspect of the campaign. He had the attention-grabbing idea of sea-kayaking solo from Darwin to Dili, arriving on the 19 May, East Timors new Independence Day.

President Xanana Gusmao was so impressed by Goz's selfless and gallant effort to raise money and media awareness for the impoverished island that he invited my good friend to collaborate with his Ministry of Sport so a bigger event could be organised in 2004. This brief interlude with the president was the beginnings of a nationwide adventure race which saw teams of four people coming from all corners of the earth to compete and raise money. The event would be called the Timor Challenge and would inspire me to bring a team all the way from the Middle East, aptly named 'Team Middle East'.

The publicity generated by Goz's efforts highlighted the value of creating awareness ... and the fact that sometimes returns were greater in the long run when the hearts of the ignorant were shaken. Having experienced first-hand the power of the media during my Melbourne Marathon I decided it was my turn to also raise the awareness of an issue that I was passionate about. I chose to do my bit to fight the oppression of women in Afghanistan by running a full marathon whilst draped in the Afghan Burkha.

With a solid four-month training regime, I would be perfectly placed for the start of the Athens Marathon 2003.

Major media attention was anticipated at the marathon as the world was intrigued to see if the local authorities were adequately prepared for the up-coming 2004 Olympic Games. Masses of people were stretching against a nearby fence or bent over limbering up their leg muscles by the time I arrived at the start line. The unmistakable aroma of sports cream emanated from those who had massaged their muscles in preparation for the enduring challenge. I stood by with the burkha draped over my left shoulder, scrutinising the sea of colourful outfits worn by my competitors. While the burkha hung, scrunched up like a towel, I was able to stand alone without prejudice or concern from those around me. This was welcome anonymity as I needed a few moments to do my own warm ups, warm ups of a mental nature.

An announcement over the P.A. system declared the five-minute warning. My heart was pounding with anticipation. I wasn't concerned about the race itself but rather the reaction of public and media alike when I put on the burkha. I didn't want anyone to think I was mocking another culture and for a moment began to question the wisdom of my decision. Slowly I moved forward with the crowd as we bunched together en masse. I wasn't interested in being up front, fighting my way across the start line. Rather I needed space to ensure I had every opportunity to slip into my regular running pace.

The thirty second announcement was made. I could wait no longer. Nervously I slid the burkha over my head. All I could see was blue. I had to feel for the small mesh opening with both hands, twisting the material around to the right so my eyes lined up with the criss-crossed eyehole. I let go of the inside and moved my hands out from underneath the oppressive garment. The hat-like portion of the burkha rested on the top of my scalp. I pulled down hard on the draping material to fasten the burkha to my head, aligning the eyehole. I sensed people around me were beginning to walk forward. The race was about to begin. I turned to the left and then to the right to regain my bearing realising I'd lost all peripheral vision.

The starter's gun had gone off whilst I'd been flapping around with the burkha. I took a few deep breaths and relaxed myself, knowing the next few hours were going to be tough. Just before stepping over the start line the man in front of me picked up his pace and stepped into a slow jog. The choke point at the starting gate was being eased as the road ahead widened. It didn't take long from that point for me to work out that burkhas were not well balanced. Two-thirds of the material hung down to about ankle height while the front third was designed to extend only as far as a woman's waist. This prevented the wearer from tripping over the material and accidentally ripping the whole thing from their body. However, the larger section that draped over the shoulders and back was purposefully tapered so the wearer could pull the ends of the longer sections towards the midriff and cover up the front of the body when they have their hands free and are not walking quickly. There was no chance that I would be voluntarily pulling the longer sections around in front of me as I would have tripped over. By leaving the burkha to drape naturally whilst running, the weight of the back sections began pulling on the rest of the burkha. After fifty metres of running the whole garment started to slide off the back of my head. I pulled down on the front section and repositioned the mesh over my eyes, grabbed a fistful of material hanging over my chest, and pulled down hard to lock it in place, but every couple of minutes I had to pull down on the front of it to counterbalance the heavy back.

At the 2.5 kilometre mark it felt more like my marathon was in fighting the burkha rather than running the race. I passed the water stand without noticing it. At the five kilometre mark I had managed to settle into a slow but steady pace, noticed the next sign indicating the water stand and moved over to the right of the road and picked up two plastic cups from a drinks table. It was difficult to swill down a drink when running at the best of times, but with a burkha and limited vision to keep balanced it was virtually impossible. I ended up wearing most of the water from the first cup on my singlet.

I poured the other cup of water over the top of my burkha and waited to feel the cool sensation filter through to my overheating head. This proved to be another mistake as I miscalculated the pour and a large portion spilled down the front of the garment. The synthetic material became so heavy it no longer flapped freely in the wind… it stuck to my skin, holding tight against my face. When I breathed in deeply it suddenly felt as though I was suffocating. The wet material felt like plastic as it blocked air from entering my hardworking lungs. I panicked, reaching quickly for the material clinging to my front to reopen my airways. Until it dried out I was forced to run with at least one arm extended out from my body to keep the burkha from sticking to my face. It was certainly living up to the conclusions I'd predicted when witnessing the garment back in Afghanistan – irritating, claustrophobic and punishing, especially when worn in overpowering heat.

As I settled into a sustainable pace and learnt how to overcome the various pitfalls, I took the time to observe those around me. By the time I had reached the half way point I realised that no one had said a word to me. Those who overtook me looked straight ahead, deliberately ignoring me. Spectators spotted me and often kept their eyes peeled on the bouncing blue sheet but made no comment. Did I exist? I felt alone and removed from the activity, quite the opposite from my run in the Melbourne marathon. The isolation and rejection fuelled my determination; the determination to see the challenge out.

At one point I noticed a photo journalist snapping away at the competitors as they ran towards his location. As he spotted the blue burkha through the lens he lowered the camera, puzzled by what he was seeing. He held the camera stubbornly by his side as I ran past. Had it all been for nothing?

The beating sun bounced off the newly paved black road as if to mock me. Other competitors ripped off their t-shirts in an attempt to quell the sizzling heat, but such freedom was not something within my grasp. Determined, I continued on in my solitary confinement.

At the 34-kilometre mark, the road wound around the base of Mount Pendeli and began descending towards the central business district of Athens. By this point I concluded the only positive aspect of my burkha burden was that it distracted me from muscle fatigue and exhaustion. Those who had been running in synchronisation with the blue burkha continued to ignore its existence, even though we had been together for three and a half hours.

"How are you going, mate?" I asked whilst overtaking a familiar body.

There was no reply. Maybe he didn't speak English. Maybe he did.

I guess we all had our sights set on the Panathinaikon Stadium, the original Olympic sports ground built in 1896, for this was the final objective. Tricking myself, I used the finish line as a motivation to pick up my pace over the last agonising kilometres. A few thousand spectators had dotted the white stands that encircled the refurbished modern day running track. Hoping for an adrenaline rush, inspired by the crowd, to kick me into an even higher gear to run the last two hundred metres, I spurred myself on. The rush of energy never came; the spectators were quiet and unresponsive to the man running down the track in a burkha. I stumbled across the finish line just seconds after the clock reached four hours.

Slowing to a walk, relieved to give my muscles a rest, I noticed that temporary aluminium fencing lined the track ahead to keep us from entering the stands on the right. On the inside of the running track a row of journalists loitered to interview runners at random. Large TV cameras on tripods captured the stories of those who had completed the revamped course in advance of the world's best. I looked through the blue mesh at the journalists, none of them acknowledged my presence. No one was interested in finding out the story behind the burkha.

Beyond the journalists was a row of long tables. Volunteers stood next to them holding up plastic bags filled with token gifts and a gold coloured medal. I thanked the lady who handed me mine but she looked obstinately in the direction of the journalists and made no comment. I removed the burkha and stuffed it into the plastic bag.

I had never felt so isolated and abandoned, a feeling I concluded was also felt by women in Afghanistan. My appreciation for what it was like to live under a burkha had been solidified but my wider efforts of stimulating conversation and interest in the issue had failed. I could not blame the journalists for ignoring me; I suppose I must have looked like a 'nut' to them.

Map of Palestinian Territories

SEVEN
MEETING ARAFAT

PALESTINE SNAPSHOT

From the beginning: *Islam, Christianity and Judaism claim significant holy sites exist for their respective religions within the area currently known as Israel and Palestine.*

1516–WWI: *The region is under the control of the Ottoman Empire.*

1917: *Administrative control of the lands to the south of Lebanon, west of the Jordan River, and north of the Sinai Peninsula are given to Great Britain.*

1920s & '30s: *Significant numbers of Jews migrate from Europe to Palestine to evade ever-increasing persecution against their faith.*

WWII: *The Jewish holocaust claims six million lives.*

1947: *The newly formed United Nations partitions the land into two separate states; one Arab (West Bank and Gaza Strip) and one Jewish (Israel). The fight for these lands begins in earnest.*

1948: *A collection of neighbouring countries come to the aid of the Palestinian people. The attacks are unsuccessful.*

Early 1950s: *A small group of Palestinians, living abroad, form Fatah (Movement for the National Liberation of Palestine). Yasser Arafat takes charge of Fatah.*

1956 and 1967: *Israel defends attacks by neighbouring Arab countries. Israel occupies the West Bank and Gaza Strip after the Six Day War in 1967.*

1970s and '80s: *Arafat resorts to terrorist style attacks to fight the occupation. The harsh occupation and settlement growth (inside the West Bank and Gaza Strip) by Israel causes the Palestinians to rise up in 1987 in what's called the First Intifada.*

1991: *A brokered peace deal is made and Arafat returns as the President of Palestine. Arafat is awarded the 1994 Nobel Peace Prize.*

1990s: *The Israeli occupation continues and Israeli settlements expand in the West Bank and Gaza Strip.*

2000: *Second Intifada kicks off. Palestinian suicide bombs rock Israel. Arafat is again labelled a terrorist.*

2002: *Arafat is cornered in his compound and held under siege.*

February 2003: *Squiz deploys to Palestine.*

"Holy shit, this guy is going to be tough" was the first thing that went through my mind when I met Mick.

Mick was a burly Brit who had been appointed to take charge of a global network of security officers working for the United Nations World Food Programme (WFP). In February 2003 I had been appointed as one of his five security officers, arriving on the Mediterranean Island of Cyprus to prepare for the unfolding humanitarian crisis in Iraq. Despite my lack of knowledge about WFP I was expected to hit the ground running.

Some background research for my role as a Field Security Officer informed me that WFP was a relatively new player within the humanitarian organisations working under the umbrella of the United Nations. The foundations were laid in the early sixties when the United Nations

Food and Agriculture Organisation created a programme to assist with the immediate food needs of vulnerable populations during or after a natural or man-made emergency. Sadly, the demands for such an organisation grew exponentially so WFP soon became big enough to stand on its own two feet. By the time I joined the team, WFP was the largest UN humanitarian organisation in terms of staff numbers, and had fed over seventy-three million people in the previous twelve months.

In order to deliver food, WFP relied on a diverse and interconnected global logistics system. There were planes, trains, ships, trucks, elephants, mules, yaks, and people carrying food items such as wheat flour, maize, rice, oil, and sugar to those who would otherwise go to bed with an empty stomach. The extensive logistics set-up required security officers such as myself. During natural disasters, when large populations were searching desperately for food to sustain themselves, it would be the security officer's responsibility to liaise and co-ordinate with local leaders on the ground to facilitate the safe and orderly delivery of food. The more difficult challenges for WFP arose when distributions were required within a conflict zone or lawless state. In these cases, a WFP security officer played a vital role in ensuring the safety of all WFP employees and the protection of equipment and food commodities. The 2003 Iraq mission would be an example of this.

The team I was a part of would sweep into Iraq about three days after the Coalition Forces to conduct an initial security assessment and, should the situation be favourable, help to facilitate the arrival of our staff and food convoys. We were each kitted out with a satellite phone, laptop, GPS, emergency trauma kit, VHF communications, NBC (Nuclear-Biological-Chemical) suits and camping gear. Just when I was starting to feel ready to tackle the Iraq war, Mick came looking for me.

"So, Squiz, how's the training going?"

"Ahhh ... good thanks. I'm really getting a lot from it," I replied.

"Okay, that's good to hear. Look, Squiz, I am in a bit of an awkward situation at the moment. I will cut to the chase. Our security officer in Palestine has just terminated his contract. I'm worried that if Saddam starts lobbing scud missiles over towards Israel like he did during the first Gulf War, we might be caught without a security officer on the ground. Would you be interested in heading that way?"

The West Bank and Gaza Strip instead of Iraq – hey, both sounded as equally challenging and I didn't want to disappoint.

"No worries, Mick."

For the first time in ten days I saw a smile on Mick's face. He was human after all.

"Great, I'll kick-start the transfer and hopefully we can get you across there shortly. Have a quick word with Charlie. Both he and I need to give you a briefing before you head off. It's quite a complex situation you're heading in to."

As it turned out, that was the understatement of the century!

Yasser Arafat's lower lip began to twitch. A tense silence hung over the room like a shroud. Everyone was poised, awaiting his next move. He was gearing up to give us a verbal bashing so I stared directly into the eyes of this infamous ruler in an effort to display my commitment to what he was about to say.

"The Palestinian people are being slaughtered in Nablus! Innocent civilians are being encircled and killed by the Israeli murderers right at this moment. How can this be allowed?"

Silence.

"When will this stop?"

Silence.

"How can the United Nations allow this to continue?"

Silence.

I sat upright, stiff as a board.

Arafat had the full attention of everyone seated at the round table in his bombed-out headquarters. Even the slightest of movements would have been enough to attract his penetrating, spine-chilling stare.

▲　▲　▲

On the day of the meeting I had been driving the lead vehicle in the convoy of three Land Cruisers heading from Jerusalem to Ramallah, the largest city in the West Bank and the unofficial capital of Palestine. The distance between Ramallah and Jerusalem was no more than ten kilometres, but depending on the circumstances the trip could take many hours. There were a series of checkpoints manned by Israeli soldiers through which we had to pass when leaving Jerusalem. Getting out was not normally an issue but rather it was the checkpoints closer to Ramallah that caused a delay as the Israeli Defence Force (IDF) monitored, controlled and searched all vehicles wanting to enter the city.

On this day we were a little lucky, aided by the fact that I had been in contact with the IDF in advance, hoping to prevent delays. We had a tight schedule and could not afford to have the important mission of senior WFP executives impeded unnecessarily. Even with a week's notice and numerous meetings with the IDF, the guarantee to move unhindered through the West Bank was not a hundred percent assured. I was therefore more than relieved when we passed through the last remaining checkpoint and were only minutes away from Arafat's compound, the Mukataa.

The rear gates creaked open to let us into a waiting bay with just enough space for three vehicles. Palestinian soldiers immediately surrounded us as the gates thudded shut. In front of us was a newly paved black road that disappeared into a jungle of twisted metal and broken cement. The devastation was from the 2002 siege on Arafat. Israeli soldiers had surrounded the compound with tanks and systematically flattened the buildings with massive armoured bulldozers. Arafat was forced to retreat into the basement of the last remaining building. Since that time he had been held inside the compound under virtual house arrest.

A man in an olive green uniform with an AK-47 slung over his shoulder approached my vehicle and motioned for me to wind down my window.

"Good morning," I said politely. "We are from WFP and have an appointment with the President. My name is Squiz. I've been in contact with Husein Husein."

He raised his left hand with his palm facing me and gave me a nod to acknowledge that he understood. He turned and spoke into a small handheld radio as I held my breath trying to look as though I expected to be accepted with open arms. Seconds later the radio made a scratchy reply and he again turned to face me.

"Go. Turn right," he commanded, pointing vaguely off to the right.

I proceeded slowly. Rubble of concrete, car bodies, logs, rocks, and general rubbish on either side of the road rose to between fifteen and thirty feet in the air. There was no chance of getting lost as the road meandered through the mess without any options other than straight ahead.

After a few bends to the left and right, the road began to straighten. The rubble diminished and the road opened up to the width of a basket ball court. In front of us stood the famous building that had been spared during the siege. It was two storeys high and about two standard rooms in width. The left hand side of the building had collapsed during the fighting and so the external walls were in fact the remains of the previous internal walls. I noticed a rudimentary set of stairs had been constructed to allow access to the new front door.

With a sense of urgency I turned off the engine and got out of the car, scanning past the stairs and across the car park looking for Husein Husein. He was nowhere to be seen. Undeterred I moved forward, relieved to observe that the remaining Palestinian soldiers all looked relaxed and welcoming.

The speed at which we were entering this highly sensitive area was quite surprising. I didn't want to stop a good thing and so I let our senior staff go with the flow. As they disembarked from the two rear vehicles a man came out and asked them to move straight into the building. My boss greeted him in a way which indicated he had obviously met him before.

That was it for me. My job was complete. Our guys were delivered safely and they were now linked up with counterparts they trusted. I waited for them to enter the building before returning to my car.

"Squiz?"

I turned. My boss's head was poking out the main door.

"You should come too," he said.

"Okay..."

I locked the car and scuttled towards the main doors. When I entered there was a soldier pointing for me to go straight up the stairwell. I took the stairs two at a time, wanting to reach the boss before he went into the meeting. At the top I could only see one door open along a ten-metre passageway to the right. There were soldiers standing every three metres or so with their hands firmly clenched to their AK-47s. One of them pointed to the open door and nodded with his head for me to enter. I paused and looked back at him. I wanted to explain that I was not here for the meeting but just needed to speak quickly with my boss. Before the words came out of my mouth I realised there wouldn't be any point – he probably didn't speak English.

I looked back down the hallway. It was dimly lit with only faint shards of light winding their way in from the outside world to this alternate universe from the stairwell and open door. Despite the lack of illumination it was nonetheless excruciatingly clear that the soldiers were hardened and poised to take action at a moment's notice.

I spotted my boss walking back to the side of a large oval conference table. I strode into the room with feigned confidence.

Yasser Arafat's welcoming smile took me completely by surprise. He was shaking the hands of the Palestinian who had greeted my boss downstairs. My boss turned to me and said, "Stand behind that seat." It wasn't really appropriate to ask him what he wanted.

On the table in front of Yasser Arafat were piles of files and documents, a box of tissues, an elaborate pen holder and a small Palestinian flag. Introductions were being made by the man who had come out to meet my boss. He didn't have a clue who I was and so simply ignored my sudden appearance. At that point my boss turned to me and whispered, "I need you to join us … to help balance out the numbers on our side of the table."

As our guys sat on one side of the table, the other side filled up with nervous-looking Palestinians. Through the conversation, I gathered they were from the Ministry of Agriculture and had helped WFP implement projects on behalf of the governing Palestinian Authority. This was a rare opportunity for them to meet their devoted leader in person.

I knew that I too should have been nervous, but there was no time for nerves. I'd literally fallen into the seat that saw me having a meeting, face to face, with President Yasser Arafat.

For the first five minutes there was a briefing from the Palestinian guys about how WFP was helping enormously to feed the affected people. This was done first in Arabic and then English. Our side replied with many polite words of appreciation for the continued support of our programmes by the Palestinian Authority and Ministry of Agriculture. Just as the translation into Arabic began Arafat moved forward, grabbed a tissue, lent back into his chair and wiped his forehead. We all watched with concern. The translation continued.

A soldier quietly moved behind Arafat and began unravelling what looked like a plastic pipe. I was totally transfixed as Arafat closed his eyes and continued to wipe his forehead. The soldier extended the pipe and placed a clear mask over Arafat's mouth and nose. As Arafat held the mouthpiece to his head the soldier knelt down to find the on/off switch. Click.

There was a dull buzzing noise and the Arabic translation stopped.

Arafat looked over at our side of the table, white and frail. I thought he was going to drop dead on the spot. He tried to apologise, but his words were barely audible beneath the mask. He started patting his chest, continuing to look at us with his deeply-set dark eyes. Then suddenly he removed his mask.

"It's my lungs," he gasped, immediately replacing the mask over his face.

I tried not to stare, unable to reconcile the image in front of me with the man's reputation. One of the world's most formidable iron leaders had been reduced to a shadowy, sickly, fragile man. Yet even suffering from obvious ailments he still demonstrated his resolute courage and determination by not being afraid to expose his condition to strangers.

We sat and listened to the buzzing noise for what felt like an eternity before the soldier who had handed Arafat the mask started to explain.

"The President has been suffering from lung problems ever since he was forced to stay inside these confined spaces. He needs to have access to his air purifying respirator at least every hour. We are so sorry that you have to see him like this, but unless the Israelis allow him to leave this dusty compound, he will continue to suffer."

We could do little but sit in disbelief witnessing a poor old man in desperate need of help.

After a few minutes Arafat removed his mask and handed it back to his aide. Leaning forward he quietly whispered, "My English ... not very good ... I will use a translator."

I was impressed with his willingness to continue the meeting under such circumstances, wondering how I might have reacted in his place.

Speaking in Arabic the President addressed his Palestinian colleagues. The language was working like medicine. By the time he finished both his volume and pace had increased to what I suspected was his normal feisty self. The translator explained he was talking about the food shortages in the West Bank due to roads being closed by the Israelis, the recent fighting in the West Bank city of Nablus, and the purported atrocities carried out by the IDF. This definitely wasn't where we wanted the conversation to go.

Our guy diverted the discussion back solely to the food situation and asked again how we could strengthen our cooperation. The translation into Arabic did not last long; in fact I was not at all convinced that the full message was conveyed.

Arafat turned to our side and locked his gaze with each us in turn. His lips began to twitch as he launched into a description of the suffering endured by the Palestinian people due to the occupation of the Palestinian territories by the IDF. This time he was speaking in English and there was no sign that he was short for words. His volume increased once more, his hand gestures becoming animated and perfectly synchronised with his voice. His twitching mouth was like a runaway freight train; apparently he had no control over it whatsoever. This man was passionate to the bone about the plight of his people and any attempt to halt the bombardment of rhetoric on our part would have been fruitless. Not only was he talking about the current situation but also explaining in detail the events of the previous ten years that had led to him being ostracized.

Again the diminutive President stared at every one of us systematically. When his gaze connected with mine I felt it burn through my entire body as if a solar flare had just plunged through my soul. I sat motionless, not wanting to run the risk of any inadvertent movement being misinterpreted.

A door quietly opened and closed behind me. I turned to see Husein Husein enter the room. We momentarily made eye contact, but his intent was clearly to speak with the President. He walked over and whispered into Arafat's ear without any concern for what the President was saying.

Arafat asked if we would be willing to have a few photos taken by the local media. After our positive reply Husein Husein returned to the door. It was no sooner opened than a swarm of journalists flooded the room. I didn't know which way to look. Were we pretending to carry on with our meeting or were we posing for the cameras? This stuff was all new to me. I took my lead from the Palestinians across the table. Even though the paparazzi were going crazy, Arafat was still firmly in control. Half of them were snapping away to their heart's content while the other half stood fast with their shoulder-mounted TV cameras.

Arafat stood up and lent forward to engage in a presidential hand-shake with our senior official. Was he going to give him the famous Yasser Arafat kiss, I wondered, but today was not the day. Instead we all had the opportunity to walk past and get our photo with the President.

When the meeting concluded we were ushered back down the stairs faster than I'd climbed them. As I drove towards the gates of the compound, I began to reflect on the previous forty-five minutes. Was it orchestrated or was it just a genuine set of circumstances? Was all of the rubble deliberately left in the compound to remind visitors of the recent siege? For me it didn't matter; it was a rare privilege to have been part of such a close encounter with a man so pivotal in shaping recent world history.

It also fired me up, something that I needed after my bleak attempt to raise awareness of the Afghan burkha in Athens. Arafat had demon-strated unquestionable passion and empathy for the Palestinian people. Whether he was a terrorist or a Nobel Peace prize winner, he had devoted his life to fighting for the rights of his people. For five decades he had not allowed obstacles or failed attempts to detract him. So when an email came from my good mate Goz, I instantly recognised an opportunity to do something personally for the Middle East crisis.

EIGHT
TEAM MIDDLE EAST

At the request of the President of Timor Leste (formerly East Timor), the international sports race [prompted by Goz's paddle from Darwin] was being organised with dual aims: to promote peace, and to celebrate the Timor Leste Independence Day on 19 May. With Goz at the helm, I knew it would be good fun, well organised and worthy. I dropped him a line to let him know that I wanted to be involved.

The three-day adventure race required mixed teams of four persons to kayak, cycle, and run through three regions of Timor Leste, spending a day of the race in each region. The race would culminate in Dili, the capital, on 19 May as the highlight of the Independence Day celebrations. My plan was to send a team from the Middle East, a team which would include both a Palestinian and an Israeli – as a simple but strong symbol of collaboration and hope. To give myself the opportunity to participate, and to give balance to the team, the remaining two team members would be UN workers currently stationed in the Middle East. With only three months before kick-off, it was time to start training, fundraising, and rousing media interest. But first I needed the team members.

The Palestinian Olympic Committee was located on the northern outskirts of Gaza City, the largest city in the Gaza Strip. Unlike Yasser Arafat's compound, access to the building by foreigners or unknown persons was tightly controlled; when I drove up to make an appointment guards instructed me to immediately return to my vehicle and move on. In this part of town there were no parked cars. There were too many high value targets, all of which were afforded the strictest of security measures. Instead I booked an appointment over the phone. The Vice President reluctantly agreed to meet me, although curiously not at the Olympic Committee Offices – he must have been suspicious of the foreign accent. Instead he agreed to meet me on the corner of two main roads. He wanted me to arrive in a UN vehicle and park alongside the curb so as he could approach the vehicle at his own free will.

I only had to wait on the side of the road for a few minutes before a small man with a large belly opened the side door and hopped inside the vehicle. He looked like an "ordinary Joe", wearing a corduroy jacket and denim jeans with a casual, friendly demeanour. I was not so relaxed, suspicious about a meeting I would have expected to be more formal.

As we drove through the streets of Gaza I explained the race and the symbolic collaboration of peace through sport. The media potential, the message of hope for the youth and the future, was enormous. His response was brief.

"While Israelis occupy our land, we will not cooperate with them in any sporting activities. We won't help you find a Palestinian team member."

It was a summary dismissal.

Disappointed as I was by his reaction, and the fact that politics made my undertaking far more complicated than I had previously imagined, my enthusiasm was renewed when a WFP colleague, Simona Palenga, volunteered to support the Middle East team. Whilst Simona sought sponsors and drummed up media interest, I continued searching for the team members.

I'd recently met a twenty-two year old Israeli called Yaron at a local rock climbing wall. He fit the criteria perfectly: he had just finished serving with the IDF in the West Bank, he loved outdoor sports, and he was saving up for a back packing trip through South East Asia. The young Israeli wasn't in the slightest bit restricted by his solid build; he was capable of running and cycling at the same pace of those who were considerably leaner. I deemed him to be competitive in any of the three disciplines, providing flexibility should we need to mix it up.

Over a meal I learned that during Yaron's three years of loyal service in the West Bank he'd grown despondent about the Israeli cause. He wasn't anti-Israel as a state, nor was he disloyal to the army that he served; instead he was annoyed that he had to put his life on the line to help protect the extremist Israelis who chose to live on the inside of the West Bank. Yaron had served most of his time in Hebron where the Israeli settlers were renowned for being particularly arrogant and brazen.

The United Nations put few physical fitness requirements on its employees, providing limited options for a second UN team member. Fortunately Marco Regnault De La Mothe, a WFP colleague, agreed to relinquish his partying regime for a few months to take up the challenge. A skinny Italian national, Marco was able to fine tune himself physically without too much effort. Finding the fourth member of the team was not so easy, not only because we were looking for a Palestinian, but also because the person needed to be female ... and one with an interest in outdoor pursuits ... who held a passport ... and who would agree to compete on a team, abroad, with an Israeli man. No problem there!

Predictably no one responded to messages left at fitness centres or to the networks I asked around at through work. Eventually I drove into the West Bank, to the city that housed Arafat's Mukataa compound, Rammallah, and systematically searched the gymnasiums on foot. At that stage any woman in a gym would have been fair game. Lucky number three came to my rescue.

In the third gym I went to I found Jennifer, a twenty-two year old from a liberal family with dual-American citizenship. When I explained my idea she was hesitant at first but nonetheless gave me her number. Unlike the other Palestinian women I'd met she wasn't cowering behind layers of clothing or too timid to ask questions about the proposed adventure. She explained to me that as she was unable to run in the streets of Ramallah for fear of being ostracised by the community, she regularly hit the gym to use the cardio machines. Curbing my enthusiasm I gave her two days to mull over her decision before calling.

"Hi, Jennifer, how's the training going?"

"Hi there, I haven't been able to reach the gym since we met as there has been a curfew imposed on Ramallah."

"Aggh shit, of course. Sorry to hear about that. Have you had a chance to make a decision about the trip to Timor?"

"Yep, I've been thinking about it a lot. I'm not really worried about competing in a team with an Israeli, or about the Palestinians who will have a problem with what we are trying to achieve. I'm more worried about my fitness level. I don't normally go to the gym for more than forty-five minutes at a time."

"Jennifer, don't worry about that. You have got so much more to bring to the team than physical strength. The same went for Marco, wait till you see him try and ride a mountain bike! We've got enough time to make sure we are competitive."

"Okay, I'm in."

I sighed with relief. We had a team, all living within thirty kilometres of each other, notwithstanding the mountain of physical and political barriers between us.

Training was a nightmare. Yaron was not permitted into the West Bank, and Jennifer needed a special pass to enter Jerusalem. Frequently we spent more time on the logistics of training together than on the training itself, including smuggling Jennifer out of the West Bank in a UN car. On two occasions I had to drive out to Ramallah in a UN marked car to pick her up because civilian movement had been restricted. The drive itself was a risk as Jennifer didn't have a UN ID card to explain her movement in the vehicle. Both Yaron and Jennifer had been anxious about meeting each other, but when they finally did it was done without any animosity. The common desire to conquer the Timor Challenge was greater than any potential inter-personal challenge.

Other team challenges were also met. Simona did a sensational job at raising cash and a press release was sent out to alert the departure of Team Middle East – the adventure team that spreads the good word – PEACE.

▲   ▲   ▲

Team Middle East was a hit from day one in Timor Leste. Goz had done a great job of promoting us in advance and so the awareness aspect of our trip was met through radio interviews, newspaper articles and a documentary on television. The team was competitive on the track, taking out first place on day one in the International Teams category and third place overall. Marco had a disappointing leg when paddling with Jennifer and so opted to take the bike during the second day. Yaron was put in the kayak with Jennifer on the second day of racing but capsized part way through the leg. The team fought back to come second in the International Teams category and seventh overall.

"There's no way I'm getting in the kayak again," said Yaron as we discussed the third day of racing.

"S'pose that kind of narrows it down to either Squiz or Squiz … 'cause I ain't getting in it either," said Marco.

"Ha ha … but if Jennifer and I do alright then it must have been you two guys who have been the weak link over the last week. Do you want to put some cash on it?" I said with a chuckle. Neither of the boys were willing to lay a bet.

On the third day, President Xanana Gusmao fired the starting gun in the main Dili stadium in front of 10,000 spectators. Yaron sprinted to the beach to tag Jennifer and myself in the kayak. The inflatable kayaks lacked a hull and therefore were very difficult to steer. With perseverance and a bit of luck the two of us managed to break with tradition and finish the leg with at least a few competitors coming in behind us. Yaron, up next to do the run leg, was rapidly falling ill with a gastro illness. He was buckled over by the time he reached the run-bike transition. It was a courageous effort that allowed the team to finish in second position for the day.

That evening we all went back to the Dili Stadium and celebrated the first anniversary of Timor Leste's Independence Day with 20,000 very happy Timorese. Goz, who had managed to pull off the adventure race without any major hitches, got up on stage to announce the results.

"… and first place in the International Teams category is being shared due to equal points between two teams … ladies and gentlemen please put your hands together for Team Australian Army and the team that came all the way from the Middle East … Team Middle East!"

I felt ecstatic and didn't want the night to end. To mix a sporting challenge with an awareness effort was a drug I wanted more of. I was hooked, and looked forward to overcoming the next big challenge, whatever that might be.

The night didn't go so well for Yaron. He continued to deteriorate physically and so left the celebrations soon after we received our award. Jennifer escorted him to our accommodation but soon found herself bailing up a taxi and rushing him to hospital. Ironically the Palestinian and Israeli spent the night together at the hospital, Yaron on an IV drip and Jennifer watching over him at his bedside.

▲　▲　▲

The team received a special compliment only minutes before we began our farewells in Darwin airport on the day after the race had finished. Jose Ramos Horta, Timor Leste Minister for Foreign Affairs and Nobel Peace Prize winner (and future President), actually approached the team when he saw that we were travelling with a mountain bike.

"Are you the team from the Middle East?" he asked.

We'd made an impression.

NINE
MESSING WITH THE BIG BOYS

For eighteen months I had lived harmoniously in the Palestinian neighbourhood of Beit Hanina, blissfully unaware that my lifestyle was creating a major problem. Unbeknown to me the fuse of a ticking bomb had been lit and would soon explode right in my face.

Only three months earlier, after the successful adventure race in Timor, I returned to the Middle East with a renewed sense of hope. Yaron and Jennifer had effortlessly proven that the issues associated with their troubled history meant nothing when people had a mutual desire to strive for a common goal. Team Middle East wasn't going to solve the crisis at hand, but it had reinforced my belief that if the political leaders made a solemn commitment to peace, the majority of citizens would support them.

Each day it gladdened my heart to see that at the grass roots level there were many examples of restraint and respect between Israelis and Palestinians. The IDF officers who persuaded their commanders to allow WFP trucks unhindered access into the restricted areas of the West Bank and Gaza were a good example of this. Even though they were at war with the Palestinians, officers and soldiers alike were willing, on occasion, to stand up against the unending rhetoric that bellowed from the Israeli political apparatuses. Most of these soldiers were like Yaron, young and impressionable individuals who were unwillingly thrust into a war zone to contain a population. They saw past the ruthless Palestinian combatants to help protect the basic human rights of the innocent Palestinian civilians caught up in the rage.

The Palestinians who continued to line up at the IDF checkpoints for hours at a time, day in day out, were also showing restraint. They were the ones who were denied access to schools, hospitals and employment, yet they stood quietly in line waiting their turn to be searched by the Israeli soldiers. Like Jennifer, for the most part they were enthusiastic and charismatic but forced to endure hardship and restrictions on a daily basis. They didn't retaliate with violence or holler expletives; rather they respected the orders of those who were unable to avoid their obligatory national service.

There was a harmony of sorts between those that lived amongst the conflict. Parents were parents no matter what their political or religious beliefs. They all wanted their children to grow up without hatred for those that lived across the road or on the opposing hill. Unofficially they talked to each other, to help reaffirm their common family beliefs and vent their mutual suffering. It was common practice for Palestinian and Israeli families to look up unfamiliar names at random in the phone book and call the homes that housed their enemy's flag. There was no anger, nor need for argument, as both sides wanted a peaceful resolution to the conflict. However the good work of those who wanted to ease the suffering, or help the peace process, was constantly and tragically shattered by the very next act of violence or persecution against the other side. Anger and distrust, as I was to learn, were easy to understand when it is oneself being directly targeted.

▲ ▲ ▲

I sat bolt upright, unsure whether I had just had a bad dream or if I had heard a disturbance outside the building in which I lived in. I looked at my watch. It was 1:15 in the morning. I'd been asleep for less than two hours and wondered why I was suddenly wide awake. I wanted to lie back down and roll over, but curiosity took hold.

My studio apartment was attached to a large Palestinian house that was occupied by a respected Palestinian family. The house was only three hundred metres from an Israeli checkpoint controlling the road that led to Ramallah. We lived on the outskirts of Jerusalem but within the West Bank if the pre 1967 borders were acknowledged. The checkpoint was like any other, a place where violence erupted without warning. Maybe something was happening at the checkpoint, after all, the noise I had heard had not rattled the whole house.

Curiosity triumphing over common sense, I climbed out of bed and put on a pair of shorts. In the time that it took to reach the front door my brain worked through a few possible worst case scenarios to assess my potential reaction in any given set of circumstances. To date I had been woken by a suicide bomb attack targeting the nearby checkpoint, and more recently the whole building was forcefully searched at gun point by Israeli soldiers who claimed they saw a person climbing on our roof with a weapon. Perhaps, I considered, something along these lines was happening again.

Like most of the houses in this part of town, metal window shutters protected my windows from flying rocks, intruders, and excessive noise. The only way of looking outside, without opening a door or raising the shutters, was to look through the peephole in the front door. As I moved my eye to the small circle of glass in the centre of the thick wooden door, I sensed that something was wrong.

Was there someone at my front door waiting for me to appear?

I couldn't see anyone in the immediate vicinity. Instead my eyes were drawn to a strong orange glow coming from the direction of the driveway. If I didn't know better I would have thought it was an orange light flickering on and off.

"Shit," I muttered to myself.

It was not a dream. Something was up, and it was too close to be ignored. I desperately wanted to open the door, but this time common sense did prevail. I knew I would be exposing myself to a very real threat. The only other option was to raise the window shutters, but those were electronic and noisy when unlocked from the closed position. Without doubt such action would draw attention from anyone within thirty metres of the building. Nonetheless, my options were limited. I pressed the up-button, and squatted low to peer through the window as the shutters loudly creaked open.

Three inches were all I needed. It wasn't difficult to comprehend what was going on. My car, a UN marked Toyota Land Cruiser, was on fire!

Instinctively I ran back to the kitchen and grabbed the fire extinguisher. It was the first time I had used it for real; all those fire drills at work were coming in handy.

Turning the key twice I burst through the front door, horrified to see half of my vehicle had already been engulfed by flames. Violent heat spewed across a wide radius as if warning me to stay away.

The pin on the side of the fire extinguisher slid from its slot without resistance. I dropped the pin to the ground and grabbed the hose dangling in front, aiming it towards the grill of the engine block. As I squeezed down hard on the handle, foam spurted over the front of the car instantly extinguishing every flame it touched. I frantically jiggled the hose to widen the spray, covering the width of the engine, able to step further forward as the heat began to dissipate.

The pressure under the handle suddenly vanished, foam spray diminishing to a mere dribble. My hand automatically began to squeeze and release the handle in the hope that it would reinitiate the spray but it was empty and flames were continuing to gush from beneath the bonnet. Where could I get another fire extinguisher? Where was the nearest water hose?

As if knowing my efforts had been thwarted, the fire began to return as quickly as I had put it out. In a moment of annoying clarity I realised flames were also emanating from the fuel tank at the back of the car. This was perplexing, to say the least. Why, I wondered, were both ends of the Land Cruiser on fire?

I ran the fifteen metres to my landlord's front door. He opened it as soon as I yelled his name but he didn't have a fire extinguisher and the flames were becoming ever stronger. There was no chance I could bring them under control any longer. I asked the landlord if he would ring the fire station as he spoke Hebrew and could therefore more easily explain our location to the Israeli run fire brigade. After that I could do little more than look on helplessly as flames stretched and roared from the front and back ends of my vehicle. Well ... perhaps there was one thing I could do.

I ran back inside my open apartment door and grabbed a video camera. Ten minutes later I filmed a convoy of emergency response vehicles arriving at location. Even though I lived a hundred and fifty metres from an Israeli suburb, the fire truck needed to be escorted when operating in Beit Hanina. The first vehicle in the convoy was an IDF jeep with soldiers ready to take up sentry positions around the house. They were followed by a police vehicle to help determine the cause of the fire. Third in line was the fire truck.

The firemen dowsed the burning car with water from a large gauge hose that extended out from the back of the fire tanker. The flames were extinguished in thirty seconds but it was too late to save the vehicle. All that remained was a charred wreck. Upon closer inspection it was evident that the cover for the fuel cap had been pried open and a rolled up newspaper had been stuffed into the fuel tank housing before being set alight. Around the front of the car was a large amount of broken glass and newspaper remains. Molotov cocktails, or 'petrol bombs', had been thrown at the front end of my vehicle from a distance.

I cringed with fear. UN vehicles and personnel were not normally deliberately targeted by Palestinians and the vehicle was clearly marked with large UN letters, WFP stickers and special UN number plates. That exact car, or a similarly marked one, had been parked in the same spot every night for the last eighteen months. It was common knowledge within the neighbourhood that it was driven by an expatriate, neutral to the conflict. This left the chilling conclusion that the perpetrators were after me as an individual.

A UN investigation team was formed to establish the motive; the results of which were far from comforting. I had apparently irritated a few of the community leaders within the Palestinian neighbourhood because I had a girlfriend who regularly visited me. She had blonde hair and wore western clothing, quite obviously not a Palestinian, and therefore, in their eyes, she was Israeli. I was sleeping with the enemy. In fact, she was an American intern that had volunteered to help a local Palestinian NGO over her summer break. To make things worse I was often seen running across the main road and into a suburb called Neve Yaacov. It was from there that I could access clean jogging tracks away from the polluted streets of Beit Hanina. But Neve Yaacov was an Israeli suburb, a place where Palestinians refused to go. A couple of the local lads were unimpressed by my apparent affinity with Israelis, and the fire bombing was their method of sending a message. The message was clear and I had no intention of arguing the point. I was faced with a simple choice, either move on or risk another personal attack.

I felt a fear that was stronger than any other fear I felt before. For the first time in my life I experienced first hand what is like to have an enemy; an enemy willing to take drastic action, and quite possibly my life, merely because they disapproved of my lifestyle. They didn't care if I was a good bloke, a humanitarian aid worker, or a naïve Australian. All they cared about was the fact that I behaved in a manner that was unacceptable to them. For the first time I really understood what it was like for the Palestinians when the IDF tanks rolled into their streets poised to shoot at any person willing to show their face, or how the Israelis felt when they boarded a public bus or entered a busy café not knowing when the next suicide bomber would strike. It didn't matter if I had good intentions or a dependant family; I was, in the eyes of those that condone violence, a legitimate target.

There was only one consolation. I could escape.

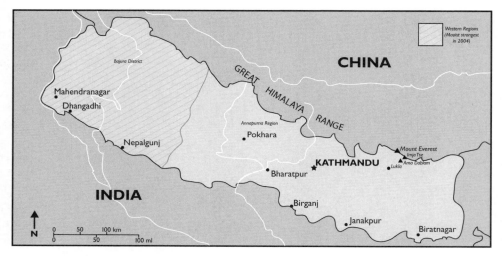

Map of Nepal

TEN
MAOIST ENCOUNTER

NEPAL SNAPSHOT

1768: *Independently ruled principalities are unified under a national monarch.*

1816–1923: *British control some portions of the Kingdom*

1950s: *The ruling monarch cedes a portion of power to a political party*

1959: *Democratic elections are held but the King only allows the political parties to run the country for a few years before he retakes control (due to supposed corruption and inefficiency).*

1980: *A referendum results in a few minor changes to the autocratic (Royal) leadership.*

1990: *A multiparty constitution is adopted after intense protests. Those in power misuse their authority. The country continues to remain horribly poor and underdeveloped.*

4 February 1996: *A small group of left wing politicians present a list of forty demands, related to "nationalism, democracy and livelihood", to the then* *prime minister, threatening civil war should they not be taken seriously.*

13 February 1996: *The demands are ignored and the authors of the forty demands head for the hills of western Nepal to commence the "People's War". The group are colloquially referred to as the Maoists and immediately begin fighting a violent insurgency against the ill prepared and poorly equipped Royal Nepalese Army (advocates of the King and his puppet government).*

Mid-2004: *The Maoist's insurgency wreaks havoc across Nepal and the King and his Government troops suffering serious defeats.*

October 2004: *Squiz is transferred to begin work in Nepal.*

By the time I reached Nepal at the end of 2004, the Maoist leaders were household names and had spread their tentacles to every corner of the country. All areas outside of the immediate vicinity of military garrisons were in the hands of the Maoists. The rugged terrain, lack of education and poverty within the farming community had provided ideal circumstances for the People's War to flourish. The Maoist Cadres were young men and women who didn't know any better and had no other option other than to inherit the primitive and demeaning lifestyle of their peasant farming parents. They came from houses that were made of mud walls and thatched roofs. Fire places were still being built in the middle of a central room without a chimney. Women were still sleeping in the animal shed when menstruating so as to avoid bleeding on the dirt floors of the house. They had nothing to lose by joining the cause.

"Squiz, we haven't had a full time security officer here in Nepal before you, as the conflict was not affecting our operations too much. About six months ago though we began to notice that the Maoists were having a lot more success and as a result started to impose their leadership on aid organisations. WFP has been hit pretty hard because we have field monitors roaming around the remote western districts of Nepal, which is where the Maoists are strongest. Our field monitors are moving between the Maoist controlled areas and the district headquarters, which is where the government troops are stationed. They are copping it from both sides.

The Maoists are forcing them to pay taxes, taking them hostage for interrogation purposes or forcefully recruiting them, and the government isn't much better. We've recently had staff detained unlawfully as the security forces have suspected them of collaborating with the Maoists," explained Erika, my new boss.

"Bloody hell, it sounds like a mess!" I added.

"It certainly is, and the situation is not made any easier when you consider that all of this is happening in the most remote parts of Nepal. There are seventy-five districts in Nepal and we have a field monitor in thirty-one of them. At the moment, around ten of the monitors phone our sub offices daily to let us know that they are okay. The others can be out for up to three weeks at a time, trekking through the hills where there are no roads or electricity, let alone a telephone. It's these guys that I need you to focus on."

"Rightio," I agreed, nodding my head.

"I need you to start tackling the extortion, detentions, intimidation and all the rest that I mentioned earlier. This is where it gets a little tricky. The only way you'll be able to deal with these problems is if you are out there where it is happening. That means that you could be walking for days, if not weeks at a time to reach the person or location of an incident."

"Hey … now that sounds alright. The walking part of it I mean," I quipped with a smile, trying to contain my excitement. I couldn't believe that a large part of my job was going to involve trekking through the foothills of the Himalayas.

"Oh, if you like being in the outdoors then you've come to the right place," said Erika.

▲　▲　▲

The three of us had been walking for two full days after being dropped at a military garrison town in the neighbouring Accham District. We were now deep within the Maoist Base Area for the Bajura District; territory no longer visited by the army and where Maoist Cadres roamed freely. The majority of Cadres did not carry a weapon or wear a uniform.

There simply weren't enough to go around but it also enabled them to blend in with the civilian population.

Every Cadre throughout Nepal was tasked with keeping an eye out for unwanted visitors. It meant we had to explain who we were and what we were doing to dozens of young men and women every day. Sometimes we were let go after a few quick questions, others, relishing the power, kept us waiting in small rooms connected to tea houses whilst they drilled us with the latest Maoist rhetoric. On this particular trip we had the advantage of being able to drop the name of Comrade Bidur, the Bajura District Commander. No one wanted to keep us from meeting with one of the most powerful leaders in the area.

Comrade Bidur had previously sent two of his Cadres with a letter addressed to our field monitor for the Bajura District, a young man called Sonesh. The letter was short and concise. Sonesh was to begin paying one week's worth of his salary, every month, to the Maoist cause. If he didn't pay then his family would suffer the consequences. In plain and simple terms it was extortion. Comrade Bidur had signed off on the letter but solving the issue was not going to be as straight forward as meeting with him and negotiating our right to work unhindered. I had to ensure I brokered a positive result without triggering an act of vengeance against Sonesh or his family after I left the district. My presence and demands could easily be construed as an imposing attempt by a foreigner to meddle with the People's War.

I had spoken to a few people who had dealt previously with Comrade Bidur and concluded that he had a solid track record of being open-minded and fairly respectful. If that hadn't been the case I would have had to go up one level and speak with his superior. In this case I decided to deal directly with him, which is why I found myself walking deep into the rugged hills of Bajura, hot on the heels of the main man for the district. All of those we came across knew very well who Comrade Bidur was, but annoyingly no one could tell us exactly where he was. We had no way of finding him other than following the suggestions of those who had seen him recently. Commonly these suggestions were as vague as, "He left in that direction two days ago." Or, "We heard he was going upstream when he left this morning."

In this part of Bajura the local population lived a particularly isolated lifestyle. This was the hilly region of Nepal where the soil was relatively fertile but spoilt by canyon-like valleys that took hours to cross. Terraces had been etched into the side of the hills many years before but the seasonal rain damage required endless rehabilitation work. Locals we came across were all knee-high in mud preparing their fields for the planting season. Often women and children were moving the mud around to reinforce the walls of their terraced platforms, while the senior male of the household manoeuvred a buffalo-drawn plough across the small fields.

According to the map I was carrying, there were a number of villages along the trail we were walking. In reality they weren't villages at all but rather names of areas that each had a cluster of five or so mud brick houses. It was common therefore for my WFP colleagues to obtain confirmation from the farmers of our location.

Sonesh was a local in Bajura, but from many valleys away which made these parts unfamiliar to him. Travelling also with us was Amrit, a trusted colleague from our regional sub office whom I would utilise both as a translator and source of information. Amrit had been with WFP in Nepal for many years and had an in-depth knowledge of our programmes and regional impact.

A charge of optimism finally surged when we heard news that we were only two hours behind Comrade Bidur, and it was believed he was planning to stay overnight at a place called Deura. The positive news encouraged us to move quickly, so quickly that just fifteen minutes into the uphill journey we came across yet another Maoist Cadre. This guy was himself walking hurriedly, but in the opposite direction to us. He followed the normal procedure and requested to know who we were as soon as our paths crossed. I quickly told Amrit, "You know the deal mate, give him a quick run down of WFP and let him know that we are planning to meet with Comrade Bidur."

The young Cadre wasn't going to let us go easily. He replied to Amrit with a lengthy spiel in Nepali that I assumed was more of the standard Maoist rhetoric. Having heard it all too many times before I whispered to Amrit, "if he is not being aggressive then try and cut the conversation so as we can keep on the move."

Amrit appeared to do a good job because five minutes later the Cadre thrust a fist high in the air as a symbol of Maoist solidarity and ran off down the road. We continued our trek to Deura, although I couldn't help noticing that Amrit was disturbingly quiet and appeared deep in thought.

I finally asked, "Was he cool with everything you had said?"

Amrit was much less responsive than normal. He eventually replied by saying, "That was a really weird conversation."

"What do you mean?" I asked, not much liking the sound of that.

"Well … after I mentioned that we were off to have a meeting with Comrade Bidur he butted in and started rambling on about a meeting that he had just had with Bidur."

"Ah, good … so he confirmed that Bidur is in Deura?"

"Yeah Bidur is definitely there, but I am not sure if we want to meet with him."

"Why?"

"Apparently Bidur has just given permission for that Cadre we just met to slit the throat of a recently captured soldier from the army."

"What?" I gasped. "Are you for real?"

I stopped walking and turned to Amrit.

"Apparently that guy managed to capture a young soldier a few days ago and had him tied to a pole in a small village called Baragaon. Before he killed the soldier he wanted to get permission from his District Commander. The sad thing about it all was that he was really proud of his capture and was keen to get back there to finish off the job."

"That is just absolutely screwed up," I muttered, still trying to wrap my head around what I'd just heard.

In my capacity as a United Nations security officer I was obliged to remain neutral, and therefore committed to avoid getting involved in any issues between the feuding sides. If I followed that line of thought my options were pretty straight forward. I could ignore the conversation and continue on our way to meet with Comrade Bidur … or do a U-turn and leave the district on the premise that Comrade Bidur was not a man we could afford to do business with.

Morally and ethically I knew this was a blatant violation of humanity, even within the context of a war. Whatever the consequences it would have been inexcusable to my conscience to ignore this barbaric situation. I couldn't help but think about the Nepali soldier who was tied to a pole, unaware that he was about to be slain like the farm animals he shared the shed space with. Fleetingly I also reminded myself that the Nepalese Army had a long history of serving on United Nations peace keeping missions. One day this same soldier could be tasked with protecting me, should I be posted to a country where an armed force was used to keep the peace and protect UN employees. My decision was made, even if I did have to somehow plan how best I could prevent the slaying without endangering my own life, or more importantly those of Amrit and Sonesh who had to work in these parts for years to come.

I pulled out my satellite phone and moved to a break in the tree canopy, all the time thinking about how I was going to present this tricky scenario. I decided to call Erika, a reliable sounding-board and clear-thinking decision maker. Taking a breath I pushed the green button to connect the call. The standard delay of an interminable five seconds dragged by before the ring tones began. After only the second tone I pulled the phone from my ear and pushed down on the red button to disconnect the call. What was I thinking? There was no time to get another person involved.

"Sonesh, mate, I want you to run after that guy and try to stall him for a few minutes. Tell him that I have an alternative option for him that might help the People's War," I ordered.

Sonesh took off immediately.

"How much longer do you think we have to walk to Deura?" I asked Amrit.

"I don't know for sure, but at least thirty to forty minutes if we walk quickly."

"If I let Comrade Bidur use my satellite phone is there any way that he could communicate with his guys who operate from the village of Baragon?"

"Probably not, there are no phones in Baragon."

My decision was made; there was no alternative other than to buy more time with the young Cadre and then convince Comrade Bidur that I could connect him with the International Committee of the Red Cross who in turn could facilitate a prisoner release. Comrade Bidur could turn this situation into a positive for himself and the Maoist movement if I could convince him to listen. Again I turned to the satellite phone for guidance, this time needing some advice on how the Red Cross organised prisoner releases and what sort of time frame they needed to take action. I ruffled through my back pack in search of my cell phone that had been turned off for the last few days. As expected no signal bars came up when I turned it on but it didn't matter; it was Hrothgar's phone number I was after, a good friend of mine who worked for the Red Cross.

I endured the interminable five second delay once more before frustratingly connecting to an engaged signal. I tried again. No joy. Glancing at my watch I realised that five full minutes had passed since Sonesh had left.

"Amrit, my mate's phone is engaged. Let's go and find out what's up with Sonesh."

My colleague silently agreed and we started back down the hill. For the first time I noticed there were a number of paths leading off the main track that we had been walking along before.

After four hundred or so metres we rounded a bend and could see Sonesh slowly trudging up the hill. His head was down and he appeared to be breathing heavily.

"What happened, mate?" I asked urgently.

"I couldn't find him. He must have been moving quickly. I don't know which track he took."

"Shit, now we're in trouble," I griped.

Should we chase after him and try to reach the village before the slaying, should we bolt for Deura on the off chance that Comrade Bidur can halt the slaying or should we just leave the whole area and protect ourselves? Over the last thirty minutes my attitude towards the Maoists had taken a 180 degree turn. Only half an hour ago I was happily walking through the hills of Bajura, feeling confident that I could deal with these people in a rational way. Now I was seriously concerned that they were nothing more than a group of callous murderers who acted without any respect for the basic rules of warfare. My thoughts were plagued by the images of a Nepali soldier tied to a pole, unaware of his own fate. I spoke with Amrit and Sonesh to make sure they were comfortable with chasing down Comrade Bidur. They both bravely said they were willing to go on. Amrit probably didn't want to indicate any sign of weakness in front of Sonesh, one of his subordinates. Meanwhile Sonesh wanted the original issue involving extortion to be solved, and definitely didn't want his security officer running back to Kathmandu with a damning report on his backyard. If it was too unsafe for me then it was guaranteed Erika would decide that it was too unsafe for him.

Without any further ado we started back up the track towards Deura, our pace much quicker than normal as we held onto the idea that there was still a chance we could prevent the killing. By the time we arrived in Deura we were dripping with sweat and knowing there was no time to lose. We could not afford to be subjected to the normal power plays. I asked Amrit to begin immediately asking after the whereabouts of Comrade Bidur as we had to speak with him urgently. According to our rough calculations we still had a short window of opportunity to exploit should there be any way of communicating between the two villages. As I could have predicted the low ranking Cadres were not swaying an inch from the standard procedures. We were asked to sit and wait while one of them headed off to secure an answer to our request. Initially we were told it would only take five minutes ... that would be five minutes "Nepalese time". He didn't return for twenty minutes. But when he did it was pleasing to hear that he wanted us to follow him as Comrade Bidur had agreed to meet with us.

The Cadre led us away from the houses and into some paddy fields. That didn't seem right at all. Why were we going away from Deura? And why was the Maoist Cadre moving so quickly, and without any concern for fact that we had back packs on? The distance between us grew to over thirty metres.

As we approached a lone house the Maoist guide turned around and pointed for us to halt. He entered the house cautiously. An old lady sat outside the front door, seemingly oblivious to what was going on around her. Thirty seconds trailed by before we were motioned to move forward and enter the open door. To conform with local tradition I bent over and untied my muddy boots, noticing there were at least ten pairs of thongs and running shoes scattered around the entrance.

I followed Amrit in through the door. Although the dwelling was virtually in blackness the presence of other occupants was unmistakable. Amrit began talking in Nepali before moving forward two steps and sitting cross-legged on the floor. I followed his lead and sat next to him. To my surprise the introductions revealed that we were meeting directly with Comrade Bidur, which by definition meant a number of the normal protocols had been waived. I asked Amrit to request Comrade Bidur to allow me to move immediately to an issue that could not wait any longer. The reply was positive.

I briefly mentioned that we had bumped into one of his Cadres who was returning to Baragaon to kill a prisoner of war and went on to explain that if there was any way he could prevent this from happening I would be willing to put him in contact with the Red Cross so that he could return the soldier in a controlled manner. At the same time he would be able to draw positive media attention from the release and hopefully set a better precedence for any Cadres that are captured by the Nepali Army. He politely allowed me to finish my sales pitch before calmly responding in Nepali. After only a few minutes Amrit turned to me with a smile.

"Squiz, he says that this man we have met is a young boy with an inflated ego. He is becoming a problem within the Bajura district because he is spreading many false stories in an attempt to bolster his self-esteem."

A wave of relief washed over me … for a moment. As time went on I couldn't shake the thought that possibly Comrade Bidur's response was a complete lie, after all why would he admit that he was responsible for such an atrocity? On the other hand, if the main power-broker of the region was telling me the situation simply never happened, how could I argue with him?

I did not feel at all comfortable staying there that evening. Although the conversation progressed positively and we managed to agree that Sonesh wouldn't have to pay any taxes, Comrade Bidur was a little overly friendly and polite. I went along with the show and accepted his hospitality, which included a meal, bed space in a nearby house, and a traditional Tikka offering (dabbing fluorescent powder on the forehead) but I couldn't shake the gnawing sense of doubt.

The next day we headed further into Bajura in the direction of the remote district capital called Maitadi. It took an additional two and half days to make the journey at the end of which we needed to get a seat on the next helicopter out. Bad weather delayed the regular flights for two more days. I used the time to pay a visit to the local army commander, wanting to know if any of his soldiers had been taken prisoner in the last week. I guess I'll never know for sure if he gave me an accurate answer as he too may not have wanted to reveal a weakness in his ranks.

His response was "No" (but he didn't look at me in the eye when responding to my question).

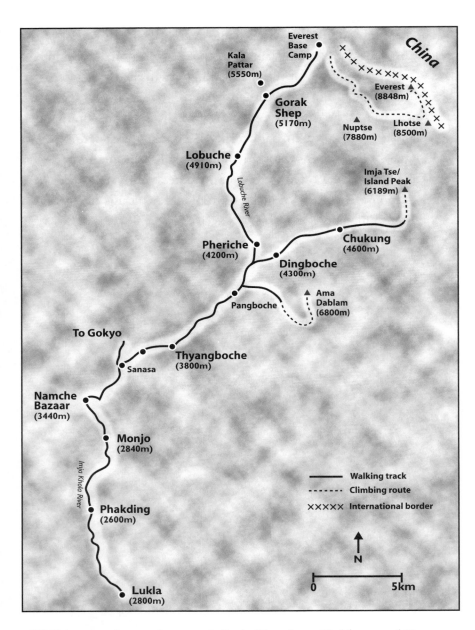

Walking tracks used to reach Imja Tse, Ama Dablam and Everest

ELEVEN
A LITTLE MOUNTAIN

After a long field trip it was always a pleasure to return to Kathmandu's relative civilisation. I called it "relative civilisation" because Kathmandu was unfortunately etched between a series of foothills that lay to the south of the Himalayan Mountains; locking in the dust and fumes that spilled from the sprawling city. The city itself was smelly, polluted and congested, but it did have a wonderful atmosphere that provided a welcome respite from the isolated and impoverished Maoist Base areas.

The heart of the city was found next to the King's palace at a place called Thamel. This was normally the first stop for tourists once they arrived in the country as it lured the weary traveller with a multitude of bars, restaurants and outdoor clothing shops, all snugly nestled amongst the budget hotels and dormitory-style hostels. All in all it was an environment that catered for the bulk of visitors; young backpackers and anxious mountaineers alike.

By early 2005 I was starting to receive positive returns from those whom I'd encouraged to come over and enjoy Nepal's Himalayan mountains. Yaron, from Team Middle East, was moving his way through SE Asia and was destined to check into Nepal whether I was there or not. He arrived in late February in desperate need of a shower, haircut and home cooked meals. Not long after arriving he began to plan a trekking trip around the Annapurna circuit. This is one of the more popular treks undertaken by those who have three to four weeks to walk amongst the spectacular mountains that lay approximately two hundred kilometres west of Kathmandu. I encouraged him to get moving quickly so as he would be back in time to join me and a couple of others on a trip to the Everest region. Encouraged by my plans to head towards Mount Everest and climb a nearby mountain called Imja Tse (often referred to as Island Peak) he took my advice. It sounded a little more challenging and fun than simply trekking amongst the valleys that surround the biggest mountain in the world.

Neither Yaron nor I had any experience at climbing big mountains but we were equally enthused to explore the opportunity as we had many years of experience in rock climbing between us. By our estimations the principles would be similar to the challenges of climbing multiple pitches on a rock face, although we were under no illusions that the colder, thinner air would magnify the level of difficulty. Almost the moment Yaron expressed interest I committed us both to the endeavour by booking the services of a local adventure company called Mountain Monarch. At the same time I added another two names to our party, even though neither had ever subjected themselves to the test of conquering a vertical piece of rock at sea level. Big Jim, my cousin from Perth, had recently finished his university studies and wanted to head overseas before undertaking his first professional job. I persuaded him to visit me in Nepal, promising endless streams of fun and adventure, using the dodgy but somewhat convincing caveat of "Trust me, I'm a Doctor". In other words, he didn't have a clue as to what he was getting himself into and therefore had ignorantly agreed to give it a go.

The other intrepid volunteer was Ingrid Burt, a.k.a. Nud, who was driven by a sense of curiosity. We were old friends from high school and had recently bumped into each other when I briefly returned home and attended a Christmas BBQ in Melbourne. I'd taken a gamble and asked her over to my enchanting place of employ so that we could "get to know each other a bit better".

My two bedroom apartment in Kathmandu was briefly transformed from a one occupant establishment to four as we neared the end of March. The close quarters didn't last long, however, as we were all keen to head into Thamel in search of plastic boots and crampons; two of the items on Mountain Monarch's list of required gear for Imja Tse. These foreign objects were a bit of a mystery to all of us, but we wanted to be properly prepared. The plastic boots were similar in nature to skiing boots in that they were coated with a plastic outer and had a thick layer of insulation on the inside. The sole of the boot was purposefully rigid to allow the crampons to remain clamped to the boot when walking. Crampons came in many different shapes and sizes but effectively all did the same thing; they provided spiky metal teeth that gripped slippery ice and snow surfaces.

The remainder of the items were nothing new to the four of us and could be commonly found in the backpack of any snowboarder or skier destined for a weekend of icy recreation. Finding the items was equally uncomplicated as Thamel had a variety of shops selling second-hand mountaineering gear, as well as an assortment of locally manufactured items that supposedly performed as effectively as the real stuff. We returned to the flat with bags full of down jackets, gloves, woollen hats, fleece pants and woollen socks and prepared to rug up like the proverbial "yeti".

Big Jim and Yaron were both strapped for cash and chose to depart Kathmandu on a bus rather than a plane. I dropped them at the Gongbu bus station on the northern side of Kathmandu at 6:00 in the morning so they could begin their day-long journey to a place called Jiri. After ten hours of sitting on top of a bus the lads were dropped in what had become a ghost town compared to its former glory. Jiri was for many years the starting point for the walk towards Mount Everest from the Nepal side, however most trekkers these days were taking advantage of the daily flights that dropped them higher up the Everest trail. This left Jiri at the end of a road with no tourist dollar to sustain the once bustling town.

While the boys slogged it out through the foothills, Nud and I continued to get to know each other and read up on the journey we were about to undertake. There was no end to the number and diversity of books available on trekking and the Everest region. The majority of these painted a pretty grim picture of the adversity we were about to face. The thin air and extreme weather appeared to play a horrific toll on all who ventured into these parts, whether trekking or climbing. It was no wonder that by the time we boarded our fifteen seat Cessna (run by a company called Yeti Airlines) that we were quite anxious about our now inevitable undertaking, and it didn't take long for the first challenge to present itself.

Landing on the airstrip at Lukla after the forty-five minute flight was nothing short of death-defying. According to the books this was a narrow and very short runway that had been chipped into the side of a mountain. As the plane approached the description appeared to be unnervingly accurate and so I quickly prepared the video camera to record the critical moment. The pilot eased off on the throttle a few seconds before the plane glided onto the uphill runway. Immediately after touch down the roar of the engines deafened the cabin as the pilots endeavoured to pull up the plane before the end of the runway. It might have looked like an impossible task for a non-pilot but these guys seemed to accomplish the task with ease.

The runway was only a quarter of the length of the one we'd recently departed, but more than adequate to land the small planes that ferry trekkers in and out of the gateway to Mount Everest. The purported "precarious" landing was an anticlimax.

We had just landed in the district of Solu Khumbu, home of Mount Everest. Before disembarking our aircraft I turned to Nud and yelled, "Let the fun and games begin." Along with the other passengers we were hurriedly escorted towards a fenced off area next to the run-down airport terminal. A series of planes had arrived minutes before ours prompting a large group of people to swarm like excited bees buzzing around a honey pot, only these drones were milling around in anticipation of collecting their luggage. Mingling amongst the passengers were dozens of small, raggedy, dirty-clothed locals, desperately seeking the attention of the newly arrived. As Nud and I joined the group, we were swamped by requests of assistance.

"Sir, you need porter?"

"Sir, I carry your bags ... very cheap!"

We both politely declined as we turned back towards the plane and focused our attention on locating our three back packs. To lose one of them at this early stage, amongst the chaotic and uncontrolled crowd, would be disastrous.

The luggage from our plane was being speedily tossed onto the tarmac while our aircraft was still "churning and burning". With deft speed I could see the ground crew refilling the cargo hold with new luggage as swiftly as they'd emptied it as a new set of outgoing passengers were quickly escorted to the plane from the terminal building.

"Nud? When you get your bag, head through the crowd and I'll meet you at that building with the red roof," I yelled.

"Okay. How about I take the camera bag as well?" she shouted above the almost deafening crowd and roaring planes.

"Good idea," I agreed, handing her the small video casing.

As the plane moved off to the top end of the runway to line up before take off, our bags were packed onto trolleys and dumped unceremoniously among us, at which point the porters became even more determined to grab our attention by promising great deals. I was more vulnerable than most as I waddled through the crowd with a twenty-five kilogram pack hanging off my back and a twenty kilogram pack cradled in my arms. As I moved away I heard Nud yell out in front of me, "Squiz, forget the red roof, turn right and you will see the sign for the Sunrise Hotel."

To my delight a right turn meant that I was headed down hill. Carefully moving one step at a time, cognizant of balancing the extra weight I was carrying, I headed down the cobblestone footpath. Only ten metres before entering the gates of the Sunrise Hotel a short man approached me from the front.

"Sir, please ... I can take your bags."

"No, mate, I'm okay. I don't need a porter."

"Sir, my name Nima, I am your porter."

"Ah, you are from Mountain Monarch?" I said with relief.

"Yes, sir," he confirmed.

Relaxing my already overburdened arms I allowed the bag to fall into his. He immediately swung it over his shoulders as though it weighed nothing and went to grab the other one on my back. I politely brushed his arm away explaining I could manage that one.

I followed Nima through the gates of the hotel and around the corner of a building to an empty set of white plastic chairs. The sun was shining, warming my face and exciting my spirit as I sat down to join Nud. A pleasant feeling of calm swept over both of us as we heard the roar of the aircraft that had ferried us to this point rise to the skies once more. It would be the last motorised transport we would hear for two weeks.

"So, have you got altitude sickness yet?" I cheekily asked Nud.

She smiled, took a deep breath, and softly replied, "Doesn't feel any different to me."

I laughed. "What are all of those books on about?"

▲　▲　▲

Lukla was a bustling village during the two trekking/climbing seasons of Nepal; March-April and September-October. It was selected as an appropriate location for the runway back in 1965 because of the short stretch of relatively flat ground it harboured, and more importantly because it was located at an elevation of 2800 metres. The altitude makes it comfortable for most people to fly into after being in Kathmandu at an elevation of 1300 metres. The general rule to avoid altitude sickness is to aim for an elevation increase of between 300-600 metres per day when climbing above 2500 metres. The higher up one climbs the more careful one has to be and every thousand or so metres there should be at least one rest day to ensure the body can keep up with the acclimatisation process. Nud had read extensively about altitude sickness as she suffered mildly from Asthma, although she'd discovered through her readings that there was no correlation between the two conditions. Her research, however, helped us both understand the strategy of climbing to high altitudes.

On the top of Imja Tse, at 6189 metres above sea level, the air contains 45% of the oxygen compared to that found at sea level. The number of red blood cells in our blood at sea level would not be sufficient to sap up the limited oxygen that comes with every breathe on the top of this mountain. To overcome this, we needed to slowly ease ourselves into the changing conditions to allow time for our bodies to produce additional red blood cells (the cells that transport oxygen around the body). Altitude sickness, formally referred to as Acute Mountain Sickness (AMS) is the first stage of two potentially fatal illnesses; High Altitude Pulmonary Edema (HAPE) and High Altitude Cerebral Edema (HACE). In simple terms, HAPE would create a fluid build up in the lungs, which would eventually drown the victim, whilst HACE would create an increase in fluid around the brain, eventually shutting down its function all together. The good news about heading into thinner air along the Everest trail was that it had been done thousands of times before and a standard itinerary had been established over the years. The generally recognised plan was to fly into Lukla and then head off that same day to a place called Phakding, which is found deep into the nearby valley of the Imja Khola River.

Nima, our porter from the Mountain Monarch crew, didn't speak a lot of English but had already proven to be reliable. Nud found him waiting at the gates of the Sunrise Hotel as per the plan given to us in Kathmandu. He immediately responded to her request to assist me with our luggage and then followed up with a hot tea before we even had time to think about it. Mountain Monarch had given us a reduced price to climb the mountain as I had offered to supply all of the climbing gear and reach the Imja Tse Base Camp without a guide from their company. For $500 USD each Mountain Monarch would provide us food and accommodation for four nights and five days, ice climbing training, guides from Base Camp to the summit, and the Imja Tse climbing permit. Nima was an additional expense that we would burden, although he was organised by Mountain Monarch so we didn't have to worry about finding a porter at the airport. He would carry the climbing gear and plastic boots to Base Camp, a pack that weighed in at twenty-five kilos. Like Yaron and Big Jim ahead of us, Nud and I carried our own personal gear.

On day one, with fresh legs and clear blue skies, Nud and I were motivated to finish our tea, pack up Nima and head for Phakding. The trail leading to Phakding was two metres wide and solid under foot from the large numbers of trekkers and porters who ferry supplies as far as Everest Base Camp. Ten thousand visitors attempted to walk the trail in search of the tallest mountains in the world each year and like every one of them we were first greeted by a forest canopy and valley walls that prevented us from seeing the monsters that lay ahead.

By midday we arrived at the riverside village of Phakding. Icy waters roared down a nearby Imja Khola river, deafening the voices of oncoming trekkers. Nud and I checked into a tea house for lunch before going any further. The menu consisted of spaghetti, curries, sandwiches and hot apple pies. I was disappointed. I'd wanted to hit the hills and experience a little adversity with Nud, to see how we responded to each other under pressure. Instead we were relaxing in front of a warm fire whilst gazing at a thundering river canyon, contemplating if we should go for a continental or Asian dish. Our time would come. With high spirits and replenished energy stocks it seemed logical to push on up stream to a place called Monjo, allowing us to regain the two hundred metres in altitude that we had just lost in the decent from Lukla hence putting us in better stead for the next day's big climb to Namche Bazaar.

At Monjo we found a tea house with a double room for two hundred rupees, about four Australian dollars. At that price we were expected to eat at the attached restaurant, which once again offered international cuisine for the throngs of intrepid foreign trekkers. As the sun disappeared the temperature suddenly began to plummet. It was far worse than we'd anticipated. Within thirty minutes we had transformed from wearing t-shirts to rugging up in down jackets. The only places to keep warm were in the restaurant huddled around the potbelly stove or cuddled up in a sleeping bag. I guessed we would soon be experiencing that adversity I'd been looking for.

The morning sun burst through our window the next morning as if heralding the adventure that lay ahead. Curtains made of flimsy cotton barely provided any resistance from the bright light that acted as a natural alarm clock for all who were sleeping in the tea house. Both Nud and I had slept well, which was a good indicator that we were doing okay with the altitude. After a hearty breakfast of porridge and fried eggs we again headed up the river trail with Nima in tow.

The valley walls swiftly became steeper and often the river waters were forced to converge through a tight gorge with small cliffs on either side. We had been crossing the river intermittently as the trail moved from one side to the other following the path of least resistance. An hour into our walk we crossed the river for the last time and began to zigzag our way up a steep valley wall. Both Nud and I began to slow our pace as Nima increased his. I told him to go ahead and meet us at the entrance to Namche Bazaar as he was barely showing any strain from the increased gradient. Other porters with seemingly heavy loads were also moving with surprising speed; I guessed they were simply more accustomed to the altitude. Nud and I slowed our pace but kept moving until we reached a resting spot (about an hour later) that was marked on the map as "Everest viewing platform".

The platform was conveniently surrounded by a rock wall that provided a welcome venue to rest our weary feet and shoulders. To the north through an opening in the trees was our first glimpse of the towering Himalayas that stood still dozens of kilometres to the north. It was a tantalising hint of what was to come. Although they seemed cold, inhospitable, and still a long way off, the lure of Mount Everest lurking in the background, barely visible amongst the multitude of eight thousand plus metre peaks, dominated our imaginations.

It took us many more hours to reach Nima who was reliably standing at the entrance to Namche, an entrance that was far from grand. A water tap was being used by the locals to fill up water cans on the right side of the trail whilst a small tin booth marked the spot as the entrance to Namche Bazaar and the last point at which the Everest park fee could be paid.

We paid our dues and continued along the path. Fifty metres later we rounded the corner of the hill where our vision was enchanted by the stunning, multi-coloured roof tops of Namche Bazaar. The village itself was tucked into a horseshoe-shaped valley and had thrived as a result of the tourist dollar and weekly market that brought in traders from across the district. The houses were constructed from local stone but covered in clay and lime to block the relentless wind that funnelled through the steep valley. Each dwelling was built on rings of terraced land, each ring wider than the one below creating an amphitheatre-like appearance. It was quite entrancing. Nud and I checked into a room at a hotel called Camp De Base, opting for one of the nicer but more expensive rooms as this would be our home for the next two nights. To move on the next day would put us at risk of falling ill from the altitude increase.

By the time we went for dinner, four hours after arriving, we were both surprised to be feeling as fit as proverbial fiddles. Admittedly we were a little weary from the steep hill climb, but the thinner air at 3440 meters was hardly causing us any grief at all. The dining room was approaching full capacity by the time we arrived and so we were asked to share a table with a young Japanese girl called Saori.

"So when did you arrive in Namche?" Nud asked her.

"I came in three days ago, and will probably leave tomorrow," Saori replied.

"Will you be going to Thyangboche?" I asked.

"No, I was planning to reach Thyangboche but will be returning to Phakding. I've been quite ill from the altitude and haven't been able to leave the hotel."

"Oh, I'm sorry to hear that. You don't think you will get better?" I queried.

"I am not sure, but I don't really care. I just want to go down now and get rid of this headache. I haven't eaten a proper meal for many days. Even worse, the rest of my group has gone on so I will not be able to join them anyway."

I sat back and reflected on my gung-ho approach to the whole altitude thing. Until now I thought the advice we had been given was exaggerating the situation. Saori was a firm testament that I was wrong.

Nud didn't take any chances after our conversation with Saori. That evening she started taking Diamox and Aspirin; two drugs that help with the acclimatisation process. While I fully supported her decision I chose to hold out, eager to discover my personal threshold. It was wonderful to have the luxury of a lazy day ahead, affording us an opportunity to eat big meals and read up on the next part of the journey. Late the following afternoon I pulled out all of the climbing gear and gave Nud a rudimentary introduction to the equipment, outlining how I envisioned it would be used on the mountain. She was sharp and attentive and I found myself relishing her willingness to leap straight into the deep end without any inhibitions.

Our brief luxurious respite came to an abrupt end with the commencement of our journey out of Namche. As we made our way past the last building my breathing had already become laboured. I knew it was time to slow my pace but instead I found myself doing the opposite as I was drawn to a large white spike piercing the deep blue sky above us. Every step I took revealed more and more of the mountain top's razor sharp ridges that ran off to the left and right. Soon the entire dramatic shape exposed itself to me, breathtaking in its immense and lofty beauty. I whipped out the map and quickly discovered that this was the famous Ama Dablam, which peaks out at 6800 metres, making it a relative baby amongst the giants that lay only a few kilometres to the north. Nonetheless it was thought by many in the early pioneering days of climbing to be an unclimbable mountain. Witnessing it with my own eyes left me with no doubts as to why this conclusion had been reached. The walls were near vertical and as smooth as silk.

For the remainder of the day we walked towards the south side of the mountain to the village of Thyangboche at 3800 metres. Most visitors were apparently enthralled by the large Buddhist monastery that dominated Thyangboche village, but I found myself more enticed by the prospect of locating the route used to climb Ama Dablam. Nud was similarly impressed but a little less inspired to focus her energies on this famed peak. She was finding the walking very difficult, despite having taken the altitude drugs over the last few days. She didn't once complain but I could tell she was finding the going tough. That night she did not sleep well as her breathing was irregular. To add to the misery, the temperature overnight was decisively colder in our room as the tea house was made of poorly insulated wooden walls and a tin roof.

By the end of the next day, when we reached Dingboche at 4300 metres, Nud was not only doing it tough with the thinner air but also suffering from a severe head cold. At that altitude it was difficult to determine if her headache was being brought on by the cold or the height above sea level. To be safe we had to assume worst case and therefore treated it as an altitude problem. Happily two tablets of aspirin soon dispensed with the headache.

The accommodation options at Dingboche were less than inspiring in both quantity and quality. A few kilometres short of arriving we had veered right and come off the main Everest trail while the majority of trekkers turned left and paralleled the Lobuche River so as to reach Everest Base Camp. Instead we opted to hug the base of Ama Dablam and head east in order to reach Imja Tse. It was at Dingboche that we were finally able to see the mountain that we had set as our objective. The western face was a two hundred metre vertical cliff section which made it difficult to appreciate that this was a mountain suitable for beginners. Although outwardly I attempted to appear relaxed, so as not to further burden Nud who was already feeling ill, inwardly I was becoming increasingly anxious. Fortunately we had another rest day at Dingboche. It was also the first chance that we had of finding Big Jim and Yaron, who should have been coming back down the Everest Base Camp trail and heading through Dingboche. We watched out for them as best we could but did not see them anywhere.

After the rest day, Nud began to perk up so we slowly made our way to the four tea houses that comprised Chukung; the final village before Imja Tse. Although the altitude gain was only three hundred metres she was again hit hard with shortness of breath, a headache and loss of appetite. And she wasn't the only one. We sat in the restaurant and watched as small groups stumbled in from the direction of Imja Tse, all appearing battle-weary and exhausted. Several of the climbers told us they had been fighting against the elements for the last twenty-four hours. Some came with stories of jubilation as they had reached the summit, whilst others sadly told of their failure to reach the objective. I couldn't help but wonder which of these groups I would ultimately end up falling in to.

The next day I watched as three Italian men packed up their equipment in the sheltered courtyard of the hotel. They had brand new equipment and matching clothing. They no sooner moved out than the rest of our foursome walked in from the west. Yaron and Big Jim had smiles from ear to ear. Glad to be reunited we sat around exchanging stories as though we hadn't seen each other for years. Both of the lads said they'd been handling the altitude okay, but Big Jim had been hampered by a bad case of giardia and was running off to the toilet every thirty minutes. In such thin air it was impossible to hold one's breath for any length of time and the unisex toilet (a hole in the ground with many seasons worth of deposits) was not somewhere one would want to "camp out" for any length of time. Once inside it was like everywhere else at that altitude, lots of heavy breathing … it even smelt horrendous for Nud whose nose was completely blocked.

Just before the sun dropped over the horizon for the evening, I spotted three men with bright red outfits moving towards Chukung from the direction of Imja Tse. As they closed on our position I realised it was the three Italians. Something must have gone wrong. They were supposed to be going for the summit early the next morning. My heart sank, reminding me of how confident and professional they had appeared when they set off. Seeing that they had been forced to turn back only eroded my confidence further, but there was no cause for alarm. It turned out that one young guy had lost a tooth filling and was experiencing immense pain. He blamed it on the thin air. They had only made it to Base Camp before returning and the other two were not interested in going any further without their friend. The whole story sounded like a big excuse to explain why they had balked the climb. I was no longer impressed by their slick image. My party of four decided on the spot that if one or more of us couldn't make it, the others would carry on regardless, unless of course we need to stay together for safety reasons.

Subhash, a Mountain Monarch guide, and an American couple in their early thirties who, like us, were Mountain Monarch customers, joined us the next morning. The walk to Base Camp was along a dusty trail that swung around to the southern side of the mountain. From here we could see the route we would be taking to the summit; two-thirds of it a rock scramble over rock scree and boulders. The remaining third was covered in snow and would involve a five hundred metre traverse across a glacier, an eighty metre climb up an ice wall, and finally a one hundred metre ridge walk.

Yaron and I were excited, the other two were not so sure. Subhash organised some hot water and eucalyptus oil for Nud so she could snort some fumes and clear her nasal passages while I retreated to the tent that Nud and I would share and began unpacking. Big Jim came over and sat outside.

"So, Squiz, do you really think that this is fun?" he chirped.

"Oh, come on mate, it's not that bad." I replied, rummaging through my bag.

"What sort of a holiday do you think this is? Look at where we are. We're in the middle of bloody nowhere, Nud's as sick as a dog, and there's not a pub within three days walk. This is bloody pathetic!"

I turned and looked outside of the tent door to make eye contact with him. He was silently laughing. My frown quickly morphed to a smile.

"Only kidding, mate," he grinned. "Can't say I'll do it again, but I am loving it."

After an early dinner in the Mountain Monarch dining tent, we all hurried back to our tents to get inside our sleeping bags. Unlike the tea houses, there were no Yak poo burning pot belly stoves to sit around and warm our souls. Yaron announced that he was inside his sleeping bag wearing every piece of clothing that he possessed, other than his spare jocks and socks.

I was awake most of the night; cold and unable to regulate my breathing, struggling to get comfortable on the half inch mat that separated my sleeping bag from the icy ground below. Every time I moved poor Nud was also forced to readjust. Eventually the trial-filled night turned to morning, the dawn heralded by the Mountain Monarch cooks firing up a gas burner to begin preparations for breakfast. The noise sounded like a jet aircraft was about to take off outside our tent. I sat upright and lent forward to unzip the front door. Through a clear plastic window on the vestibule I could see the cooks going about their work.

"Hey, Nud. Before you open your eyes, do you want the good news or the bad news?"

"The good news," she replied quietly.

"It looks like the boys are getting ready to give you some hot tea in bed."

"Oh, that sounds great. What's the bad news?"

"Well, actually, there is some more good news. It's been snowing, which has covered everything with a beautiful layer of white crystals."

"Ah, sounds gorgeous. Now, what's the bad news?" she asked again.

"It snowed inside the tent … not outside."

With that Nud rolled over, opened her eyes, and started laughing.

"What the hell has happened in here?"

"I don't know. Have a look at the crystals hanging off the roof and check out the sleeping bag. No wonder I was cold during the night. Did you sleep alright?"

"Hardly a wink."

A few minutes later Subhash came over and squatted down in front of our vestibule, explaining we should have left an air hole opening in our tent to allow our moist breath to escape overnight. It was that which had turned to ice overnight, and if we didn't shake it all off before the day thawed our frozen exhales the entire tent would soon be filled with water and run the risk of turning our down jackets and sleeping bags rotten. Turning to the essential task at hand, I quietly hoped Subhash wasn't going to let us learn any future lessons the hard way.

A few hours later we were pleasantly surprised as our guide gave a very thorough demonstration and explanation of the technique used to climb an ice wall. He had taken us down onto the Imja glacier and found a twenty metre slab of ice angled at seventy degrees which would serve as our rehearsal for the eighty metre wall just below the summit of Imja Tse. Subhash had one of his guides skirt around the back so as he could clamber onto the top of the ice block and put in a "fixed line". A fixed line was a strong bit of rope that hung down from the top of the ice wall to the starting point at the base of the climb. The rope was used to help us climb and also to act as a safety line in case we fell. This was achieved by placing a mechanical device, commonly referred to as a 'jumar', on the rope that only slid "one way" up the rope. When pulled downwards, metal teeth within the jumar gripped the rope and the device was held firm. As the jumar was tethered to our body harness by a short sling, it was able to hold us in place should we fall.

The jumar itself was held by the climber's master hand whilst an ice axe – a sharp pick attached to a handle – was carried in the other hand. With pointed crampons attached to the plastic boots, the climber moved up the wall by sliding the jumar upwards and digging in with the crampons and ice axe. Assuming the jumar was correctly attached and the rope was properly secured, the process was relatively safe. Subhash asked me if I would like to have a go first. I approached the fixed line and attached the jumar. Subhash watched to make sure that I did everything correctly. I looked up towards the top of the wall. Twenty metres of smooth ice, almost vertical, stretched threateningly upwards towards the deep blue skies. I slid the jumar up the rope as far as my hand could extend and raised the ice axe, slamming it into the ice next to the jumar.

"Squiz, not so hard," Subhash called. "Remember that you have to pull the ice axe out again. You will waste a lot of energy if you can't easily pull it out."

I looked down and raised my right leg before kicking it into the ice wall at knee height. It didn't hold. I kicked harder and then pulled up with my arms.

"No, Squiz! You should step up with your legs rather than pull up with your arms. Think about how many more stairs you can climb as compared to chin ups you can complete. Your legs are the key," he explained. I should have known better, the same principle applied when rock climbing.

Before he could finish his sentence my foot fell off from the ice wall. As soon as I released the weight from my arms, the crampon fell out of position. I could see now the other important reason for leading with my feet rather than with my arms. I started again and soon found my rhythm. Standing up on the points of the crampon put enormous strain on my calf muscles, forcing me to keep on the move. The tempo of my breathing rapidly increased and the back of my throat began to burn as my body gasped for air. I suddenly felt extremely hot and uncomfortable. I was wearing thermal underwear, a pair of fleece pants, and an outer layer of gortex. The sun was beating directly down from overhead and the wind had been silenced by the block of ice. It felt like I had gone from a freezer to a solarium in the space of a few minutes.

The rest of the team yelled out words of encouragement and I eventually stood again on horizontal ground at the top of the slope. I rappelled back down to the start point, thoroughly disillusioned about the whole experience.

"Well done, Squiz. That was very good for your first try," Subhash said cheerily.

"Mate, that is hard work. I don't think I will be able to do the eighty metre wall if it is anything like that," I gasped between breaths.

"Don't worry, Squiz, we will get you to the top. Okay, Nud? Do you want to go next?"

Nud came over and went through a similar experience to me. The rest of the team all had a go and successfully "summited" the glacier ice block. After a few more attempts with some additional obstacles, such as an unplanned knot in the rope, we all proved to Subhash that we had the skills to give Imja Tse a run for its money. The American couple weren't convinced, however. By the time we had all walked back to the Base Camp, they decided their journey was over. Subhash encouraged them to stick with the plan but they had made up their mind. The Imja Tse Base Camp would be the highest point in their journey. We said our farewells and slowly moved off in opposite directions. Subhash, two other guides and a cook departed Base Camp along the same path as us. As we moved away he pointed in the direction of a trail and said, "Just head up that trail until you see some tents. We will be waiting."

It all sounded so easy.

▲　▲　▲

The Mountain Monarch guys bounded off like it was a Sunday walk in the park while we slowed to a snail's pace, the steep gradient sapping our energy and triggering another breathing frenzy. Big Jim and Yaron appeared to get into a rhythm, slowly but surely pulling away from Nud and myself. Poor Nud and I were both forced to stop every few minutes in an attempt to calm our oxygen-deprived muscles. By the time we reached the tents, Yaron and Big Jim had already settled in for the night. Nud and I really had to move like we had a purpose, as indeed we did, to nestle in because we'd been advised to bunker down at the

Attack Camp, at an altitude of 5470, until 2am. At that time we would then climb for the rest of the night, aiming to summit sometime in the morning in order to avoid the gale force winds of the afternoon.

A euphoric feeling of delight swept my body when I was finally able to lie back and rest in the tent. The uncomfortable struggle to operate at these altitudes was making the simplest form of relaxation feel like pure unadulterated paradise. When the cook came around with hot noodles and bread I should have been similarly ecstatic at this regal banquet, but sadly I felt ill just thinking about trying to eat.

Nud sensed that I wasn't feeling right and suggested that I take some Diamox. I probably should have acquiesced immediately, but stupidly I wanted to believe that if I could have come this far without any drugs I could make the remaining eighteen hours without any chemical assistance. I lay back and thought about it. My mouth began to salivate, sadly a sensation not originating from my taste buds being aroused by the sensuous aromas emanating from Nud's bowl of noodles. No, this was something else all together. I sat up and rolled over onto all fours, hurriedly poking my head outside of the tent door to get some fresh air. Big Jim spotted me immediately.

"What's up, Squizzzaa? Feeling a little sick, are we?" He started laughing, no doubt thinking it was his chance to have a go at his older cousin who was normally dishing it out to him.

It was a false alarm. I moved back inside.

"Okay, I surrender. Give me some drugs!!" I said to Nud. "I think I need to have some anti-nausea tablets first."

Nud found the right drugs and I swallowed them down without hesitation, able to raise my head again just as the sunlight began to disappear. As the tent turned completely dark I listened to the gusting winds howling outside. The side of the tent flapped hard and I found myself wondering, almost hoping, if the blustery weather was bad enough to make it unsafe to proceed.

Relaxing my body was impossible due to the heavy breathing. Resting my mind was equally impossible as by this stage anxiety was beginning to set in. Thinking back to Big Jim's earlier words, I began to muse over where the fun in all this really was. By 2am, Nud and I had hardly slept yet again. I was feeling weak from the nauseous sensation in my stomach. As scheduled, Subhash came to our tent and unzipped the vestibule.

"Hey, Squiz, Nud, it's time to get moving," he yelled.

"Are we going up or down?" I asked.

"Up. We will summit today. There aren't any clouds in the sky, so we should be okay," he replied.

"What about the wind?" I asked.

"It will drop by early morning. Should not be a problem. Okay, so we leave in one hour. Make sure you eat before we go."

I didn't lie around and think about it any longer. The decision had been made and it was now up to me to do my bit. The first task was to determine if I needed to have a poo. Once the layers of clothing and climbing harness were fitted, it would be a lot of hard work to "snap one off". Determining it was safe to proceed with donning more clothing, I pulled on a set of gortex pants and jacket over the thermals, fleece pants and top, woollen hat and down jacket I was already wearing. Next was the climbing harness and then plastic boots. The thought of eating was still making me feel ill. Nud was able to eat a bowl of porridge but the best I could manage was an attempt at drinking a cup of warm sugary lemon tea. We both packed up the sleeping bags and kit that would remain behind, from that point on we would only need to take one small pack between us. We checked the contents over and over to make sure we had the necessary items but more importantly to ensure we didn't have any extra items that would weigh us down. Extra weight wasn't something anyone needed to be burdened with on this leg of the journey.

Just before 3am, Nud and I were ready to go. Before squeezing out through the tent door, I rummaged back through my big pack that would remain behind. I found the Victoria Bitter singlet that had helped me get through the Melbourne marathon. I needed it again, to give me inspiration. I forced it over the top of all the other layers of clothing that had doubled the size of my torso, put on a pair of gloves and moved outside.

Looking down towards the direction we had come from yesterday I could just make out six small lights bouncing around in the darkness. These were headlamps being used to light up the trail for another group bravely attempting the summit. They had chosen to launch their bid from Base Camp, which meant they had an additional two hours of climbing. Having not been able to sleep or eat at the Attack Camp, I was wondering if we should have done the same but it was no point trying to second guess the situation. They were on their way and the sight of them inspired me to get on with the task at hand. I would make it to the summit before them. No longer was I sulking around feeling sorry for myself.

"Come on boys! Let's go. The competition is hot on our heels," I called to the gang.

Yaron and Big Jim had gear and clothing spread throughout their tent. They were both flapping around trying to get on top of the situation when I looked back down the slope and watched the fast approaching lights drawing closer. I took a deep breath and reminded myself to calm down. It wasn't a competition and if we departed ten minutes later than planned, it wouldn't make a lot of difference. Before long the other group moved through our position. At least it provided me with a good opportunity to see how others were dealing with the challenge. They were breathing heavily and looked straggled. Like us they were most likely beginners as Imja Tse was defined by the Nepalese authorities as, "A Trekking Peak" and promoted by local guiding companies as, "A non technical climb suitable for trekkers with a little more determination than most". Over half of those who sign up fail to reach the summit.

Our intrepid band moved off from the Attack Camp at 3:15 in the morning. Subhash led the way informing us that he would set the pace in order to reach the summit at 9am. It was a good feeling to be moving, not only psychologically but also because it helped get some warmth back into our rapidly freezing bodies. The pace set by Subhash was not very quick but fast enough to bring on heavy breathing. The strain of the climb was alleviated by the distraction of needing to concentrate on the unstable rocks underfoot. The rocks were flat shards of slate that ranged in size from a few centimetres to a metre. The bigger ones were the most difficult when they were lying on top of smaller rocks. Balancing became an art form hindered greatly by the awkward and stiff plastic boots.

We marched in single file, unable to talk comfortably over the strong winds that whipped up from below. The other group kept ahead of us but failed to make any further ground other than the lead they had already established. As the first glimmer of light began to turn the black sky above to a sullen grey-blue colour we came to the first fixed line. In this instance we didn't need to apply our jumar, instead a carabiner was needed. A carabiner is a "D" shaped metal ring that can be more easily attached to the fixed line and tethered to the climbing harness to act as a safety line. The difference between it and the jumar was that it could slide up and down the rope, whereas the jumar took a little extra time to attach and would only slide one way. It was advised in this case to use the carabiner because the rope was not in place to protect us from falling back the way we came, but rather off to the left where there was a one hundred metre drop. The enormity of the cliff was not immediately evident as the lack of light prevented us from seeing any further than a few metres. Within fifteen minutes however there was enough light to look back down on the tents at Attack Camp. Between us and them lay a massive mountain of rock scree that steepened as it reached the narrow rocky outcrop that we were negotiating.

The other group was perched thirty metres ahead on a narrow platform of rocks, preparing to move on to the ice glacier. As we slowly moved towards them Subhash negotiated with their guides for us to be given some of the limited space. We all sat precariously close to the cliff's edge, still attached to the safety line. The howling wind was replaced by a gentle breeze. I took a position next to Nud, looking forward to a conversation at a regular pitch.

"How's it all going, Nud?"

"I'm really starting to feel tired. I don't have any energy left," she answered quietly.

I felt a pang of guilt.

"I know what you're feeling. At least we can see the end now. Do you feel like some chocolate or a drink?" I whispered gently.

"Okay. Maybe a drink will do the trick," she smiled.

I started emptying the back pack and passed Nud a drink bottle that was still warm from the hot water that the cook had boiled up in Attack

Camp. I also handed over her crampons and then started to put on my own, which involved taking off my gloves to thread the straps through a buckle. My fingers immediately began to go numb.

"Nud, can I have that water bottle back? My fingers are freezing!"

I looked across and noticed that Subhash had already put on his crampons and was now preparing the pink climbing rope that we would soon be attached to. He was organised and looking comfortable. I lent forward, cuddling the warm water bottle, wishing that I had spent a little more money on getting a decent pair of flexible inner gloves that could be worn under mittens, rather than a bulky set of fake North Face ski gloves. Two clients and a Sherpa from the other group picked up and shuffled past us. They were heading back down. Although there wasn't a lot of communication going on between them it looked like one of the lads was seriously ill. By the time the remainder of the other group pushed onto the glacier Subhash was ready to start hooking us up. One by one we walked over to him so that he could attach the rope to our harness. Yaron went first followed by Nud, a Sherpa, myself, Big Jim and then the other Sherpa. Subhash moved in front of Yaron and stepped onto the glacier. We all followed at the appropriate time; when the slack in the rope disappeared.

Crunch … crunch … crunch, the crampons dug in providing "rock solid" traction. There was virtually no snow on the wind blown glacier so the surface we traversed was dry, slippery ice. Subhash hadn't given us much information about why we were all tied together but the book I'd read before leaving Kathmandu had explained in detail the technique of using each other for safety when crossing a glacier. If one of us fell into a crevasse, a wide opening in the ice, we could all dig our crampons and ice axes into the snow to prevent the falling person from plunging further into the chasm.

After fifteen minutes we came across just such a crevasse, about a metre in width. It had an aluminium ladder placed across the gap that acted as a bridge. Subhash ignored the ladder and lunged across from one side to the other. We all followed suit. By now the sun was beginning to rise above the monstrous peaks that lay to our east, the heat bringing no comfort whatsoever, in fact the heat made me feel decidedly uncomfortable. Subhash pushed on for another twenty minutes before we were able to untie and shed the outer layers of our outfits that were causing considerable grief. Two fixed lines were hanging down the eighty metre wall above us. I turned to Nud.

"Hey, mate, this is the wall. Are you up for it?"

"I am not sure. I am so drained of energy," she answered softly.

"It's virtually got steps the whole way up. This will be a breeze compared to that training wall. You've got to keep going now."

The wall had been climbed many times during the season, the result of which was a deep set of stairs had been dug into the side of the wall. Subhash had also cleverly neglected to tell us that the incline was more like sixty degrees. It was a good tactic as I was more confident than ever that we would all be able to make it after having trained on the harder wall. Nud smiled at me and I somehow knew in that instant that she wasn't the type who cracked or gave in easily.

Yaron stepped forward and connected his jumar to the rope on the right. The Team Middle East "machine" took off without any delay, closely followed by one of the Sherpa's on the other rope. Subhash called for Big Jim to go next. He too stepped forward, connected and then made his way up the rope on the left. I gave Nud a quick kiss and moved towards Subhash. I found it far easier to climb than the training wall, hardly needing to use the ice axe at all as the steps and jumar provided enough stability. I found I could take about eight or nine steps at a time before needing to rest and regain my breathing composure. At the half way mark I looked up. Yaron was off the wall and following the Sherpa up the ridge walk. Big Jim was nearing the ridge and looking strong. I didn't want him to get too much ground on me or I would never hear the end of it. After another few steps I looked back down and saw the three remaining climbers battling up the wall. Nud was really digging deep to find the reserves to keep going. I was proud of her for being so determined.

By the time I came over the lip of the wall sweat was pouring from my brow. It was a relief to feel the strong breeze coming up from the other side of the mountain as I slumped down and sat on the edge of the wall. Big Jim had his back to me only a few metres away, having a piss.

"Bloody hell, mate, I'm flaming glad that's over!" I exclaimed, gasping for air.

"There must be something about that wall that makes people want to go to the toilet. Check out all of the dumps over here," Big Jim called back.

Glancing briefly in the direction he'd indicated I could see a brown curly deposit not far from Big Jim's size 12s. It was encouragement enough to keep on the move.

The ridge climb was the only thing left to do. The summit was only ten minutes away, the knowledge of which gave me a sudden surge of energy similar to that which I'd experience in the last few hundred metres of the marathon in Melbourne. All the pain and suffering suddenly vanished, or were at least masked, by an injection of heart-pumping adrenalin. I picked myself up and told Big Jim that I would see him on the summit. The ridge was about two metres in width and gently sloping off to the left. On the right hand side, the wall we had just climbed propped up a cornice, a lip of ice protruding from the side of the ridge. The fixed line gave no flexibility in the path to be taken. After five minutes of slow walking I had to stop and allow the rope to be used by those descending. The group of three, who were ahead of us, had only spent five or so minutes on the summit. It was impossible for them to rappel down the rope whilst I used it to jumar up so I gave them right of way and only once they passed did I again head up the ridge.

My breathing continued to labour even though the adrenaline-charged surge of enthusiasm kept me determined to keep moving and join Yaron on the summit. Nonetheless I suddenly started to feel weak and began violently gasping for air, dropping onto my knees and slumping forward. I was overcome by a feeling of weakness and could feel my stomach getting ready to vomit. My whole body convulsed but nothing came out. I spat out saliva and convulsed again, this time vomiting yellow bile and clear fluid. I spat again. My eyes were watering as I felt a gentle pat on my back.

"Are you okay mate?" Big Jim asked.

We had stirred each other a lot over the last few days but Big Jim realised this was not the time to mock me. I felt weak and defeated. There was only five minutes of climbing left and I was on all fours at the complete mercy of the mountain.

"Come on, mate, let's get this last bit over and done with," Big Jim said kindly, helping me to my feet.

At exactly 09:20am Nud, closely followed by Subhash, stepped onto the summit of Imja Tse, and I was waiting there with open arms. We embraced for what seemed like forever as I thought over and over again how proud I was of her for accepting my challenge and pushing herself through the relentless adversity to reach the dizzy heights of 6189 metres.

After our group all congratulated each other and passed on words of praise to our three Nepali friends who had made it all possible, we posed for photos and took a moment to soak in our surroundings. White capped mountains surrounded us for as far as we could see. The vomiting, headaches, giardia, head colds, sleepless nights and frozen fingers were all momentarily forgotten. We were on top of the world.

Subhash shattered the magical moment, crashing us back down to reality with a thud, when he mentioned the need to get off the mountain before the winds and possible bad weather rolled in. No one argued knowing there were many dangers and physical challenges yet to overcome. Moving down off the ridge and wall was an individual effort as it involved rappelling down the fixed lines. The glacier, however, was again negotiated as a team with a single rope interconnecting our party of seven. Negotiating our way down the rocky section and scree slope was like moving across new territory. The daylight revealed a series of precarious sections that involved movement along narrow trails that had sizeable cliffs dropping away for dozens of metres at a time. I remember feeling surprised that this part of the mountain did not claim more casualties during the night time ascent.

The cook was waiting for us back at the Attack Camp with a late and warmly welcomed lunch. Even I could stomach a small bowl of noodles at that point. It helped restart our motors for the journey back to Base Camp; in fact we felt so energised we toyed with the idea of packing up our gear at Base Camp and stomping back to Chukung for a warm fire and foam mattress. Obtaining consensus amongst the group was not difficult. We hurriedly sorted through our kit and packed up Nima for the mad rush back to Chukung before the sun once again disappeared.

We must have looked a sorry lot by the time we dribbled into Chukung, a bunch of walking zombies. But looks didn't matter. We'd done it. I was immensely proud of our team who had approached the mountain with no prior mountaineering experience and a mix of borrowed clothing or dodgy imitation gear from Nepalese manufacturers. Against the odds we had helped to improve the 50% success rate, thwarting the infamous Imja Tse from claiming any new victims on this day. Furthermore my gamble had paid off. In a short period of time I had been able to witness and savour Nud's wonderful strength of character and her warm, witty personality. Over the next two days, as we walked long days to get back to Lukla, I thought relentlessly about how best to approach "the big question". Before getting on the plane to Kathmandu I sat Nud down and asked…

"Hey, Nud, do you want to come and live with me in Nepal?"

Above: : In the Army (left) before heading overseas to do aid work.

Above: My Indonesian colleagues and their chance meeting with a 'fierce' Australian soldier.
Budi is far left and Guntur is second from right.

Above: Amadeo, his ten children and wife in front of their house
that had been and destroyed by a grenade.

Above: New Years Eve 2000– Celebrating the turn of the century and freedom for East Timor in Dili with General Cosgrove, commander of the Australian led Stabilization Force.

Above: On the water clogged Albanian roads with Mercedes and horse drawn carts.

Above: Bluffing the Albanian cops after being caught for speeding again, just days before being taught a lesson at gunpoint.

Left: The designated 'Manure thrower', cleaning his hands with bull's urine in Southern Sudan.

Below: My little mate Joseph, the orphan who ran with bare feet, outside the UN camp on the Kenya-Sudan border.

Above: Playing on an old war relic near Herat, Afghanistan.

Above: Changing money in Kabul, Afghanistan.

Above: Running the Athens Marathon underneath an Afghan burkha.

Above: Meeting with Arafat.

Above: Team Middle East gets ready to pounce in East Timor. L-R Squiz, Jennifer (from the West Bank), Marco (the Italian Stallion), Yaron (the Israeli machine).

Above: Team Middle East avoided the carnage in the first minute of racing by clearing this wave.

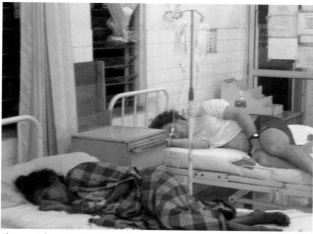

Above: After the final race Yaron was admitted to the Dili hospital. Jennifer was the first to be by his side.

Above: Jose Ramos-Horte and Team Middle East as we depart East Timor.
L-R Jennifer, Squiz, Ramos-Horte, Simona, Marco, Yaron.

Above: Squiz's UN car just minutes after being firebombed outside his Jerusalem flat.

Above: The damage after being firebombed.

Above: Checking out a Maoist built tunnel in a remote district of Far West Nepal.

Above: Three women, beneficiaries of WFP, walking home with their rice.

Above: Food preparation in the non-touristic districts of Nepal.

Above: Negotiating with Maoist leader, Comrade Bidur, after tracking him through the Himalayan foothills for days (white sweat marks evident on blue t-shirt)

Left: Nud practicing her ice climbing skills.

Above: On the summit of Imja Tse L-R Big Jim, Squiz, Nud, Yaron.

Above: Route climbed on Ama Dablam.

Above: The biggest limitation of scaling Ama Dablam without the support
of an expedition – massive packs!

Above: Moving across the ice bridge just after Camp Two on Ama Dablam.

Above: Squiz is dwarfed by a massive wall on Ama Dablam.

Above: Squiz and Andy after climbing Ama Dablam (background).

Above: Route climbed on Mount Everest.

Above: Practising in the Icefall with Pommy (Squiz on ladder).

Above: Coming across a ladder in the Ice Fall, Everest.

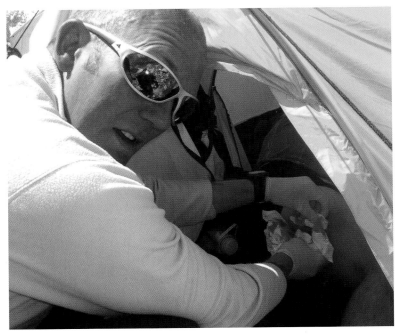

Above: Pommy draining fluid from Tims leg.

Above: The rescue of an Italian climber
(taking up the resources of 10 sherpas).

Above: Squiz using a shemagh to protect against
the intense UV rays in the Western Cwm, Everest.

Above: The Lhotse Face with early morning climbers.

Above: At Camp Four with Pommy (in red) before departure for the summit, both with masks that were about to fail.

Above: Looking back down towards Camp Four and the Balcony on summit day.

Above: The Hillary Step and Summit. Taken from the South Summit just after being told to turn around.

Above: On the summit with the Fight Hunger Flag (Pommy in red).

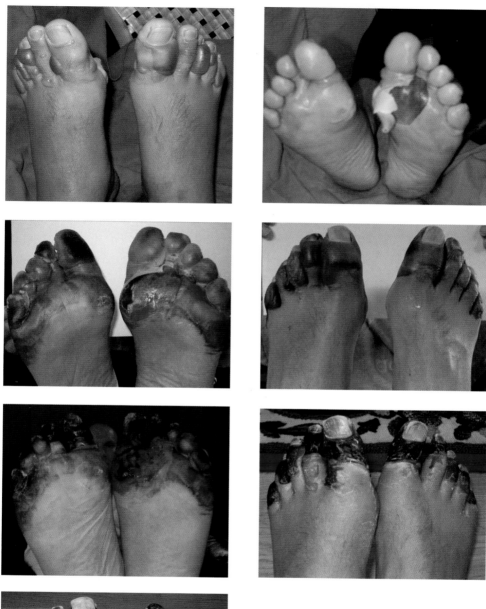

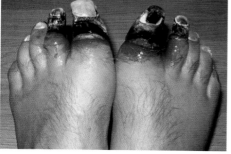

The progression of frostbite on Pommy's feet over a nine week period. Beginning with them after a courageous walk off the mountain (top), then 3 weeks later, then 6 weeks and then 9 weeks. Four toes fell off a few weeks after the last photo (left) was taken.

Above: Arriving back at work in Kathmandu after Everest

Above: Short security job in Somalia with guns blazing

Above: The Squirrell family back in Australia.

TWELVE
A BIGGER MOUNTAIN

By the time we reached Kathmandu the only things we craved were hot showers and cold beers. Big Jim found it difficult to decide which of the two he wanted to indulge in first so, deciding no decision was actually necessary, he grabbed a beer and took it with him as he headed for the shower. I turned on my mobile phone for the first time in two weeks and started inviting a few people over to help us celebrate our monumental conquest. The first person I made contact with was another Aussie bloke called Andy Mitchell. He was working in Nepal for a French NGO and had lent me a pair of gortex dungarees for the climb. Being an avid mountaineer, Andy was excited for us from the outset and I was certain he would be equally eager to hear of our success. Sure enough Andy and a few others came over that evening to watch the poorly filmed video I had endeavoured to shoot over the course of the two weeks.

At the point in which I filmed the magnificent slopes of Ama Dablam, Andy asked me to put the tape on pause. He was keen to inspect the most commonly climbed route, the South West ridge, as a few of his climbing friends had mentioned they might give it a crack in the post monsoon climbing season, a few months away, and he was thinking about joining them. The four of us gave him our unified response.

"You'd have to be crazy!"

The memories of freezing nights and debilitating breathing issues from the altitude were all too fresh in our minds yet, undeterred, Andy remained adamant that it was definitely something he was considering. Having listened previously to his modest accounts of success on a variety of arduous and technically demanding mountains, I had no doubt that he was the type of person who would have a decent chance of pulling it off.

A week later I sadly resumed my bachelor lifestyle in Kathmandu. The Maoists continued to grow in numbers and strength, which in turn caused a steady flow of WFP related incidents that required intervention or follow up from myself. Week after week I would hit the hills in the western part of Nepal in search of a Maoist commander that had extorted, threatened, detained or stolen from one of our staff members. It was a blessing that Nud had opted to delay her acceptance to my proposal by eight months. She too had some heavy work commitments back in Melbourne.

As time went on my recollections of the time spent on Imja Tse drifted from the cold and painful moments to the enormous satisfaction of successfully achieving the challenge and standing on the summit with Nud and the boys. By way of distraction I began to wonder if I could go higher than 6189 metres, or if I could scale a mountain with greater technical demands. The yearning for more mountain challenges quickly turned into a passion and I built up the courage to approach Andy about joining him on the Ama Dablam expedition. At first he was reluctant because of the burden that I would potentially pose to him and the rest of the team. However, after a brief discussion he soon realised that I was able to give him a few of the things that the rest of the team could not provide at that moment in time. Firstly, I was willing to make a one hundred percent commitment to the expedition. Although there were only three months before the proposed departure date, his climbing mates were still procrastinating about the price of airfares and time required to take off work. I was also in the unique position to help Andy with the administration and logistics issues he had been delegated, simply because he lived in Kathmandu. He decided to let me into the fold.

Andy wanted to climb the mountain without any external assistance other than Base Camp support. Many nights were spent trawling through the outdoor shops in Thamel for second hand or new gear to ensure that we could be self sufficient once we departed from Base Camp. Similarly, for my own personal kit I went through every item with Andy to make sure that I was not caught out with 'amateurish' gear. In the early mornings and weekends our focus was on training. Our tack was to cycle and run for many hours at a time to build up our cardio vascular system, and rock climb to build up our technical climbing skills, strength and teamwork. As much as I enjoyed the training, the pressure was on me to perform. I had to prove to Andy that I was worthy of being on the team and up to the challenge.

My Aussie mate was patient and coached me as best he could, always increasing the tempo as soon as he noticed any improvement. If I succeeded on a climb, he made me repeat it whilst wearing the cumbersome plastic boots. Once that had been achieved, which could have taken many weeks, I was required to do the climb whilst wearing plastic boots and a heavy back pack. It was a relief when the owners of the climbing gym banned us from wearing the plastic boots as they were worried of cosmetic damage being caused by our non-stop assaults.

With his wife living in Paris, Andy and I came to know one another extremely well, our lives intensely and mutually focused on Ama Dablam for three months before departure. It turned out to be critical that we got along like a house on fire because one by one his other mates slowly dropped out of the expedition. On the 11 October 2005 the two of us boarded a plane in Kathmandu, bound for the small runway of Lukla.

We landed safely and moved away from the aircraft towards the crowd of porters and trekkers, all eagerly awaiting the appearance of packs and bags. I naturally slid into the role of our tour guide as it had been less than six months since Nud and I had landed in Lukla. Not breaking with tradition, we soon found ourselves at the same tea house in Monjo, huddled around the same fire place and being served dinner by the same family. The experience for me, however, felt very much different. Last time I was naïvely exploring a new environment with like-minded friends, without any expectations or benchmarks to go by. This time I was moving through the hoops with a veteran and was about to face a challenge that was way beyond my level of experience. But I was a willing participant and desperate to learn new skills and gain knowledge from Andy.

▲   ▲   ▲

For the next few days Andy and I moved along the Everest Trail before turning east towards Ama Dablam, just short of Dingboche. We spent ten days preparing ourselves and acclimatising to 5600 meters on a smaller mountain called Ombigaichen. On the walking trails my enthusiasm often found me separated from Andy who chose to walk at a snail's pace to prevent heavy breathing. I, on the other hand, chose to suck hard on the thin air and move at a normal walking pace so as to get the job over and done with quicker.

It was to be a poor choice of strategy. The cold and dry air irritated the back of my throat, forcing me to cough hard every time I exerted myself. By the time we had reached Ama Dablam Base Camp, ready to begin our reconnaissance trip up the mountain before our attempt on the summit, I had nearly used up all of our throat lozenges. Over the next few days, as we camped at Advanced Base Camp (an intermediate site between Base Camp and Camp One, usually referred to as ABC) the cough developed into a serious impediment. I found myself having to stop what I was doing and relax my breathing in order to cut the coughing frenzy. By the time we reached Camp One I suddenly realised that I'd sucked dry our supply of lozenges. The night before, while staying at ABC, I had noticed some rubbish bags wedged between two boulders that had been pecked at by birds, exposing some of their contents. Subconsciously I recalled seeing what looked to be a few lozenges still in their wrapping paper.

"Andy, I'm heading back down to ABC to search through the rubbish, just in case my memory is serving me correctly," I said

In desperation I was willing to take the risk of subjecting my throat to another four hours of strain, wishing I had followed the example set by Andy in the earlier days when he consciously moved at a controlled pace to protect his throat. By the time I arrived at ABC I was overcome with desperation to find any relief for my debilitation and so quickly skipped around the tops of rocks to find the rubbish I'd previously spotted. I lunged towards an open bag the instant I found it as though I'd just unearthed a priceless buried treasure. There was a menthol sweet on the ground next to the bag. I untwisted the two twirled ends of the wrapper and plopped the tablet into my mouth. Drawing back, I could immediately feel it soothing my raw throat. "You bloody ripper," I quietly murmured to myself.

With the first wave of relief in place I began searching through the rubbish to see what else I could find. It was midday and warm enough that the rubbish gave off a putrid smell from festering cans of tuna and baked beans. It didn't worry me one bit; I delved headlong through the rubbish without any hesitation whatsoever. Happily the more I searched the more I found. Scattered amongst the rubbish were twenty or so individual menthol lozenges. Most of them were dirty from the remainders of the rubbish but they were protected well enough by the outer wrapping to be safely used.

I returned very slowly to Camp One, a very happy man. For the next few days my strategy was to go easy and repair my throat before our big assault on the upper parts of the mountain, knowing that from Camp One the real fun and games were about to begin. We had a quick foray out towards Camp Two with light day packs to get a little more elevation and reconnoitre the first few challenges. The route moved across the side of a rocky slope that dropped off to our right at varying angles for a kilometre. After moving across the side of the slope for two hundred and fifty metres the route climbed up on to a ridge; doubling the exposure factor as there were now drops on either side of us.

I had been anxious as to how I would deal with the exposed sections of the climb that left us perched on thin ledges of ice or rock with hundreds of metres of air below us. Although our half day sojourn was only a taste of what was to come, I was pleased to see that I remained focused on the rock ahead and did not suffer significantly from vertigo. Andy led as we climbed along the exposed ridge, all the time connected to a fixed line via a carabiner. Eventually we reached the most significant rock section of the mountain, a thirty metre rock pitch known as the Yellow Tower. We looked at it and agreed; it was going to be a challenge when we came back to begin our climb in earnest. We took solace in the fact that we had for the time being reached our goal of 5900 metres and needed to return to Base Camp to sleep, eat and strategise.

Relativity is a wonderful thing. Base Camp suddenly felt like paradise. We ate three square meals a day and slept comfortably on the flat plateau floor. Andy visited the other expeditions to ascertain when they were planning to be high up on the mountain whilst I sorted through our kit and prepared our rations. As luck had it, the group we had linked in with for Base Camp support was heading out of Base Camp the following day. None of the other expeditions appeared to be aiming for the day after that, which opened an opportunity for us. Andy negotiated with the expedition leaders to have one of their tents left at Camp Three. It meant that we would have a little less weight and therefore could hopefully climb from Camp One to Camp Three in one day, the risk being that if we didn't make it to Camp Three we would be left high on the mountain without a tent. The advantage being that we could avoid using Camp Two which had a reputation for being exposed and too small to cater for everyone.

From Camp Three we were intending to move up to the summit and return all the way back to Camp One on the same day. In total that would have us on the upper parts of the mountain for only two full days. That part of it at least sounded appealing.

On the morning of our departure from Base Camp we anxiously waited to see if any other climbers were heading up towards the mountain. A few smaller groups headed off but we were pretty certain they were moving up to acclimatize only. We were hopeful that the South West route would be unclogged and that the weather would hold for our two critical days. It took the best part of the day to move up through ABC and across the rocks to Camp One. Although we had slept at Camp One before we no longer had a camping space as we had taken our tent back with us to Base Camp. Camp One was precariously located on the side of a sharply angled rock slope with only limited rock platforms suitable for pitching a tent. Andy and I found a space not more than a metre wide and began extending the platform as best we could with large rocks to give ourselves more room. Once complete we squashed the tent onto the jagged rock space and tied it down to nearby boulders. I began laying out our gear inside the tent while Andy headed off to collect fresh snow to melt for water. The last time we'd stayed at Camp One the recent snowfalls had made it easy to collect snow, which in turn gave us an ample supply of water. On this occasion, however, a few days had slipped past since the last dump, and many more people were vying for these vital supplies on the lower parts of the mountain. Andy spent over an hour finding a suitable clump, ultimately moving along the slope to a rocky pinnacle that provided a perfect viewing point for the whole of the South West route. From that vantage he could see that the group that had gone before us had not climbed as quickly as previously anticipated. They would still be on the mountain the next day when we had our epic climb from Camp One to Camp Three. Although they would be coming from the other direction, we would have to give them priority on the ropes.

Also watching from the pinnacle was a well known expedition leader called Henry Todd. Andy had heard and read a lot about Henry as he was an acclaimed leader on mountains above eight thousand metres, including Everest. On this occasion he had a couple of small groups climbing at different points on the mountain.

Andy and I were forced to sleep very close to each other, thanks to our dodgy makeshift platform. It was extremely uncomfortable and probably played a significant role in getting Andy out of bed by five the next morning. Peering outside, it was motivating to see a perfect cloudless and deep blue sky emerge from the blackness of night. There was not a hint of wind in the air as we boiled some water for porridge and packed up our gear to get moving by 6am. Andy and I worked like clockwork and departed the camp feeling confident about the first of our two big days ahead.

As we walked past the rock pinnacle, Andy yelled out to a tall burly man quietly watching the climbers above, "Hey, Henry, have your guys started moving yet?"

"Looks like they are just about to push off," Henry called back.

"No worries. Might see you in a few days," Andy cheered.

159

"Alright. Good luck to the both of you."

I looked over and gave him a smile, only just stopping myself from saying, "We need all the help we can get!" Andy was already gaining ground on me. No longer was he moving along at a conservative pace, indicating to me this was crunch time. We had twelve hours to climb up through a rock section, then a mixed section consisting of both rock and ice, and finally an ice section that led to Camp Three. There was no time to waste.

▲　▲　▲

Moving across the rocky slope and along the ridge to the Yellow Tower was a lot more difficult the second time around. It should have been easier as we were familiar with the route but with additional weight on our backs and the rigid plastic boots, the climbing was slow and very strenuous. I concentrated as hard as possible to move quickly across and up the ridge so as to keep within range of Andy. Eventually I caught up with him at the Yellow Tower. He was beginning to attach a jumar to a blue and black rope that hung from the top of the cliff. This was a particularly difficult section for Andy from a pride perspective. The thirty metre vertical pitch above him was something he could easily scale if at a lower altitude, wearing proper gear, and without a fully laden pack, but none of these circumstances prevailed. We didn't have time for him to climb the pitch and then haul his gear up. If we wanted to make Camp Three by nightfall we had to take advantage of the fixed line, a manoeuvre Andy had been contemplating for the last few days. The difficulty Andy was facing was not the task of 'jumaring' up the rope but the fact that he was utilising a fixed line to aid his climbing. Andy had only ever climbed mountains or rocks in the purest of fashions. His strategy was normally to climb unassisted, free from any previously placed ropes or artificial aids. As he stepped up and raised his jumar, he turned to me and said sarcastically, "Bloody hell, we should have just brought a ladder."

I watched as Andy awkwardly climbed the rope with his big pack threatening to flip him backwards at any moment. I didn't need to be psychic to know he wasn't enjoying any part of this exercise, and indeed using a jumar in this fashion wasn't something Andy was accustomed to at all. As soon as he hauled himself over the lip of the rock face I began my own ascent. In addition to the jumar I attached a thin cord known as a prussic. This essentially did the same job as a jumar but was not attached to my harness. It hung to just below my groin and formed a loop big enough to put around one of my boots. I could step up and take the weight off the jumar so as I could slide it up the rope another arm's distance. The thin air and heavy pack made the task exceptionally difficult and by the time I heaved myself over the ledge I was gasping for air and sweating profusely. The exertion forced me to sit with my legs hanging over the edge for many minutes trying to regain my composure. Looking back down the pitch I saw the small ledge at the base of the Yellow Tower, and below that hundreds of metres of exposed cliff, none of which daunted me in the least. The overwhelming enormity of the effort required to climb vertical rock at this altitude was far more overpowering and distracting than any potential plummet to doom.

In the time it took for me to fathom that between me and Camp Two lay a few small pitches of varying degrees of difficulty I worryingly lost all sight of Andy. With a new surge of motivation I got moving again, at one point looking up to find a hand hold in order to climb over a series of large boulders. Taken completely by surprise I was suddenly overwhelmed by a strong smell of faeces. I immediately withdrew my hand from the top of the rock, fearing that I had placed it on another climber's morning dump. Examining my appendage for human waste I was relieved to see the hand was clean so I reached up again and pulled myself up through the boulders, not wanting to even think about where the offending odour had originated from. Immediately in front of me was a small yellow tent and a few metres beyond another two tents were squashed between the rocks. I had arrived at Camp Two.

The area was no bigger than a single car garage space. It was literally perched on the side of the ridge with spectacular cliffs falling away on either side. The tents were jammed amongst the spiky rocks that covered the small area. And there was my answer. In the heat of the day the smell of human excrement was rife, providing ample encouragement to move through the area as quickly as possible. So tight was the area that the occupants had no option other than to relieve themselves right next to their tent. Congratulating myself on the hindsight to not utilise Camp Two, I hurried straight through the contaminated and cramped camp.

Cautiously moving down and around a rock bollard that stood between Camp Two and the first piece of ice hanging off the side of Ama Dablam I found Andy standing there with his arms crossed.

"Where've you been mate?"

"Oh, you know mate, just hanging about on some ropes. That bloody Yellow Tower was a killer," I spluttered between heavy breaths.

"Yeah it wasn't the easiest, and it doesn't look like it's going to get much easier."

With a sombre expression he gazed ahead.

"You're right there, mate, but at least we might have some ice to play with," I suggested.

"Yep, this looks like the crampon point," Andy agreed, kicking a loose bit of snow with his boots and crampons.

"Geesus, mate, you got those crampons on pretty quickly."

"Well I'm not sure if I should have bothered rushing as we won't be moving for at least another hour … have a look at how slow these guys are moving," Andy replied.

I looked ahead and watched a stream of climbers slowly rappel down a massive wall of ice and rock. They didn't seem to be moving with the same urgency and vigour that we had been earlier that morning. There was little to do except take advantage of the forced break to pull out some chocolate and high energy sports gel. It was difficult to swallow even though it was just before midday and I hadn't eaten anything since 5:30 that morning. My body was no longer prioritising time for digestion; it was more concerned with the breathing difficulties and the overwhelming demands of the physical exertion.

Nausea swept my being once more as we moved off from the crampon point an hour after arriving. My body was attempting to adjust, preparing itself for the next bout of strenuous climbing. To reach the wall I followed Andy across a very thin ice bridge, looking the whole time at where my feet were placed in an effort to psychologically trick myself into not noticing the two devastating precipices that dramatically fell away on either side of the bridge. It wasn't until we arrived at the base of the Grey Tower that I felt my anxiety level calm a little. At last I had something solid to grasp in my hand.

Andy was already well on his way up the multiple pitches that lay ahead by the time I reached the base of the climb. Fortunately there were a couple of fixed lines to choose from and so I could also begin to head up as soon as I connected my carabiner. For this section it was easier to use a carabiner as the climb ahead was chunky rock, mixed with patches of ice and snow. Although the angle was near vertical, there were plenty of hand and foot holds. The difficulty, however, was amplified when we were forced to use the crampons while climbing through the rocky sections. I was grateful for the times I had spent with Andy on the local crag in Kathmandu. He had helped me understand the adjustment required in climbing technique, as well as the mindset needed when forced to climb rock with crampons attached. Instead of searching for large platforms to step up onto, the crampon spikes allowed wafer thin cracks to be utilised as standing positions. The larger platforms, usually sought after when wearing climbing boots, were potentially dangerous as the crampon spikes easily slipped unless pressure was evenly applied across the crampon. The concentration required, once again, distracted me from the hundreds of metres of vertical rock that lay directly below.

The wall eventually topped out and another precarious ridge walk was required. Andy continued to climb at a much quicker speed than I was able to achieve. He would often turn to yell back advice or snap off a photo. I didn't expect him to slow as there was little assistance he could provide other than to warn me of potential problem areas. It was as much of a constant challenge to consciously prevent myself from getting flustered at the opening gap between the two of us as it was to conquer this massive task in the first place. But that widening gap did encourage me to hurriedly move forward ... even, perhaps, at the risk of reducing my safety measures.

By late afternoon the route dropped over onto the left hand side of the ridge, which was the wall that made up the western face. Climbing along and up this face was all done on snow and ice. No longer was there any exposed rock. Fortunately the technical skills required to traverse across the walls of ice and up through the three walled ice chutes came back to me quickly. With only the few hours of training on Imja Tse, I found the movement across these ice sections relatively straight forward. Nonetheless it was both frustrating and troublesome to see Andy powering ahead like a freight train.

As the sun began to lower in the sky I noticed cloud cover building up below us. The Base Camp tents and lower portions of the valleys were no longer visible. It was incredible to think I was climbing above the white fluffy clouds I usually looked up at. The surrealism of the moment provisionally helped me savour the true natural wonder around me, as well as the satisfaction of achieving even this much of the challenge, before the agony of the constant physical strain struck home hard again. The good news was cloud formation was not unusual for that time of day and certainly did not indicate bad weather was on its way. To the contrary, as there were no signs of fast moving cirrus clouds high in the sky we were most likely set to enjoy good conditions again the following day. The concern at that moment was the impending nightfall that would bring sub-zero temperatures and gale force winds. We had to get off the exposed ridge and into the sanctuary of a tent or we risked being exposed to blizzard-like conditions.

The snow platform that housed our tent (left by the group that we were sharing Base Camp facilities with) was part of a large mushroom-shaped ice block that bulged out from the side of the vertical western wall. To get onto the ice block I still had to cross over and move along the snow ridge we had been chasing for the better half of the afternoon. While comfortably perched on a wide section of snow on the eastern side of the razor sharp ridge I dumped my pack on the snow in front of me. My long-suffering shoulders immediately relaxed as the blood began freely flowing again to my strained muscles. I quickly opened the top flap of my pack and found my down jacket and head torch, quietly giving thanks that I had pre-empted the needs of the late afternoon by placing both of those items at the top of my pack.

As I popped back up on to the ridge to clamber along the other wall I spotted Andy, motionless, and pinned against the base of the mushroom formation ahead me. He had one hand hanging from the jumar and the other from his ice axe. His feet were unable to get purchase on the ice as the wall mushroomed in towards the mountain.

"Hey Squizza, where are you mate? I need you to give me a hand," he yelled.

As if to deliberately make matters worse, the wind from the west suddenly whisked up making verbal communication almost impossible.

"Andy ... I'm on my way," I yelled, in case he could hear.

All I could do was watch as Andy made a desperate lunge with his ice axe to gain more height. He swung his leg around to push over the lip of the ice ledge. By the time I reached the spot the sun had dropped over the horizon and darkness was rapidly ratcheting up the dangers upon us. Through the narrow beam of light from my head torch I studied the three metre gap in the ice that would require both skill and strength to overcome. I didn't have the time to pull out a prussic cord to help provide a footing for my feet, nor would it have been sensible to take my mittens off to attach the cord. With my energy levels at an all time low I had to get this done the first time around.

Instead of pushing high with the jumar, I opted to swing as high as possible with the ice axe. Mustering all the strength I could harness I jumped up and locked both arms onto the ice axe handle. It held. I quickly reached for the jumar and rushed it towards my mouth. With no weight on the rope, from above or below, the jumar did not slide along the rope. I placed the rope hanging from underneath the jumar inside my mouth and immediately pushed the jumar away. It slid along until I felt the connection to my harness prevent it from sliding anymore. Relaxing my arms, I allowed the harness to take my weight through the jumar.

My breathing was uncontrollable. The pack on my back continued to pull backwards, forcing me to tense my abdominal muscles. I kicked for the wall but my thighs were the only parts of my legs that hit anything solid. I again lunged forward after swinging the ice axe out in front of me, kicking up with my left leg and pushing forward. I was over the lip, laying motionless, sucking hard on the cold air but feeling warm within a temporary state of euphoria.

Complete darkness descended around me as strong winds filled my ears with a piercing whistling. I told myself to keep moving or the cold would quickly sap what was left of my strength. The fixed line was no longer just a safety line; it was providing me with the critical direction in which I was to move. If I shone the light from my head torch to the left or right it disappeared into black velvety nothingness for there was nothing there to reflect off. I had to focus on the rope ahead.

Every twenty or so metres I bent over to unclip the carabineer from one rope to the next. It was difficult to judge the angle of the slope and distance covered as the only reference was the rope in my hand. After doing this several times I again bent over to unclip, only this time I found myself digging in search of the next line. It was gone. I couldn't find it anywhere. The sickening realisation sunk in that there was no more rope to guide or protect me.

I stood there, thinking hard about what to do next. Was I on top of the mountain? How could I be sure that my next footstep wouldn't be my last?

Looking as carefully as possible at the four metres of snow that my head torch allowed me to see, I convinced myself that the angle of the slope was tapering off. I stepped forward and continued walking as best I could on the same bearing. Thirty seconds later I saw a large orange glow appear in front of me as walked over a gentle crest. It was the glow from a tent. I had made it to Camp Three. But where was Andy?

THIRTEEN
CAUGHT HIGH IN THE HIMALAYAS

Kneeling next to vestibule I yelled, "Andy, is that you inside?"

For what seemed like an eternity I anxiously waited for a reply.

"Yes mate," a faint voice from the tent finally called to me.

I unzipped the vestibule and tent door to see Andy, deep inside his oversized sleeping bag. I quickly threw my pack into the vestibule area and sat inside the tent backwards so as to leave my boots and crampons outside, leaning forward to zip the vestibule back up to prevent the spindrift from blowing into the tent. The wind continued to mercilessly pelt the side of our flimsy dwelling, belting it ceaselessly with a loud flapping noise. I lent back and relaxed every muscle in my body.

"Shit man, that was flaming out of control!" I gasped.

"Mate, I'm glad you made it because I am absolutely frozen. I wasn't looking forward to going back out there to look for you," Andy murmured, devoid of any expression.

"Well I'm bloody glad I got over that mushroom ledge the first time or I'd still be there now."

"Yeah, look mate, I probably should have stayed to make sure you were alright, but I was watching you all day and knew you could make it. I thought I'd try and get to the tent before the sun went down 'cause I couldn't be arsed putting on a down jacket. Bloody wish I had've now," he said with almost an ironic laugh in his voice.

"Shit, you were out there in just a fleece? You must have been bloody frozen by the time you made it to the tent."

"That's why I'm in my sleeping bag … I was going down … bloody quickly. I kept on thinking we were just around the corner. That flamin' last twenty minutes felt like three hours. If we hadn't been delayed by that other group we would have made it in good time."

Before I took my boots and crampons off I headed back out into the cold to collect some ice for our cooking and drinking supply, taking Andy's sleeping bag cover to carry the ice and an ice axe to cut out the chunks of frozen water. By the time I arrived back inside the tent Andy had set up the stove and begun to prepare our dehydrated satchels of food. There was still a significant level of wind gusting under the vestibule, which forced us to place the stove on the inside of the tent, so once lit we had to be damn certain not to accidentally knock it over.

During the twelve hours of climbing we had gained over five hundred metres in altitude. Camp Three was located at 6230 metres, which put us slightly above the height of the Imja Tse summit. To get there had been far more demanding than the Imja Tse climb, yet I hadn't vomited. The training, altitude drugs, and longer acclimatisation period had all undoubtedly helped to prepare me for this much greater challenge, hence despite the cold and exhaustion I was quietly feeling excited that we had made it this far.

Andy was adept at replenishing his energy stores. He managed to eat and drink just as he would at lower altitudes, while I found it very difficult to take in anything other than a few mouthfuls of vegetable pasta and an energy bar. It irritated me as I knew I would need the strength for tomorrow, but my body stubbornly refused to accept any further nourishment. By 8:30pm we turned off our head torches and shut our eyes, leaving me only able to hope my energy reserves would be sufficient for the challenges ahead. For the next ten hours I lay horizontally and tried to sleep. It was simply impossible. The winds continued all night, flapping and distorting the tent. My breathing was laboured, preventing my chest from relaxing. My mind was racing, thinking back over all the precarious moves of the day and predicting the challenges of the day ahead. Was I up to the challenge? Would I have enough energy to keep on the move?

▲　　▲　　▲

A crap night's sleep had done nothing to help me prepare for another massive day of climbing and descending, and Andy didn't seem to be in much better shape. Despite this we both knew that complaining about it wouldn't help with the next challenge.

We had until 8am before we needed to be ready to step outside. At that time the winds should have slowed and the sun would have risen high enough to beam down on the western face of the mountain. Leaving beforehand would have meant unnecessarily exposing us to extreme cold. The plan was to climb up to the summit and return, without any packs and hopefully within 4-5 hours. We could then pack up and rappel off the mountain to Camp One in the afternoon.

Just as we were about to step outside and put on our crampons we heard voices. I unzipped the tent door and saw a guy in his thirties yelling back towards the direction we had come from last night. We soon worked out from his conversation and lack of pack that he had slept at Camp Two for the better part of last night and then climbed up to Camp Three early this morning. Andy and I looked at each other, bemused, somehow knowing we were both thinking, "Why on earth did we choose to haul our packs all the way to Camp Three? That guy probably had a much better sleep than we did at the lower altitude, even if it was among a faeces-filled nest."

By the time we were out of the tent the other climber and his partner were fifty metres up the first ice wall. They were both moving quickly and looked energised. I hoped that I too would move more graciously now that the heavy pack had been removed from the equation.

In daylight we had a chance to check out the surroundings of Camp Three. Above us was the most prominent feature of Ama Dablam, a massive overhanging glacier literally stuck on to the side of the sheer western face. It towered over us like a roof, ready to crash down upon us at any moment. It was probably a good thing that we hadn't seen it in daylight before we entered the tent last night. The ledge that we had slept on consisted of ten square metres of horizontal ice. From our tent the massive block of ice gradually rolled away from the mountain, conforming to the shape of its description, that of a mushroom. The 180 degree view of the snow-capped mountains and deep valleys of the Himalayas would have been soothing had I not been facing a climb of over six hundred vertical metres.

Andy again took the lead as we headed off from Camp Three to a route that inched up the ice wall that lay beneath the overhanging glacier. The more we climbed the steeper it became, and as we entered the shadow of the glacier we began angling off to the right so as to move around, rather than over, the colossal piece of ice. We manoeuvred around and then back on to the top of the glacier before I suddenly realised that I was climbing at the same speed as Andy. How did that happen? I guessed the reasons weren't as important as the fact of the matter so I just let it go. My confidence level was returning.

Stopping for a short break afforded me the opportunity to take in the enormity of the snowfield above us. From the point where I stood to the summit was a three hundred metre wide ice-field creating the spiky spear-like appearance of the mountain. The seventy degree slope was ribbed with vertical ice flutes from top to bottom, and the only hope of approximating a correct perspective came by observing the two climbers in front of us who were fast becoming miniscule dots.

Andy asked me if I wanted to take the lead. From there the climbing was nothing other than mechanical. It would be a hard slog, but in relative terms a straight forward climb so I didn't hesitate and stepped past Andy to take point. An hour up the chosen ice flute I came alongside the only bare rock in the whole of the ice field. Up close it was about the same size as a small truck and only then did I realise that this was the 'famous rock'. Six months before, when Nud and I had first spotted Ama Dablam we were ecstatic to see a climber on this high section of the mountain. As the day went on we noticed that the climber was not moving up or down and was possibly in a lot of trouble. Two days after that we concluded the motionless black spot was probably nothing more than a rock. Now I was able to confirm for myself it was not a rock, but rather a massive boulder.

The climbing was not significantly easier without the packs; it did mean that we could move more quickly but we still gasped for breath during the entire venture … and the two climbers above were still annoyingly moving quicker than we were. They eventually disappeared from sight, which I hoped meant they were standing on the summit. Although Andy and I were moving together we didn't speak a word, needing to concentrate on the mental challenge as much as the physical ordeal. In the next moment I noticed the other two climbers coming back down the ropes. It was a good sign as surely this indicated we were not too far away from the summit. As we stood to one side to allow them pass, we exchanged greetings.

"Much further to go, mate?" I found myself asking.

"Oh, you're about three quarters of the way."

I knew I shouldn't have asked. Every time we reached a point that looked like the crest in the slope, it opened up again for another long stretch. It seemed so long ago I had believed we were almost there that I stopped myself from even thinking that we were getting nearer. Even when I saw a colourful prey flag fluttering on the ground as if to whisper, "You really are nearly there this time, mate," I ignored it, refusing to suffer the indignity of another anticlimax. I became robotic, moving forward as if in a trance. It was Andy who suddenly snapped me back to reality.

"Yeah, baby … we've made it!" he cheered.

Did I hear that right?

There was no longer a wall of white snow in front of us but rather a series of white capped mountains, in fact the biggest mountains in the world. These were the giants; Makalu, Lhotse, Nuptse and Cho Oyu who stood haughtily in the shadow of the grandest of them all. The almighty Everest towered supremely in the background with its very own plume of white cloud bellowing off to the north.

Glancing down deep into the valley below I saw Imja Tse, it no longer looked challenging.

We had taken a lot longer than anticipated to reach the summit, proven by the fact that the midday sun had reached its zenith in the sky just above us.

"Alright, Squiz, let's get some photos and then get the hell out of here," shouted Andy.

We took turns to stand with our back to the largest mountains in the world whilst the other captured the moment on camera. I, in particular, wanted a photo taken whilst holding up a special t-shirt I'd been dragging up the slopes in anticipation of success. The t-shirt was from WFP's global awareness campaign, designed to alert the world to the ongoing hunger disaster affecting over 840 million people. The campaign simply titled 'Fight Hunger' requested individuals to don one of the Fight Hunger t-shirts and walk a small distance on a designated date. Although our climb failed to line up with the designated date for the 2005 Fight Hunger Campaign, it was a particularly unique backdrop that could be a helpful stimulus for 2006.

Ecstasy didn't really come close to describing my sensation in that moment, a moment I knew I should fully savour as in the next 24 hours the same perils we'd faced on the way up were about to be replicated on the journey back to Base Camp.

It took us two and a half hours to reach the tent at Camp Three.

"So, mate, how the hell are we going to get off this mountain before dark?" I asked between puffs of heavy breathing.

"I'm not sure; I don't think we can make it back to Camp One today."

"What about Camp Two?" I asked hopefully.

"Even that might be pushing it, and there is every chance that there won't be any spots available."

I shut my eyes. On the one hand I wanted to stay at Camp Three for another night as it meant that we had no more down-climbing for the day, but it also meant that we would have to spend another night perched on the ledge at over 6200 metres. Andy and I ultimately concluded it would be suicidal to pack up our gear and attempt to move further down the mountain in the state we were in. We both lay there, our boots and crampons still attached but placed outside the tent in the vestibule for over an hour. It felt really good to just let the body relax.

▲ ▲ ▲

Only a few short hours after turning the head torches off my body woke up. I was again breathing heavily due to the thin air. My muscles felt sore when I rolled over to find a more comfortable position but I had enjoyed a full two hours of uninterrupted sleep as a result of fatigue. For the remainder of the night I would toss and turn with little more than fifteen minutes of rest at any one time.

At 8am the next morning, Andy and I packed up the tent and headed off the mushroom shaped block of ice that had been our home for the last two nights. Moving with a renewed sense of urgency, and with hope that the day ahead would involve a leisurely series of rappels down the fixed lines that we had used to scale the mountain, we once again permitted hope to become our companion. That was a mistake.

After thirty minutes or so I began to feel fatigue again. The rappelling was particularly difficult as the packs we were carrying were threatening to flip us backwards and the ropes, being only 9mm in diameter, made it hard to control our rate of descent. Ironically we came into Camp Two a bit after lunchtime, which was the same time as the group that had delayed us when we were climbing up. I understood now why they had been travelling so slowly. I sat on a rock, released the straps on my pack, and lent forward to begin taking off my crampons. As my pack lowered itself onto a small space next to the rock it triggered a stench from faeces. I was too tired to care.

A relatively fresh turd was smeared along the bottom of my pack. I leant over, picked up a rock and began wiping off the gooey remains not even realising I didn't care about the smell; I just wanted to get off the mountain.

I set off before Andy but it didn't take long for him to catch me up and we continued down the mountain at the same pace. We both instinctively knew it was important to stay with each other during this last section due to our fatigue and diminishing morale. By the time I reached the bottom of the Yellow Tower I sat down and looked across at the small tents that made up Camp One. Although our objective for the day was within visual sight I found myself grappling with the mindset that I could not go any further. My body was telling me that I had reached my physical limit. If it were not for the fact that I still sat precariously on the side of a sheer cliff, without any possibility to pitch a tent, I would have convinced myself that this was as far as I could go. Then I remembered the time when my Under-13 football coach started screaming at the team for not trying hard enough at training.

"What you boys don't understand is that you are far from reaching your limit! If there was a tiger chasing you around this oval everyone of you would be running quicker," he'd holler.

He was right. I did have enough in me to reach Camp One if I changed my focus. I began concentrating on the tents and the comfort they would bring rather than the immediate pain of each step.

It worked.

Andy and I safely returned to the relative security of Camp One as other teams and couples were preparing for their attempt to reach the summit. I didn't envy them one bit. We both must have looked like we were on our last legs as we slowly began unpacking our sleeping bags, finding snow and sorting through our kit. I was not only moving slowly but also constantly trying to restrain coughing fits that left me doubled over.

Later that night I began to reflect on the achievement and relish in the euphoric feeling of accomplishment.

Over the days ahead, as we made our way back down to Base Camp and on to the main route travelled by trekkers heading up to Everest Base Camp, I started feeling elated and proud of our achievement. I couldn't thank Andy enough for the crash course in mountaineering. Neither of us realised at the time just how important the experience would be for me over the coming six months.

FOURTEEN
PREPARING FOR EVEREST

Erika was extremely glad to see me return to work after my three week sojourn climbing Ama Dablam. The civil war was spiralling out of control and our staff needed their security officer more so than ever. Without any time to settle back in, I was sent in to the hills once more to trek down a Maoist district commander that had stolen a satellite phone from one of our staff.

After a weeklong hunt through the remote hills in the west of Nepal, I successfully found the perpetrator and retrieved the phone. When I called Erika to tell her of the good news I was immediately assigned another mission as a Nepalese Army commander had unlawfully detained another staff member in a nearby district. The commander was claiming that our staff member was an informer for the Maoists and therefore committing treason against the state. I immediately set off to speak with the commander in an attempt to secure a release.

My work was quickly becoming intense and demanding as both sides increasingly applied pressure on the aid workers who operated in the army and Maoist-controlled areas. Although it was tiring and delicate work, I felt somewhat comfortable with the challenges that were being thrown at me, having now notched up a level of experience dealing with militants and scenarios of this nature. Aside from the experience already under my belt in this region, the issues were similar to those I had been dealing with over the years in the various hotspots that I had been posted to. To put it crudely, it felt like it was *the same shit but a different bucket*. While I knew no-one could ever fully be on top of the situation when two or more sides were warring, I had gradually become accustomed to what worked in different scenarios and how best to deal with the various actors on this macabre stage. The innocence and naïvety were gone, replaced with a pragmatic "let's get the job done" attitude.

My latest mission was accomplished with little effort, yet despite the satisfaction of achievement there was a niggling sensation in my gut. The root of the sensation had nothing to do with my day to day work but was nonetheless undeniably and very distinctly Nepalese. It had nothing to do with the Nepalese conflict, nothing to do with any doubts about my mission in life; no, the sensation originated from a far more fundamental question burning in my mind ... did I have what it takes to climb Mount Everest?

The more I thought about it the more I became obsessed, so naturally the first person I chased down for advice when I returned to Kathmandu was Andy. He didn't laugh when I told him, which was a good start; in fact he assured me this may not be such a ridiculous undertaking at all. He advised that the journey would be completely different from that which we had just experienced on Ama Dablam because I would be required to climb with people of varying standards and experience, and furthermore they would not be climbing partners of my choice. He also warned that the mountain itself attracted a lot of egocentric individuals who were simply climbing Everest to get the tick in the box. That last comment hit a little below the belt because, if I was going to be honest with myself, I too was only harbouring this burning ambition because Mount Everest was the biggest peak in the world.

I thought long and hard about whether I would be as motivated to climb Everest if there was another mountain that held the record for being the biggest. I did know for certain that I wanted to try and climb a peak over 8000 metres, so from a risk and financial perspective a mountain just a few kilometres west of Everest, called Cho Oyo would be the better choice.

Over the next few weeks I started to research the options over the internet and spoke with climbers in Kathmandu who had climbed over 8000 metres. The obvious step before climbing Everest appeared to be Cho Oyo or at least another 8000+ metre peak so as to be tried and tested in the extreme thin air. The optimum time of the year to climb an 8000+ metre peak in Nepal was April-May. I had only five months to go if I wanted to have a crack at it during the 2006 season. As the majority of Everest expeditions were planned years in advance with tens of thousands of dollars required for a deposit upfront, I began focusing on what it would take to climb Cho Oyo. Only a few days into my research it seemed I was to be thwarted.

I received some information at work that threw my plans into complete chaos. WFP announced that the 2006 Fight Hunger Campaign, the worldwide drive to encourage people to walk a small distance on a particular day in the name of alerting people to the global hunger problem, was to be held on Sunday the 21st May. I stared at the message in disbelief. How could this be?

The optimum and most likely window of opportunity to summit Mount Everest fell during the last two weeks of May each year. The timing of the Fight Hunger Campaign could not have been better. If I was to be successful on Everest I would most likely summit within a week of the 21st May. For a few hours I could not think of anything else. It was a gilt-edged invitation that was simply too good to dare to refuse.

I called Australia and spoke with Nud.

"Hey, Nud, guess what?"

"Ummm … what?"

"I have a bit of a crazy plan but I need you to promise me that you will keep it quiet for the time being."

"No worries, you know it will be safe with me," she answered with an excited tone of curiosity to her voice.

"I think I might give Everest a crack next year!"

"Oh, I knew you were going to say that sooner or later. That's awesome."

"I'm not sure if it is awesome or just bloody stupid, but I can't seem to get it out of my mind. I still need to do a little more homework before I make a one hundred percent commitment, so hold back from telling anyone yet."

Nud understood and convincingly told me she'd support me whatever my decision was. With that kind of encouragement and my new goal fervently developing in my mind, an unrelenting rush of energy gave me crystal clear focus in to my immediate future. I would need all of the vigour I could muster if I was going to pull this off in less than half a year while working amidst an escalating conflict. Before I was willing to even think, let alone say, that I was going to climb Everest I had to find an expedition that would let me in at such short notice ... and I needed to secure two months leave of absence from WFP.

After a couple of conversations with seasoned climbers in Kathmandu I found myself emailing Henry Todd, the British bloke who had watched Andy and me head off from Camp One to tackle the heights of Ama Dablam a month earlier. Henry had been running expeditions on Everest for many years and had a particularly high success rate. He used a strategy, unlike the majority of expeditions, which gave him much greater flexibility to take on climbers at the last minute. He did not formulate a team and have them train and climb the mountain together. He signed up individual climbers and allowed them to more or less use his guidance, Sherpas and permits to climb the mountain as individuals.

Henry was very careful in ensuring that he only took on climbers with a proven track record, and with the right attitude. His reply to my initial email came with a series of questions that I paid very careful attention to in answering. He wanted to know about my previous mountaineering achievements and my reasons for wanting to climb the biggest mountain in the world. With just a few sentences describing my frugal climbing history I made sure that the Fight Hunger Campaign was understood as the main catalyst for moving quickly onto Everest rather than another 8000+ metre peak. He replied that he was willing to accept me on the trip on the proviso that I accepted his ground rules. He was expecting to be in Kathmandu early in the New Year to finalise the administrative arrangements, which would allow us to have a one-on-one meeting, and he generously quoted me his minimum rate of $25,000 US dollars, non refundable should I be unsuccessful for whatever reason. It was a bargain compared to the other expedition companies as they were charging $40,000–$60,000 US.

With the positive response and confirmation of the expedition fee, I put together a spiel outlining my training schedule, sponsorship package, media plan, and anticipated budget to try and win over the various decision makers at WFP. Erika was right behind the idea; fired up by the potential opportunities. So too were the organisers of the Fight Hunger Campaign for 2006. The campaign used the motto '*Walk the World* on the 21st May to help Fight Hunger'. My *walk to the top of the world* fit in perfectly with the campaign lead up.

My application for two months leave without pay was tentatively approved, although a replacement for my position would have to be found. By the end of December it all began falling into place; I could see the plan was coming together. My training to this point had focused on rebuilding the weight and strength I'd lost on Ama Dablam. I ate and drank a great deal in an attempt to put the weight back on, and concentrated on core body exercises, such as chin ups and sit ups, to rebuild some lost strength. During the month of January it was time to focus on building my lung capacity through intense aerobic conditioning. This necessitated getting out of bed at five in the morning to go for a mountain bike ride or run on the outskirts of Kathmandu before work. Dragging myself out of bed at that hour was hard enough on the frosty mornings, but the wrench was made infinitely more difficult once Nud joined me to live in Kathmandu. She wasn't up for the early morning activities, although she did join me on extensive bike rides during the weekends.

All was going well until 14th January when my training plan was forcibly put on hold. The Maoists had attacked a number of government buildings and police posts on the outer perimeter of Kathmandu. These were the very places where I had been conducting my training and were now off limits for UN staff. The forecast on the war front was not very pretty. The Maoists announced the attacks were just one of many disturbances that urban centres across Nepal would be enduring in the lead up to the 8th February, the date that the King had set forth to hold national municipal elections.

True to their word the Maoists covertly infiltrated the urban centres, including Kathmandu, in an attempt to muster local support and to initiate a series of 'bandhs' (or strikes). On a Maoist declared bandh day all shops had to be closed and no form of motorised transport was allowed to be used. A marked increase in tension strangled the activities of those living in the capital city as bandhs increased in frequency, although I was soon to realise they were in fact a blessing in disguise. For the first time I could run through the streets of Kathmandu without any crazy traffic or fumes.

Election Day was eerily calm, resulting in little violence due to low attendance at the polling booths. The Maoists appeared to be slowly changing their strategy from one of violence to one of disruption and protest on behalf of the people. The transition was well thought through as the general population was increasingly disappointed with the lack of economic and political progress being achieved by the King. The ensuing chaos being created around the country doubled my workload, which in turn put even greater pressure on my fundraising and media awareness efforts. I felt as though I was being pulled in two directions and needed an army of clones to achieve everything required of me in the limited time. Fortunately Nud was able to come to the rescue by shouldering some of the responsibilities leading up to my face-to-face meeting with Henry in February.

▲ ▲ ▲

It wasn't hard to spot the tough Brit. When Henry entered the café where we'd agreed to meet he towered over the average-sized Nepali. I waved to get his attention, a gesture greeted with an open hand and larger than life smile from the man who was about to direct my upwards ascent.

"Hi, Squiz. Good to see you again," he cheered, approaching my table.

"G'day, Henry. Likewise."

"So, are you feeling up for the challenge?"

"Well, I've been doing a fair bit of training and I'm starting to feel the results of that, which is making me feel a lot more confident."

"Well don't train too much because there is no point turning up in April and being tired. In fact what is more important is that you turn up as relaxed as possible and with a few extra kilos than normal because you will need them as a reserve when you get up high. The other really important thing is to make sure that you don't get sick. Just a common cold has been enough to prevent people from summiting in the past. And whatever you do, don't rush to Base Camp. It is really important, just like the rest of the climb, that you take your time when gaining altitude."

"Yeah, I really learnt that one on Ama Dablam as I enthusiastically raced forward each day on the way in and ended up getting a horrendous cough."

"There are a couple of other things that I need to let you know so there isn't any confusion on the mountain. I have some very experienced climbers coming on the trip this year and also a couple of guys who have had limited time in the mountains like yourself. Regardless of the experience level, everyone is expected to get themselves to Camp Four. You will of course do that in small groups, with the other climbers, but I am not providing a guide or any personal Sherpa service. I will remain in Base Camp or Camp Two and control you remotely via a radio. Does that make sense so far?"

"Yep. I think I would prefer to do it that way rather than clamber up as a large group."

"Well that's the purpose. It gives me a lot more flexibility as I can adjust your schedule depending on how you are going. Now ... you will carry all of your personal gear but I will get my Sherpa teams to go in advance to set up the tents and fix the lines. If you are successful enough to reach Camp Four, which is at the South Col, I will link you up with one of my experienced Sherpas who will climb with you to the summit. It is important you understand that when you are going for the summit the Sherpa will be carrying the radio and will be communicating with me down at Base Camp so that we can make any decisions on your behalf. You will need to focus all of your energy into getting to the summit if we should be fortunate enough to be given a decent break in the weather."

"Rightio, it sounds like it is going to be quite a challenge."

"Well it certainly isn't easy but if you listen to my Sherpas then you won't get yourself into any trouble. The climb itself is not as steep as Ama Dablam so you shouldn't have any troubles with the gradient. And considering that we start using supplementary oxygen at 7200 metres, you only have to be able to climb 400 metres higher than the summit of Ama Dablam."

I thought back to how exhausted I was on the summit of Ama Dablam and knew I didn't ever want to feel that shattered again. But I was ready to do whatever it took to make sure that this trip was successful, and the meeting with Henry bolstered my belief that I would be in the hands of the professional who offered me the best and safest opportunity to achieve that success. It was a timely shot in the arm too, as there were less than six weeks before I would once again board a flight for Lukla. Joining me aboard the flight would be Nud, my parents, and a friend of the family named Sandra. I had encouraged the trio to join Nud and me on the walk to Everest Base Camp even though they didn't have a clue what that really meant … which is probably why they agreed to give it a crack.

During the month of March I began to focus my training on building up endurance. I achieved this by going for long walks with a fifteen kilo pack on my back, sometimes just walking up and down the same the hill for hours on end. To help build some of the reserve that Henry had mentioned I ate large quantities of fatty foods and gulped down lots of beer. It didn't feel much like I was in training but there wasn't any other way to stockpile a few extra kilos in such a short period of time. Also during the month of March I went on a field trip to a remote rural district called Dailekh which, unbeknown to me, would provide added incentive to face and overcome the undoubted adversity ahead.

I arrived at a rural school in Dailekh just on feeding time and watched on as the children received their daily food ration from WFP. On first glance the meal itself didn't look all that impressive, consisting of a few handfuls of a mix which could have been dried porridge. In fact each small portion was a rich composition of vitamins and minerals that were critical for the children's development. It provided their parents with the encouragement needed to release them from the duties of the farm, which in turn gave the children the opportunity to get an education.

As I looked around the school at the impoverished little faces the grand design that had been driving me to this point crystallised with poignant clarity. The majority of children wore tattered clothing, had no footwear, and relied on this meal as their primary food source for the day. The classrooms were empty of furniture, the floors were made from dirt, and there wasn't any glass in the window frames. The pitiful desolation experienced by these poor families hit hard to the core of my soul. In that moment I was more determined than ever to make sure I raised the Fight Hunger and WFP flag on the summit of Everest on behalf of these children and the remaining millions that endure famine each day.

When I returned from Dailekh there were only two weeks left before departure. The final fortnight was frantic because I had to handover the responsibilities of fundraising and publicity to those working on the Fight Hunger Campaign, orientate Chris McCann (who had arrived to carry out my work duties) and finalise the purchase and packing of all clothing and equipment. The latter was made particularly difficult as I was counting on a large overseas shipment of high altitude clothing and sleeping bags coming from a manufacturer that had promised to help kit me out for the expedition. When the boxes finally arrived I eagerly tore into them only to discover they had sent items barely suitable for a mild winter night in Melbourne (i.e. 5 degrees Celsius). This left little time to buy the necessary extreme weather gear that would be required to survive the howling winds and blizzard conditions synonymous with the high altitudes of Everest.

I rushed around the shops of Thamel, no longer haggling over prices, to purchase the final few items that were missing from my list of essentials, and collected plastic barrels to be used for transporting my equipment before heading to a restaurant to meet Henry for dinner. As soon as we made eye contact his face lit up with another monstrous smile and open hand. He certainly had a way about him that somehow helped ease apprehension.

"Welcome, Squiz."

"Hi, Henry. How are you?" I asked, shaking his hand.

"Very well thanks. Can I introduce to you Pommy, and Aussie Tim?"

I turned to shake Pommy's hand as he stood up. He had a shaved head, tattoos covering both forearms, and a set of shoulders that any rugby player would have been proud of.

"'Ello," he said, preparing to sit back down.

I mused over how Pommy's firm hand shake and brief greeting matched his thuggish appearance as I turned to the other leaner man.

"G'day, mate. You can call me Kahuna. It's just these Pommy blokes who call me Aussie Tim," he explained, with a welcoming smile plastered across his face.

"No worries mate. I hear that we are the only two Aussies on the team."

Before Kahuna could answer, Pommy said, "Yep, and that's two too many as far as I'm concerned."

Henry and Kahuna laughed at Pommy's sarcasm. It was a good ice-breaker, proving from the outset that our group enjoyed a good joke and could hold themselves in a relaxed manner.

"Don't worry about this bloke, Squizza. He's just a little uptight because he knows how much stronger we Aussies are when we hit the mountains, or any other sporting challenge!" Kahuna teased.

"Hah … no flaming chance of that, you little git. What about the 2003 Rugby results?" Pommy shot back, taking a swig of his beer.

"Bloody hell, Pommy, how many times have I heard that over the last few weeks? Is that the only thing we have ever let you guys win?" Kahuna asked cheekily.

It was quite obvious that the two lads knew each other quite well. They had just spent the last two weeks together on a trek in the Annapurna Region of Nepal as part of their acclimatisation and fitness preparation, and were now relaxing in Kathmandu getting ready to begin their walk in to Base Camp. The boys would have to fill in some time on the trail as they were hitching a ride on the cargo flight that was dropping our equipment in Namche Bazaar in a few days. Henry later reminded all of us that we were not to arrive at Base Camp any earlier than 12ᵗʰ April as he would not have the latrines, mess tent and kitchen set up before then. This worked well with my schedule as Nud had booked our flights for a departure on the 4ᵗʰ April, allowing just the right amount of time to reach Base Camp.

▲　▲　▲

"Whoooo hoooo, Mark darling ... it's time to get out of bed!" a voice whispered from the darkness.

I sat up knowing that gentle command could only have come from one person – my mum. Hardly anyone else called me Mark anymore and I don't think anyone else will ever be able to replicate that familiar way of waking me up. It was finally time to forget about all of the preparations and start focusing on getting the job done. It was Tuesday the 4ᵗʰ April and poor dad was feeling a little sick as he had eaten something that didn't agree with him. Quietly Nud and I couldn't help but laugh; this was not the best time to be constantly in need of a decent toilet.

On the way to the airport I gave a quick brief on the unorganised carnage we were about to experience at the terminal and held all of the tickets intent on getting the five of us seats on the same plane. The cloudless sky could have deceptively filled the unsuspecting with optimism that all passengers would be able to make it on this day but I knew better. I was anxious right up to the last moment when boarding passes were issued. Once those vital permits to fly were safely in hand I felt obliged to advise dad, "This is a forty-five minute flight, and for sure there won't be any toilets on the plane. You might want to take advantage of the airport toilets."

He headed off in the direction of the men's room as I turned to mum.

"He doesn't have a clue what he is heading into you know."

Dad returned a few minutes later with a smirk on his face.

"That was disgusting. I couldn't tell the difference between the toilet and the floor. The whole place was a putrid mess."

"Welcome to Nepal, dad," I grinned.

A few minutes later we were hurriedly boarding a light aircraft with other trekkers kitted out in all of the latest outdoor clothing. As the aircraft reached the end of its taxi and soared into the Nepalese skies it was as though all the pent-up pressure leading up to this moment vanished like melting snow. The journey was about to begin.

Although this was my third landing at Lukla in twelve months every nerve still sizzled with excitement at the prospect of heading out into the great unknown once more. Nud and I helped lead the others to the Sunrise Hotel so as to avoid the teeming porters at the airport. A number of the more ambitious would-be baggage handlers followed us as we clambered down the steps, anticipating that we would eventually surrender. They were mistaken. Between the five us we only had three back packs weighing a total of fifty kilos; this time around I was only interested in carrying the bare essentials in a small day pack, the rest was shipped in advance with Henry's cargo.

We were no sooner on the ground when Dad's radar telemetry sought out the nearest toilet facilities while the ladies set about ordering some tea. Glancing around the now familiar scene I spotted a group of waiting porters gathering at the front gate. I bargained to have two of them join us and then saddled them up for our journey.

The first thing I noticed when we moved off towards Monjo was that Mum, Dad and Sandra moved at a particularly slow pace. Looking a bit gawky and aged in my eyes, they each carried ski poles to aid with the unstable and at times steep track. Their pace was actually convenient as I was making a concerted effort to minimise my work rate to prevent heavy breathing. At these lower altitudes it wasn't so critical but I thought it would be good practise for when the thinner, colder and drier air would begin to eat away at the back of my throat. I couldn't afford to have a cough in the first few weeks or the remainder of the trip would be unbearable.

Many other trekkers, some in pairs and some in groups of up to ten, cruised past as the day wore on. We eventually reached Monjo at 4pm, just as the sun began to drop behind the towering ridges above us. I dropped my pack at the gate of the Tea House that had previously provided us with such good service and accommodation and left Nud at the gate for the others who were only a few minutes behind us. I grabbed a fleece jumper from the top of my pack and headed towards the dining room to book in our accommodation.

As I opened the door the warmth of the room embraced my body. The room was already quite full and alive with a positive vibe from small groups that were either exchanging stories from the trail or playing cards. A large lady with a familiar face exited the kitchen through the drapes with a round of hot mugs in her hands. After she placed them down at a nearby table I approached her and asked if she had space for five more guests.

"Sorry, we are full. Many, many groups at this time of year."

"Okay, no problem. Thanks anyway."

By the time I had walked back outside, Nud was welcoming the trio donned with ski poles.

"No joy here folks, all the rooms are taken."

"Damn, that's a shame," Nud answered, trying not to sound overly despondent.

"You guys stay here and I will quickly see what I can find up the track," I announced optimistically.

Darting from one side of the track to the other I entered and departed the neighbouring tea houses one by one. Every one of them was full, except for some space at the dinner table after 9pm when the other trekkers would have retired for the night. It was not the way I wanted to start the trip. With only two tea houses left unchecked I was feeling less than optimistic about securing a private room. In desperation I began to explain how I needed to find accommodation for my elderly parents and therefore would prefer to avoid the dining room floor. Happily one of the "inn keepers" took pity on my situation ... I knew it was a flash of inspiration to invite Mum and Dad along!

The owner of the second last tea house offered us his prayer room. I checked it out before heading back to pick up the others, just in case there were any problems with it. As the owner gingerly led me up three sets of rickety wooden stairs just wide enough for one person I kept reminding myself "beggars can't be choosers". At the top of the last flight there was barely sufficient illumination to see a small door immediately on the right. He opened it, asking me to watch my head as I entered. I crouched low not wanting to pre-emptively imagine what it would be like inside.

Aladdin's Cave! I entered a room opulently filled with every lavish colour of the rainbow and encased by large glass windows. A massive statue of Buddha adorned the main wall in front of me with vibrant prayer flags criss-crossing the roof. It was better than perfect; it was truly an oasis in the desert. The owner's exceptional generosity was rewarded with a liberal tip the next day. Anticipating accommodation problems again, I sent one of the porters ahead to secure us five beds in Namche Bazaar. It would be a strategy we would have to employ if we were to be certain of obtaining private rooms in future.

I reached the Everest viewing platform around midday with a few moments to stare alone at the imposing summit before Nud caught up. I pulled out my map to reconcile the distance between me and my daring objective. The base of the mountain was around thirty kilometres away and the summit more than five and half vertical kilometres straight up from my current position. Memories of freezing temperatures, blizzard conditions and nausea unwelcomingly returned to my mind.

When the others arrived, Nud and I helped them find Everest through the trees as I pointed out the distances I'd just calculated.

"You'll be right, son," Dad said, always ready to back his son.

At the gates to Namche Bazaar we were greeted by our porter who was sitting, waiting patiently for our arrival. He happily informed us that he had secured three double rooms at a tea house next to the German Bakery. Good news indeed.

With that potential dilemma out of the way, and to help with the acclimatisation process, we all headed further up the hill for just a few hours to briefly breath-in the air at a higher altitude. Nud and I took a detour on the way back to visit the original Hillary School at Khumjung, established in 1960. It was school holiday time so the grounds were devoid of children and the classrooms locked up, but this did nothing to diminish the magic of the place. I peered through one of the windows and saw neat rows of desks facing a large chalkboard. The walls were covered in colourful paintings from the children and a cylindrical ball with a map of the world rested on the teacher's desk. The rooms and learning environment were significantly better than those I had seen in the not so touristy parts of the country. It was a pity that the abundance of tourists who visited Nepal every year could not see the dire need of those who were isolated by the centralised government and rugged landscape. This fact was yet another reminder to myself about why I was really doing this.

For the following couple of days I had the pleasure of recounting the challenges of Ama Dablam as we all walked around the sheer faces that help comprise its western flanks. Mum unsurprisingly commented that she was glad she had not fully appreciated the severity of the slopes when I was on the mountain a few months before or she would have been wracked with nerves for the duration. Dad moved slowly as he was finding his energy stores were insufficient to keep up with the ever-thinning air. He laboured every breath, but continued on with good ol' fighting Aussie spirit. We all ensured that he was encouraged throughout the day by having regular breaks and keeping hydrated.

The next mountain to the north of Ama Dablam was Imja Tse. Only an hour after having a full view of the mountain that helped bring Nud and me together we hooked left and entered the valley that housed the Lobuche River. This wide and dry gorge would lead us all the way to the glacier that was home to Everest's southern Base Camp. Not more than a kilometre along the valley was the village of Pheriche, the second location in which we would have a two-day stop over. At 4200 metres, it was critical that our bodies had the opportunity to adjust to the ever-thinning air.

The air outside had become particularly cold, prompting me to start wearing a facemask more commonly used to protect oneself from fumes in a polluted city. The mask captured the moisture in my breath when exhaling which helped to moisten the dry and cold air that I sucked in. It seemed like overkill at the time but I was motivated to keep disciplined every time I saw a coughing trekker coming back down the valley.

After our first night in Pheriche, Dad failed to get out of bed for breakfast. Concerned I went to visit him, sitting down at the end of his bed. He had not slept well and was feeling particularly weak after many days of being unable to hold on to his food. He looked pale but was still able to smile and crack a joke. We both decided that he should abort the acclimatisation walk and rest in bed for the day. Twenty four hours later I found myself once again walking into his room. He had slept a lot better but was still feeling weak. When my father said he did not feel up to pushing further up the trail I knew I had to take him seriously for he was not one to complain or quit easily. I went and had breakfast with the others and then returned to say 'adieu'.

"So, Dad, we are going to head off now. We've paid for the food and lodging up 'til now so you should only have to pay for any expenses from this point forward."

"Okay, thanks. I should be able to move back down the trail in a few hours," he said hopefully.

"Well don't push it; you have lots of time to slowly cruise back. But if you do decide to head off today then the owner of the tea house said he will organise a porter for you."

"Alright, well be safe now and don't forget that you've got a lot to look forward to when you get back down," he smiled, opening his arms wide. I moved forward and gave him a farewell hug.

"Thanks, Dad. I'll speak to you when I get a chance."

With that I left the room before either of us ruined our machismo with a display of teary emotions.

Half an hour later, as we walked away from Pheriche, Sandra stopped to gather her breath. She called out for mum, which in turn caused me to turn around.

"I'm not sure if I will be able to continue," she yelled between breaths.

"I know what you mean ... it's pretty tough on the lungs," Mum agreed reluctantly.

We all walked towards Sandra. With a tough of resignation in her voice she explained she was feeling exhausted from the thinner air and only dared to think how difficult it would be when the valley's incline increased. Although this was the first time she had verbally communicated the difficulty she was experiencing, inwardly her resolution had already been reached and was firm; this would be as far as she would go. We were fortunate that the porter we had sent in advance had not been asked to carry any of Sandra's clothing. Purely by coincidence, the porter walking with us had all of her gear and most of Mum's; it was therefore a simple logistical exercise to offload Mum's gear into my day pack so the porter with us could return with Sandra. Emotions ran high as the two ladies farewelled one another as they had helped each other through the difficulties we'd faced to that point. In the larger scheme of things it was probably a good thing because she would be able to provide company for dad.

Lobuche, at 4910 metres, was less than four kilometres from where we farewelled one friend and one porter. I slowed the pace as we moved off and actually dropped behind Mum and Nud when I too began to breathe heavily on the steep sections. The temptation to remove my mask reached an all time high as clouds rolled in to the valley not long after 11am. Visibility was reduced to thirty metres and the temperature suddenly dropped under ten degrees Celsius. We decided to keep moving with few breaks so as to reach the sanctuary of our destination for the day, the little village called Lobuche.

Gentle sprinklings of snow fell on our shoulders just minutes before the first tea house at Lobuche emerged through the fog. Our porter was nowhere to be seen but I was not expecting to see him sitting in the cold waiting for us. Peering into the first tea house it was plain to see it was full to the brim, and there was no sign of our porter. Approaching the second tea house an uneasy sense of deja vu tried to meddle with my mind before our trusty porter appeared at the door to usher us in. By that point we were all covered in snow flakes and ready to get out of the cold.

The porter had managed to get us bed space in a dormitory room, which we soon learnt was something to be grateful for. Lobuche only had four tea houses and they were not as spacious as those found at lower altitudes. Frankly all any of us cared about was to be near a warm fire and protected from the ever increasing pillaging winds. The dormitory room, while gratefully welcomed, was bitterly cold so we remained in the dining room until retiring for the evening. Rest didn't come easily for Nud and I, partly because one man sharing our dorm snored so loudly it almost reverberated off the walls, and partly because of the thinner air.

When dawn eventually broke, I sat up and peered between the curtains next to our bed. It was still snowing outside, padding an ever-thickening white blanket across the ground in a perfectly picturesque postcard scene. From a snapshot perspective it really looked quite idyllic. I, of course, knew otherwise.

Over breakfast others warned us it would be unadvisable to push on if the snow storm prevailed, which was fine by me. Nud and I were really keen to stay another night in any event, as we needed the time to get acclimatised to this altitude. Surprisingly, Mum had slept like a baby and was feeling no side affects from the increased altitude whatsoever, in fact she seemed to be getting stronger as the trip went on!

Very few people dared to move from the safety of the tea houses that day. It was an enormous relief when the snowfall slowed that afternoon and the clouds gradually began to dissipate.

Nud and I slept more comfortably the second night at Lobuche, which helped to ease us out of bed early the next day to get started out on the trail to Gorak Shep. We again sent the porter out in front, but this time with a different mission. He was asked to deliver my pack to Base Camp, which was another two hour walk past Gorak Shep. We had decided to hold on to the bed space that we occupied at Lobuche as there was no guarantee of accommodation in Gorak Shep. If we were unable to find accommodation it would have been impossible to find space in Lobuche again, as the delay caused by the snow meant that greater numbers would have been coming up from Pheriche.

Veteran porters broke the snow trail in advance of our walk to Gorak Shep, but with only a few porters and trekkers ahead of us the trail was still icy and very slippery underfoot. Mum's ski poles became the envy of my eye for the first time. By the time we reached Gorak Shep clouds again began to roll in from lower down in the valley. Tantalised with a brief glimpse of the place that would be my home for the next six weeks, Everest Base Camp, we all knew it was not worth risking entrapment by Mother Nature in a fresh storm. Accordingly the last part of the walk was called off.

"It's a rotten shame I can't quite say that I made it to Base Camp," Mum mused, glancing towards the colourful tents dotted like sprinkles on an ice-cream in the distance.

"Well, if it makes you feel any better, Mum, you can say that you made it to the 1953 Base Camp. Apparently Hillary's expedition used Gorak Shep as their Base Camp," I explained, noticing a faint plume of pride puffing in her rosy-cheeked face.

As we turned and carefully began the walk back towards Lobuche on the icy trail, I felt so proud of Mum for coming this far on my journey. She had reached her 'summit' as far as I was concerned and could now happily retreat to the lower altitudes with a profound sense of achievement.

Nud and I slept considerably better the third night at Lobuche. Sunlight through the curtains however eventually put an end to the last comfortable sleep I would have for many weeks.

After paying for our lodging and food the three of us moved thirty metres down a small slope to the trail. I gave mum a big hug for which I received a smothering of kisses in return. She bravely planted a huge smile on her face as she repeatedly told me that she would be thinking of me the whole time. I then turned to Nud and gave her a big hug.

"I love you," she whispered softly.

"Not half as much as I love you," I choked back. "Have fun with Mum and I'll see you shortly."

"Okay, be safe now," she smiled bravely.

As we pulled apart I saw the unmistakable glint of tears welling in Nud's blues eyes. My heart began to pound. I took in a deep breath of air.

"See you later," I said with a controlled smile.

She nodded; turning to Mum's side to walk away.

I also turned away but only took a few steps before stopping and turning back. Mum and Nud kept walking until they neared a turn in the track, which was fifty metres away. They both turned, waved, and then disappeared around the corner. I moved off the trail and squatted. I needed a moment by myself.

There had been one possible outcome of this endeavour I had steadfastly shrugged off since making the commitment to give Everest a crack. Hundreds of would-be mountaineers on Everest never returned.

Even with the help of better equipment and accurate weather forecasts, it was not unusual for the number of deaths and injuries to reach double figures on Everest in any one season. I didn't want the farewell to be the last time I would see two women that that I dearly loved.

I made a promise to myself right there and then. I was going to give this challenge my all but no matter what, I was coming home in one piece.

I stood up, took a deep breath and started walking towards Base Camp.

FIFTEEN
GAPING CREVASSES AND MONSTROUS BLOCKS OF ICE

As I made my way back along the trail to Gorak Shep, my mind continued to revisit the dreadful thought that I had just said goodbye to Nud and Mum for the last time. I tried to stomp on the emotion every time it reappeared to prevent it from eroding my confidence but for the most part with little success. By the time I arrived at the point where the three of us had stood the day before, the clouds had lifted from the valley in front of me and I could once again see the colourful tents of Base Camp. The tents lay on what appeared to be the last piece of horizontal ground on the earth's surface. Near vertical walls rose up on all three sides of the area housing the tents, creating an amphitheatre style appearance.

Seeing the tents fired me up. I became engrossed with the challenge ahead, no longer reflecting on the emotional farewell of that morning. I was desperate to find the route that we would be taking to reach the summit of the mountain; the mountain that I could, for the first time, see in full from top to bottom. The western flanks of Everest dropped down sharply to form the right hand side of the amphitheatre that I was walking towards. It did not appear to be scaleable from this distance prompting me to ponder about the courageous teams that chose to tackle that route. I was to be climbing the classic South East route that followed the exact same course as the first successful expedition, back in 1953. The final approach to the summit was made along the notoriously exposed South East Ridge, however the early stages of the climb involved manoeuvres near to or underneath the Western and Southern slopes.

As I walked towards Base Camp it became evident that after reaching Base Camp the route would take a ninety degree turn to the right, towards the slope of least resistance. This slope fitted the description of the renowned Khumbu Icefall, that of a frozen waterfall abundant with deep crevasses and overhanging seracs – sharp ridges or pinnacles of ice among the crevasses of a glacier. My eyes remained peeled on the Icefall as I meandered my way along the trail that connected Gorak Shep and the 2006 Everest Base Camp. Yak herders had found the optimum route through the craters of melting ice, across the small streams and around the slippery slopes of the glacier during the previous weeks of March. The hoofed beasts had etched a distinguishable, yet thin trail whilst dropping off the tents and equipment necessary to build Base Camp.

Half an hour after leaving Gorak Shep, the summit of the world's tallest mountain disappeared behind its own bulging sides. I was truly moving underneath the belly of this massive giant, feeling dwarfed by its enormity but fired up by the realisation that the challenge I had set myself a little under six months ago was about to begin in earnest. I had to temper my enthusiasm in order to arrest the temptation to walk quickly, which in turn would force heavier breathing.

Before reaching the first tents at Base Camp, the path ironically led all who had come to climb on this side of the mountain past a symbol that revealed first hand the potential dangers that lay ahead. The remains of a helicopter lay on the icy floor of the glacier, still propped up on its underbelly without the back end of the aircraft attached. The cockpit and portions of the fuselage remained in good condition, frozen in time, an icy grave for those who had come before. At 5400 metres it was particularly difficult for helicopter blades to get sufficient purchase in the thin air to remain stable when taking off and landing; as a result emergency helicopter rescues were only carried out for critically ill patients and with minimal weight on board to maximise the chances of a successful flight. These particular helicopter remains, which symbolised the gates to Base Camp, were sadly only three years old. The helicopter pilots had been unable to control their landing and had speared out of control, crashing into the glacier and killing three on board.

Continuing along the trail I eventually reached the first cluster of tents and yelled out to a Nepalese man, "Namaste, Henry Todd's expedition?"

"That big red tent over there," he replied.

His immediate response reassured me that Henry had managed to get things in order and was, as he had previously suggested, linked in with other expeditions. I was indeed fortunate to have him as my expedition leader. I soon spotted a large red dorm style tent with the words 'ICE8000 Everest Expedition 2006' written across the front door. I dropped my pack at the entrance and yelled out, "Hello, anyone home?"

From inside I heard the reply, "Yes, come on in."

I opened the flap door and peered inside. Henry was sitting at a long trestle table that ran the length of the tent devouring a bowl of soup but immediately stood up when he recognised my face.

"Ah, Squiz, welcome to Base Camp," he cheered, moving towards me.

"Thanks, Henry. It's nice to be here."

We shook hands.

"So, can I get you some lunch? There is some being prepared for me at the moment."

"Yes please, that would be great."

Henry left the tent for a few minutes before returning and asking me to join him at the table. As we both sat, he asked me how my walk in had gone.

"Dad and a family friend had run into some difficulties around Periche and so didn't make it much further, but Mum and Nud did really well and made it to Gorak Shep yesterday."

"So you said goodbye to them this morning?"

"Yeah I did, which was fairly tough to do."

"There is no doubt about it; the mountains are an emotional place. They can help you get clarity on many of your feelings."

Over lunch, which consisted of a bowl of soup followed by noodles, Henry explained that the lower parts of the mountain had already been prepared with fixed lines and that the Base Camp was, as of yesterday, fully functional. The green tent was set up for latrines, the red tent was for dining and socialising, the cooks were working from the tent that was reinforced by rocks, and we all slept separately in the yellow dome tents. He suggested that I select a yellow tent, settle in and rest up for the next few days. After lunch I rummaged through a pile of bags and barrels to find my luggage (that had been sent in advance) as well as the pack that the porter had dropped off the day before. As I carried the first of my heavy loads past the dining tent to reach the yellow dome tents, a voice yelled out from the far right.

"Hey, Squizza, ya Aussie git."

"Is that you Pommy?" I called back.

"Nah, mate, it's the Queen's Mother. Who do you bloody think it is?"

"Oh, sorry mate, I wasn't expecting to hear your voice this far up the trail!"

"Ha ha," he chuckled sarcastically.

Pommy crawled out from his tent. He had arrived only a few hours before me and stood at the entrance to his tent as though he was the proud owner of a new house.

"This is the best location around," he announced, going on to explain that the ice would eventually melt during the course of the climbing season and therefore it was critical to be as high up as possible to avoid any runoff.

I had a good look at the other tents that were awaiting occupation. None of them seemed more suitable than the one pitched directly next to Pommy's latest abode so I returned and broke the good news.

"Hey, Pommy, I'm taking this one, 'cause it's one of the closest to the dunny."

"Yeah, but it's also the closest to me," he feigned a grumble.

"I suppose I will have to take the good with the bad," I quipped back, thinking how much I really enjoyed Pommy's sarcastic wit. Somehow I knew that it would be a good distraction when the pressure and stress began to build later on down the track. In the end, as Pommy had no doubt fathomed, the main factor in selecting my tent was knowing I would be next to someone I could have a laugh with.

Tim Calder was the only other climber to have reached Base Camp earlier that day. He had climbed significantly in the Himalayas and was returning to Everest after an unsuccessful attempt the year before that saw one of their party suffer a fatal heart attack while going for the summit. At over 8300 metres, Tim and the remainder of the team were forced to retreat after the sudden collapse of their climbing partner, and after a turn in the weather that complicated matters even further. As I was to learn, returning to conquer the beast, even after death and other adversity, was not at all an unusual occurrence.

As the remainder of climbers on Henry's expedition started to arrive over the next 48 hours it became evident that five out of the eleven of us had attempted to summit Everest previously, a fact that made me feel like an apprentice when we sat around in the dining tent swapping stories of previous climbs. Along with Kahuna, I had the least amount of mountaineering experience, and we were the only two who had not ever gone higher than 7000 metres. We would both have to prove our worth while climbing as we had little chance of competing with the dinnertime stories.

After two days of sorting through my kit, getting to know the other climbers and acclimatising to the new altitude, Henry called Tim, Pommy and me into the comms tent to suggest we head over to the base of the Khumbu Icefall and 'play around a little'. Tim naturally took the lead as he was familiar with the challenges of the Icefall.

"Hey Pommy, are you taking an ice axe?" I asked.

"Yeah mate, I'm taking the lot ... just in case."

"Just in case what?"

"Umm ... just in case there's a bunch of groupies who want to see the Pommy in action," he laughed.

"Man, the altitude is really giving you are a hard time."

I grinned, packed my climbing harness, crampons, ice axe, cold weather gear, sunscreen, camera bag, chocolate and water bottle into a day pack, and was thankful that I had taken the time over the last few days to get everything in order. Tim was already waiting at the dining tent by the time I arrived. A massive field of ice lay three hundred metres away from where we stood. The base, wider than any other part of the Icefall, spanned at least twelve hundred metres across. It was difficult to determine the angle and length of the slope as a whole because the incline angled away from where we stood. The whole area looked like a half eaten piece of toffee, complete with teeth marks and bulging shards that jutted out from the main body. It was a mess and I could hardly fathom a route to the top where a saddle separated the western shoulder of Everest and the northern slopes of her neighbour, Nuptse.

"So, Tim, how the hell do you know where to start?" I asked.

He began pointing towards the Icefall. "Well, see those little black dots in a line about a third of the way across from the left hand side?"

"Yep."

"They are people, either coming down or heading in to the Icefall, we need to get over there and look for the entrance."

Those words helped put the Icefall into perspective. It was a mountain in itself. We skirted around the other camps that lay between ours and the general vicinity of the Icefall entrance, noticing that small trails from the various camps began to join together and lead to a point on the glacier where the undulations became more prominent and the rock debris began to thin out. The trail ran parallel to a large mound of ice for forty metres and then turned sharply to the right, rounding the corner of the mound. Ahead only twenty metres were a couple of large rocks and a small plastic flag on a thin rod embedded into the ice.

"Here we are boys ... the start," Tim announced.

We sat on the rocks and began to pull out our harnesses and crampons as a group of four Sherpas appeared from over one of the mounds that lay ahead. They were moving quickly and appeared sweaty even though they were wearing light clothing. I watched them closely, eager to learn any tips. As they moved past I was amazed to see they hardly stopped to remove their crampons, laughing and joking the whole time. To these guys it was just a walk in their own backyard.

We moved off, treading carefully, over a well-trodden path as solid as concrete. Tim took point, navigating easily using the flags that were every forty metres or so. For the first ten minutes it felt as though we were amongst sand dunes of ice, the path zigzagging through the mounds of glacial frost until eventually we were left with no other option; we had to scale one of them.

A fixed line had been put in place so we decided to hook our jumar on, even though the slope was only five metres in length. None of us wanted to risk an injury at this early stage. I moved quickly to the top to join Tim who was already beginning to set up for an abseil down the other side. I started breathing heavily, my lungs catching up with the sudden exertion, and looked back to see Pommy slowly plodding up the slope. Quickly I reminded myself to slow down; it was not a race.

At the bottom of the five metre abseil was a small stream, no more than three metres wide, frozen solid. Even though the sun had been up for many hours it did not appear to have thawed in the slightest. If it were to unfreeze, which was likely on a clear day, it looked deep enough to swallow an average sized individual up to their knees. Obviously I was not the only one who thought that, because a ladder had been laid down from one side of the stream to the other. It was a perfect training spot for Pommy and me to get familiar with this type of crossing. I knew that we would be required to cross many horizontal ladders when climbing through the Icefall as they were the primary means of crossing the large crevasses. They were all aluminium and firmly secured to the ice. Tim informed us that two safety lines were also attached to the ice in case we fell off the ladders. The safety lines were secured to the ice at ground level on either side of the crevasse with enough slack to prevent the user from having to crouch over whilst moving across the ladder. Tim also told us the best way to become confident was to have someone pull up hard on the safety lines at one end, helping to make them tight and raising them to waist height. In doing so the ropes felt more like hand rails for the person crossing the ladder.

For the next hour the three of us took it in turns to move from one side to the other, sharing the responsibility of tightening the safety lines for the person moving across the ladder. Although the ladder was less than a foot from the ice below, it was unnerving to place a heavy boot, with crampons attached, on the narrow rungs. The crampons often wedged hard onto the rungs, making it difficult to lift them off. Calm and concentration were critical.

Tim took safety very seriously. He had us hook on to both safety lines with carabiners to get into a routine, even though we had no distance to fall should we come off. I agreed as I firmly believed that routines such as these helped to overcome laziness when fatigue set in. We pushed on for another twenty minutes past the first ladder before deciding that it was enough for the day. The dune-like formations were becoming steeper and sharper which meant that we were heading into the Icefall in earnest. In keeping with tradition we were not to venture high onto the mountain until we had received the blessings from a Tibetan Lama monk. These were received during a puja ceremony, which in our case had been booked for the 16th April, two days away.

On our return trip I began to feel a renewed sense of enthusiasm for the challenges ahead. The short foray into the Icefall had helped to erode some of the anxiety and nerves that had been building over the last few weeks and it felt like the siren at the start of a football match was about to scream out the all clear … the game was on.

The night before the puja our mess tent was filled to the brim. All of the eleven Everest climbers had arrived at Base Camp as well as five climbers who were intending to climb the neighbouring mountain of Lhotse. They would climb on the same route as us until we reached Camp Three. Only one of their party was yet to arrive.

We were requested to bring our crampons and ice axes to the puja ceremony, which was due to commence around 10am at a makeshift temple built from the rocks by the Sherpas. I placed my gear by the rock-strewn holy place and stood back to watch the proceedings. The Lama monk arrived dressed in a dirty jacket and worn pair of trousers, quietly taking a seat with Henry and his senior Sherpa in front of the temple. As food and drinks were placed between them and the temple the Lama monk began to chant and throw rice in all directions. For the next two hours we all sat behind these three strategically placed men, dodging handfuls of rice. At intervals of around ten minutes offerings of food and chang (local rice wine) were handed around for consumption. I'd previously promised myself to keep off alcohol until the end of the trip but thought it would be bad karma to refuse the offering on this particular occasion.

As the service came to an end we all filed past the monk and handed him a cash donation in appreciation of his efforts to safeguard our trip. The ceremony was ultimately brought to a close with the whole group throwing handfuls of flour into the air. At the time I was standing next to Kahuna. Pommy, who was standing behind us, took the opportunity to 'accidentally' throw the white powder straight at the two of us and make a quick get away in anticipation of our retaliation.

"Bloody Pommy," Kahuna muttered, dusting off his down jacket.

"Don't worry mate, we'll get him back," I said.

During the evening meal Henry announced that six of us, including myself Pommy and Kahuna, should prepare for a three hour acclimatisation and orientation climb the following day. He had lined up Pedawa, one of his experienced Sherpas, to take us as high into the Icefall as possible in the time allocated. It would be the only time that he would be allocating a Sherpa to guide us on the lower portions of the mountain. We were to depart at 8am.

As the thick blackness of night began dissolving into daylight at 5:45am I could no longer lie about in my sleeping bag. I quickly wriggled out, donned three layers of clothing in an attempt to hold the warmth I'd generated overnight, and headed over to the green latrine tent. Experience had taught me this was the best time to visit the toilet as the normal putrid stench was numbed by the frosty morning.

I was the first to have breakfast that morning. Kahuna arrived not long after but to my surprise, as 8am neared, a few of the others were only just casually walking into the mess tent in search of nourishment. Although I held my tongue I felt annoyed and frustrated that our departure time was not being respected.

"I'll be back in a few minutes lads; just need to snap one off in the toilet," Pommy announced with an all too familiar need to share superfluous information.

"Ha, have fun mate," Kahuna replied.

Pommy was no sooner out of ear shot than I whispered to Kahuna, "Mate, let's stick some rocks in his pack to sort the old fella out."

"Yeah … good idea," he agreed.

I immediately began opening Pommy's pack while Kahuna looked around for a decent sized rock. The first one he collected weighed around twenty kilos. Giggling like a kid he dropped it, realising it was too heavy, and went for another one about half the size. We both helped to place it inside and quickly tighten the straps. Saying nothing I stood back and watched carefully as we all saddled up for the trip. Pommy strained initially but soon swung the pack onto his shoulders. For a second or two he stood still, clearly not willing to pull his waist band tight, a look of bewilderment spreading across his face.

"What the fook's going on?" he muttered under his breath, taking his pack off and opening the top flap.

The rest of the group started walking off, following the lead of Pedawa. Kahuna and I paused before walking away, not wanting to miss Pommy's reaction.

"You guys think your so bloody smart, hey?" he growled, pulling out the rock and depositing it on the ground.

We couldn't hold it any longer. Kahuna and I started belly-laughing throwing high fives at each other.

"You'll never outwit the Pommy, you bloody Aussie gits," he rumbled threateningly.

"Sure, Pommy," I grinned as we all moved off.

When we arrived at the entrance to the Icefall I hurriedly dropped my pack and began putting on my crampons. After putting on the left one I looked up to see that Pedawa had already put both of his on and was looking around to see if anyone needed some assistance. Paranoid about being seen as the weakest link I fervently avoided eye contact and swiftly fixed the other crampon in place. Similarly, when we began moving through the Icefall, I kept within a metre of the person in front of me. There was no way I was going to be the one who was lagging behind. To my surprise, after only five minutes of walking at a fairly modest pace, gaps began to separate the group. Pedawa was not setting a cracking pace, yet even at these initial stages we struggled to walk together as a group of seven.

The first ladder brought us all back together as we took turns to go across. Pedawa didn't need the practise so he just skirted around the ladder on the frozen stream before turning to watch us all move across. He again said nothing but observed intently. Pommy was the last to move over the ladder as I held the ropes up, pulling them taut to help his stability. Moving onward we eventually passed the point Pommy, Tim and I had reached a few days before. The pace slowed from there as the incline increased significantly. The trail began meandering around massive blocks of ice, some the size of houses and paralleling crevasses that were up to ten metres wide. It was difficult to see how deep the crevasses were as the trail kept a few metres away from the edge of the opening, which I didn't doubt was a good thing. My breathing was laboured but I still managed to keep up with the pace, even though that maddening tickle was returning to my throat. It took a constant and conscious effort to refrain from coughing, but at that moment I'd have rather turned blue fearing one cough would trigger the first bout of a never-ending coughing problem. Happily around another bend a new aluminium ladder provided a short respite to get my breathing back under control ... or so I thought.

The crevasse that was to be crossed spanned five metres wide and required two ladders, lashed together, end to end, to breach the gap. This was no training ladder. It was the real thing. Pedawa, like a true professional, leaned down, hooked onto just one of the safety lines and then skipped across the double ladders. Although he made it look so easy the rest of the team was not so confident and all helped encourage each other as we moved slowly across the ladders, one by one. Pommy went across before me, which meant that he was tasked to hold up the safety lines for my passing. As I hooked my carabiners to the two safety lines I stood only a footstep away from the edge of the crevasse. As I peered into the void I could not see anything other than a blue sky-like image plummeting into a black abyss. The depth was so great that sun rays were unable to reach the bottom.

"Alright Pommy, I'm good to go. Keep these lines tight now," I yelled out.

"Don't you worry about me, just get on with it."

I stepped forward with my left foot and placed the front spikes of the crampon just over the lip of the first rung. The rest of the crampon locked in comfortably when I placed my weight on the boot. I began to lift up my right foot and move it forward to the next rung. The temptation to place it next to my left foot was nearly overwhelming as it felt unstable when standing on one foot on a horizontal ladder. I focused on the rungs ahead as I placed one foot in front of the other, trying not to look through the ladder at the gaping expanse below. As I neared the join of the two ladders in the middle of the bridge, I noticed that the join allowed quite a bounce to occur if I started to get shaky or unbalanced. Suddenly, the ropes that I was pulling on became slack and my whole body twisted and flinched to regain my balance. My arms began to swing wildly as the ladder began bouncing up and down in reaction to my legs shaking.

I looked up and saw Pommy, dropping the camera that was hanging from his neck and grabbing again for the safety lines. He pulled on them tight once more, which in turn gave me the necessary stability to haul myself under control.

"Pommy! What are you doing?" I yelled.

"Sorry mate, I thought it was a great spot for a photo," he replied calmly.

"What, a photo of me hanging in a crevasse?" I yelled back sarcastically.

My heart was pounding and body temperature rising from the adrenaline rush. I really wanted to get off this ladder. I moved quicker than before and with little hesitation, missing the last three rungs and lunging for the solid ground on the other side of the crevasse.

"What's going on with the jelly legs, Squizza?" Pommy quipped in an attempt to deflect the conversation.

"Oh, you are friggin' kidding me, aren't you? You'd better not get me to help you over the next ladder, mate, or you might end up underneath it."

"Ha! No chance of that, you little git. I'm not the uncoordinated one."

Although I looked to blame Pommy for the incident it quickly became apparent that it had helped build my confidence and understanding of how best to get across the ladders. Instead of trying to move slowly to maintain stability it was easier to walk at a normal pace, accepting that there would be some bouncing. It meant less time exposed to the dangers of the crevasses and ultimately less time in the Icefall.

▲ ▲ ▲

Pedawa continued to lead us high into the Icefall for the next two hours, quickly moving from one precarious predicament to another. If we weren't breaching a crevasse, we were darting around a perilous block of ice or climbing a ladder to scale a vertical wall. It was exhausting both mentally and physically but I was pleased to note I did not feel entirely inappropriately skilled to deal with the adversity.

At 11:15am Pedawa announced that we had gone far enough for the day and should begin our descent. It was a welcome relief for most of us as the going had been quite testing. Moments after the relief temporarily washed over us our morale was dampened as Pedawa informed us that we had only made it about two thirds of the way through the mammoth Icefall. So much for progress, I thought. At least we'd made it that far injury free, perhaps dowsed with the good luck endowed upon us from the puja ceremony the day before. The next few days were to quickly prove otherwise.

Two of the Lhotse team withdrew from their expedition. One was feeling love sick and the other pulled a muscle in his back. Meanwhile Tim was put out of action from a severely infected upper leg. A few days before arriving in Kathmandu he had slipped from a ladder and suffered a hairline fracture of his right thigh. His determination to complete the job that he couldn't quite finish in 2005 was enough to override any sane contemplation of resting; he instead opted to move very slowly in an attempt to allow the fracture to heal. The mountain, it seems, could play with a man's logic making him believe he could, well, climb mountains even with a fractured bone in his leg. Of course this was not the case. With the altitude placing an additional strain on his body, Tim began to deteriorate rather than recover. His leg had developed a Haematoma; a huge internal infection. On the 18th April he woke with a swollen leg that threatened to put him out of action for weeks to come. Luckily for him a few of the climbers were doctors and therefore able to cut an incision to help drain his thigh of the pus and excess blood. Pommy volunteered to play nurse for the day and helped to squeeze out the fluids. Twenty-four hours later poor Tim was still showing no signs of recovery and the decision was made to move him down to a lower altitude. Courageously, he gathered the strength and will power to walk on what looked like a terribly sore leg.

In addition to the loss of climbers, the whole expedition began to suffer from a loss in climbing time. On the 18th April, the six of us that had climbed high into the Icefall were supposed to be preparing for a two day trip that would see us sleep at Camp One. We could barely get out of our tents let alone begin to tackle the Icefall. An unseasonal snow storm blew in and dumped three feet of snow over two and a half days. The ropes in the Icefall were buried and the trail was no longer discernable. Team members from the Jagged Globe expedition came over to visit Henry as they had some of their clients stranded at Camp One. Their climbers were running low on cooking fuel as they had planned to be away from Base Camp for only 48 hours but were now into their third day. Fortunately for them Henry had cached some spare fuel at Camp One that he could donate to keep them going.

Even when the snow stopped falling on the 20th, the Icefall was still off limits. A full day would be required to dig out the ropes and reset the ladders. Henry sensed that a few of us were becoming restless with all of the waiting and so sent us back down the trail to Gorak Shep. It was particularly slippery underfoot because of the icy snow, although the conditions hardly slowed Kahuna down at all. The two of us headed off before the rest of the team, maintaining our own pace. Kahuna took the lead at a velocity that was quicker than I would normally walk but I kept up with him as I'd decided that it was he who I wanted to partner up with when we started to get on with the serious climbing. The return to Gorak Shep was uneventful and from there we moved to the nearby peak of Kala Pattar with relative ease. The previous acclimatising climb through the Icefall helped significantly with our breathing.

From Kala Pattar we had a bird's eye view of the Icefall and the next part of our climb: the Western Cwm (pronounced: Coum), a three-walled valley that housed the glacial ice before it tumbled down the Khumbu Icefall. The walls of the valley were sheer and extended as high as any in our view. This was the king of the giant valleys that could only possibly exist in this part of the world. The walls comprised of the southern side of Everest, the western face of Lhotse, and the northern cliffs of Nuptse. From where we stood the glacier that covered the valley floor looked like a smooth blanket of marshmallow starkly contrasted against the jagged edges of the Icefall.

On our way back Kahuna spotted Rob, one of the three remaining climbers attempting Lhotse, walking towards us from the direction of Base Camp. Rob had already summitted Everest once and had also been a part of the unsuccessful attempt in 2005. He was the last member to arrive at Base Camp, just after the puja service. He was not only an invaluable source of information for the two of us but also a doctor by trade with a wealth of knowledge about acclimatisation, frost bite and other extreme weather issues.

"Hey guys, how are you going?" Rob said.

"Great, mate, and you?" Kahuna replied.

"Well, I am not bad but I have some pretty nasty news."

"What's that?" I asked.

"Three Sherpas were killed this morning in the Icefall."

SIXTEEN
PUSHING TO NEW LIMITS

Both Kahuna and I were shocked as well as saddened to hear of news of the tragedy.

"Bloody hell, that's shit news," Kahuna gasped. "Were they from our expedition?"

"Nope, they weren't our guys. It's not clear which expedition they were from. Apparently there was a team of seven Sherpas moving through the Icefall and three were buried alive when a massive block of ice rolled onto them. The other four were all injured and are being evacuated back down the Icefall at the moment."

Throughout the two hour walk back to Base Camp we could talk of nothing other than this tragic news. Unsurprisingly when we arrived back at Base Camp a sombre atmosphere gripped the group. Our Sherpas were huddled away in their tents as they had each lost friends or relatives in the tragedy. The Sherpa community was very tight and interconnected. Sadly, it was always the Sherpas who faced the greatest loss each year, as statistically they always had the largest numbers on the mountain. Given the prevailing atmosphere it took me by surprise when Henry announced in the afternoon that eight of us were to begin preparing for a trip to Camp One early the next day. I expected the tragic loss of life would have brought all climbing to a halt for a period of mourning, but apparently not.

It wasn't easy to prepare for the next day with the tragedy constantly flashing into my mind. I decided to give Nud a call on the satellite phone. News of the Sherpa deaths had already reached Kathmandu, even though there was turmoil of another nature brewing within the capital city. She had been locked inside our flat for a few days as the government attempted to quell a nationwide uprising. The Maoists had gathered the support of previously disloyal civilians and the resulting chaos was turning the country upside down. Reluctantly ending my call to Nud I couldn't help wondering whether the puja ceremony that we had held a few days ago had brought us, the other expeditions and the country of Nepal any good luck at all.

Before going to sleep I reminded myself of the two key strategies that Henry employed to minimise our exposure to the risks presented by the Icefall. The first was to travel in small groups at the fastest pace possible. He didn't like the idea of having a group of ten people move through together at the pace of the slowest person. Secondly, we were told to begin our journey at first light and try to finish by midday. This meant that we avoided the most unstable periods, i.e. the thawing that occurred in the afternoons and freezing in the first half of the night. Henry was a veteran and as such I had complete confidence that his strategies would protect the daredevil and the foolhardy among us alike as we pushed forward.

The sound of my beeping alarm brought me to consciousness at 4am sharp. In the pitch black of my tented night I immediately felt for my head torch, which I'd deliberately placed on top of the pack that lay next to me. Sitting up in the closest thing to a bed that could be found on the mountain, I began putting on a down jacket. All of my clothing and equipment had been laid out in a systematic fashion the night before to ensure a smooth transition from my sleeping bag to leaving the tent with all of my equipment for the two day climb ahead. Shoving my pack outside I squeezed through the opening, my plastic boots leading the way. As I stood up the icy snow underneath my boots crunched loudly, almost as though the mountain might have been gnashing its teeth. Savouring the pristine and motionless night I looked up to take in every aspect of the cloudless sky above, illuminated by thousands of stars twinkling like diamonds around a bright moon. Despite the immaculate beauty of it all the cold found its way through my multiple layers of clothing; I had to begin moving or my circulation would seize up.

Pommy's tent was illuminated from within so I quickly said 'g'day' before heading to the latrine tent for an aerobic exercise of "avoid the frozen toilet seat". Anxiety had softened my stools and so I managed to get the job done quickly. By the time I reached the mess tent Kahuna was already inside, donning his climbing harness and doing up his boot laces. I quickly began to do the same, not wanting to be last to be ready. By 4:30am I sat at the dining table to chow down on a warm bowl of nourishing porridge. Fighting my stomach's resistance to accept food I forced the essential supplements down my gullet knowing my next meal wouldn't be until well after midday at Camp One. Enviously eying Rob, who somehow managed to gulp down two big bowls while looking completely relaxed about our trip ahead, I tried in vain to eradicate the terrible news of yesterday from my mind.

Our departure time had been set at 5am. Henry, the Sherpas, and the rest of the climbers were still in their tents at that time so it was up to the eight of us to organise ourselves and take the initiative to leave on time. We would climb without any escorts on this occasion, but with a radio link to Henry should we need any guidance or advice. With ten minutes to spare I sat watching a few of the late-comers casually eat breakfast and prepare their kit, again astonished at their laid-back approach towards time-keeping. Didn't these people know that the schedule had been determined for our safety, and not because our guide enjoyed the sound of his own voice?

At 5am I slung my pack over my right shoulder and pushed open the mess tent flap at the end of the elongated structure. The dark sky had turned grey in the short period I'd been inside as night began to turn to day. I wriggled my left arm through the pack strap, did up my waist belt and started putting mittens over my inner gloves.

"Shall we go?" I asked Kahuna, who had followed me out of the tent.

"We could wait a few minutes, it looks like the others will be ready to go soon."

"Alright, how about we just slowly walk across to the crampon point and catch up with them there?" I suggested.

"No worries," he agreed. "Let's go."

Before heading off, I quickly stuck my head into the mess tent to advise we were heading over to the crampon point at the entrance to the Icefall. In the distance I saw dots of light from headlamps bobbing up and down as climbers from other expeditions walked in the same direction. It encouraged me to walk faster, as if it were a marathon and we were to begin jostling for the closest spots to the start line. By the time we reached the entrance a team of ten or so were just standing up to move off. They had beaten us to the starting line on this occasion.

Almost as soon as Kahuna and I had put on our crampons the remainder of our group, except for Rob, had arrived. Rob had told us the night before that he would travel through the Icefall separately; although it didn't appear to be a wise decision it did conform with the way Henry ran his expeditions. Until the final summit Henry allowed us, as individuals, to work out who we wanted to climb with and at what speed. With this in mind we put away our head torches and headed into the Icefall as early morning light brightly welcomed us to the new challenge. As a group of seven we headed off for the first rope.

I skirted around the first ladder, taking advantage of the cold morning to walk confidently on the frozen stream. The others did the same, knowing full well we couldn't afford to dawdle. The trail we walked had become a three foot trench as a result of the recent snowfall, which in turn added three feet of additional roofing to the towering blocks of ice above us. Before Kahuna and I reached the second ladder a gap of over thirty metres had opened up between the two of us and the remainder of the group leaving me pondering the wisdom and ethics of sticking together as a group versus moving quickly to escape the dangers of the Icefall. As I was about to yell to Kahuna to suggest we slow I turned back and noticed that another party of climbers were overtaking our fellow climbers below.

"Kahuna! Check this out," I yelled.

We both stopped and watched as the new group of climbers moved briskly towards us at a speed much quicker than we had been walking. As they neared Kahuna and me it was evident they were a group of Sherpas, mostly carrying loads that looked particularly heavy. I could do little other than to gawp in admiration. I realised that Kahuna and I, although moving quicker than the rest of our group, had actually been moving pretty slowly. The Sherpas were hardly slowed by the ladder crossing, and some of them didn't even take the time to clip onto the safety line. This was just another day at the office for them.

Before heading over the first ladder I mentioned to the remainder of our group that Kahuna and I would be pushing on ahead by ourselves. A few of the slower ones in our clan didn't look impressed and even showed signs of animosity as they were not expecting the group to begin splitting at such an early stage. It was even harder for them to accept our decision as both Kahuna and I were the least experienced and therefore not supposed to be the first to reach Camp One. Part of me felt I was somehow being disloyal to the team.

"Hey, Kahuna, I think there might have been a few dudes who weren't happy to see us split away."

"Stuff 'em, mate. It's not our fault they didn't train as hard as us. After yesterday's loss I'm not sticking around in this place any longer than I have to."

I again reflected over Henry's methodology for getting his clients to the summit safely. It was really working well for us today. Kahuna and I felt strong and were determined to push through the Icefall at our maximum pace moving at twice the speed we had been climbing when we first went through the lower sections of the Icefall with Pedawa. Less than fifteen minutes after splitting from the remainder of our group we came up behind the ten or so climbers that had set off from the crampon point as we'd arrived at the entrance to the Icefall. They were moving slowly under the control of an American guide who led the troop like a slow moving caterpillar, weaving around and over the undulating ground in silence.

Kahuna and I picked up our pace and pushed through the single file. I smiled at the other climbers who were pausing to allow us to pass as a gesture of thanks. Some returned the smile whilst the others ignored our passing, whether they were too tired to acknowledge us or indignantly snubbing us I will never know. I was just quietly grateful to be a part of an expedition that gave us so much freedom.

Kahuna continued to lead the way for the next few hours. We were both surprised at how much quicker we could move in comparison to the time we had climbed up with Pedawa. Our bodies had acclimatised over the last few days and we were both feeling strong. Although it was difficult to remember every section of the Icefall, as there were many crevasses and blocks of ice that looked the same, I could discern our previous turn around point which meant that we were stepping into the unknown from that point up. Following a rope and well etched trail in the snow, I felt a surge of excitement moving into brand new territory. Our enthusiasm was tempered when we came across what appeared to be a small field of jagged ice. The area was no larger than a tennis court and relatively flat compared to the surroundings but the trail in front of us was not well worn. Kahuna stopped to survey the area.

"This must the spot where the Sherpas were hit yesterday," he said solemnly.

"Yeah, it looks like it. Bloody hell. We are going to have to walk straight over the top of them," I said quietly.

"There's no alternative, mate."

It was an eerie feeling as we crossed the jagged ice field. There were no visible signs of the bodies as they lay under many metres of ice and snow, but their presence was strong nonetheless. I couldn't decide if they might be wishing us well or cursing us for tramping over their final resting place, and concluded it was probably better not to try. Instead I offered my condolences silently as a sign of respect to the brave and the fallen beneath me.

Our pace was slowing, partly due to fatigue but mainly as a result of being at a higher altitude than we had previously reached. Glancing at my watch I noted it was 10am. We only had an hour to reach the top of the Icefall within the timeframe that we had set. Looking up I could see nothing but towering blocks of ice. The sun would soon be overhead and although the majority of the trail was still protected from its rays by the blocks of ice in front of us, we wanted to clear the dangerous part of the Icefall before the sun had a direct beam over the whole of the mountain. If we couldn't reach the top in time we would be forced to stop and shed our cold weather gear while still among the ever threatening ice field. I turned around in an attempt to gauge our distance from Base Camp. Around forty metres below a familiar peaked cap was closing on our position.

"Hey, Rob, how are you mate?" I yelled out.

"Bloody great. Hey boys, you're moving along nicely."

"Thanks mate. We are starting to slow now though. Do you know how much further we've got?"

"You've done most of the hard work. It should flatten out pretty shortly. But you need to keep on the move as the threat from avalanches coming off the western shoulder of Everest still exists until you get further up the cwm."

Rob soon reached the two of us and tagged along behind, hardly even looking tired. The three of us continued together for another fifteen minutes before climbing over the last steep section of the Icefall. No longer were there any ice blocks towering above us. Instead we had a wide open field of smooth snow that stretched for a kilometre in width between the near vertical walls of Everest and Nuptse. The depth of the massive valley was not visible from this point as the glacier gradually rose up in front us, blocking the lower sections of the Lhotse Face. We all sat down to begin shedding our outer layers as the rising sun was no longer masked by Everest or the ice blocks. Sweat beads were forming on my brow even though the air was still cold, dehydration prompting me to reach into my pack and swallow down half a litre of water.

Rob headed off first, negotiating the large crevasses that were preparing this part of the glacier for its inevitable drop into the Icefall. Although the incline reduced significantly, the trail zigzagged across the glacier adding many more hundreds of metres to our journey. The number and width of the crevasses did, however, drop off the further we moved from the Icefall, the trail then meandering out into the centre of the Cwm, a full five hundred metres from either of the walls that lay to the north and south and therefore well out of reach of any avalanche.

Ahead, only three hundred metres away, was a cluster of dome shaped tents. They were all pitched among narrow bands of snow that stretched up to two hundred metres in width, and thirty metres in the air. These bands of snow were the initial stages in the formation of crevasses. They looked like monster waves, frozen in time just as they were about to come crashing down.

We kept walking until we found four yellow tents with ICE 8000 written in black on the outside fly. This would be our home for the next two nights. Kahuna and I placed our ground mats on the inside of the tent and laid there with our legs and boots hanging outside. It was good to get our breathing under control and hide from the ever glary sun. After a twenty minute rest the three of us shovelled fresh snow into the vestibules of all four tents to provide sufficient drinking water before turning to the task of unpacking our gear.

The remainder of our group stumbled into camp three hours later. By that time Kahuna, Rob and I were both well established and rested, and hence happy to offer them hot cups of tea to boost their morale, wondering if we'd really looked that tired and dishevelled when we'd arrived. Pommy took up our offer and joined us in our vestibule.

"Fook me," he choked. "That was bloody hard going, hey?" He slumped on the snow we had previously collected.

"Bloody oath mate," I agreed. "It sorted us out alright."

"What the hell took you so long, Pommy?" Kahuna asked.

"Don't bloody ask, mate. We had a few 'heart' problems, if you know what I mean. No 'balls' to just keep moving through at a solid pace. We even lost Raj. He decided to pull the pin about half an hour after you guys left us. He said that he wasn't in the right frame of mind. I think he just got a little spooked by the three deaths yesterday."

"Yeah, mate. We didn't want to leave you but there was no way we were going to hang around in that place any longer than we needed to," Kahuna commented.

"Well next time I'm coming through with you guys," Pommy asserted firmly, sipping on his tea.

By 7pm Kahuna and I had boiled enough snow for the following day and eaten as much as our stomachs could take. At 6100 metres, Camp

One was slightly lower than the summit of Imja Tse so it came as no surprise to me that I was not able to eat a full meal. Hoping for the best we turned our head torches off and said goodnight.

▲   ▲   ▲

After a miserable night's sleep, interrupted by the need to breathe heavily, I greeted the new day by preparing for a day trip to Camp Two. Although we planned to depart at 7am I decided to put a thick layer of sunscreen on my face, neck and ears, thinking we were already facing an adequate sufficiency of physical ailments without adding sunburn to the list. I had to squeeze the plastic container with all my might as the sunscreen was frozen solid. I guessed it had never been designed with these temperatures in mind!

Henry had warned us that the sun was particularly strong when walking through the Western Cwm. Even by eight in the morning, only shortly after the sun had found its way over the top of Lhotse, the temperature was slowing our progress. With advance knowledge of the conditions, I was wearing a thin pair of white thermals, deliberately purchased for this leg of the journey to help combat the heat. Not only were we physically closer to the sun than normal, but rays from the fireball were reflecting off the white walls of snow magnifying the intensity to the point where I suspected it could burn a hole in a sheet of paper held in its path. Even though our expedition was traversing ice and snow it felt more like we were struggling through a desert savaged by unbearable heat ... and there was a huge mass of open space still to be covered in front of us. At least the undulations in the glacier had disappeared and the incline had all but flattened out to a gentle rise. Ropes were no longer needed as we moved slowly towards the end of this huge valley. Lying ahead, over two kilometres in distance, was the Lhotse Face. Now in full view, I started to study the western slope of Lhotse to see if I could spot our future route. Sherpas were working on fixing the lines, which made some parts of the route discernable.

Three hours of monotonous plodding later we arrived at Camp Two, about 800 metres in distance from the base of the Lhotse Face. We found a couple of our Sherpas putting up a small dining and cooking tent as this would be the place we would call home for quite a few nights over the coming weeks. As our "home" it was equipped with all the "comforts": a latrine tent, a cook, and a radio base station. After a 30 minute break we returned to Camp One, having completed our acclimatisation walk for the day. That evening I found it painful to take so much as a spoonful of food. The inside of my mouth felt as though I'd gulped down boiling water. As I hadn't eaten anything warm since dinner the night before the source of this irritation was a complete mystery to me, but nonetheless it was there. Another fringe benefit in the long list of delights associated with this escapade.

The next morning, after a much better night's sleep, my mouth was even worse. It was uncomfortable to eat a muesli bar for breakfast, so I ate some chocolate instead. Similarly to the day before, I slapped on a layer of sunscreen and lip balm before exiting the tent. Then it hit me. As I applied the lip balm it dawned on me that my sore mouth was caused by sunburn! For over four hours the day before I had been huffing and puffing, with my mouth wide open and tongue hanging out. The inside of my mouth was the only part of my body that I had left exposed and without sun protection. It took another two days before I could comfortably eat and drink again. That was one side effect that I hadn't been warned about.

Getting back down through the Icefall that morning was a lot easier and less daunting than when we had climbed up it two days prior. Looking down over the ice blocks, rather than up at those above, took away a huge amount of the psychological pressure. Many a time I have experienced, and heard others comment, that it seemed to take an age finding a place that was unfamiliar, only to be pleasantly astonished on the return journey. So it was with our return; moving across familiar territory seemed to make the journey go that much quicker.

For the next three days we relaxed in Base Camp, giving our bodies time to recover from the strains caused by the recent climbing, and also to allow for the generation of additional red blood cells. We would need all the help we could find as the next time we set off we were expected to climb from Base Camp to Camp Two on the same day. Camp One would remain set up for the next few weeks as an emergency measure but Henry was keen for us to move directly to Camp Two to speed up our acclimatisation programme.

The night before we were due to head off, gusty winds started swarming up the valley. Sleep was nigh on a luxury and rapidly becoming a total stranger to us as the tent flapped around in the wind and ice was blown against its sides. By 4am, when my alarm went off, there was no sign that the weather was even thinking about abating. Always wanting to remain positive I proceeded to get ready, just in case our climb was still going ahead. It turned out to be both a prudent and fortuitous move, as after Henry had consulted with the Sherpas he decided we would indeed continue with the climb.

On the lower sections of the mountain the winds were unlikely to pose an additional danger other than the reduction in temperature. Comfort was irrelevant. If one wasn't up to the heat (or in this case cold) one should stay out of the proverbial kitchen. I just knew the blustery weather was going to make the Icefall a torturous experience. By this stage in the expedition small groups were forming, driven by personalities and climbing speeds. Pommy, Kahuna and I opted to head out of the mess tent door at the same time and aim straight for the dreaded Icefall. It took me a full fifteen minutes to regain feeling in the tips of my fingers after putting on my crampons at the entrance to the Icefall, having to take turns in placing my mittens underneath my armpits as we walked. The wind was blowing spindrift, reducing visibility to less than ten metres. We had to yell hard to communicate and keep on the move to help generate heat. It was a lonely and chilling experience.

We all looked like armed bandits about to execute a bank heist as we slowly moved through the obstacles with bandanas tied across our faces and balaclavas to help protect our throats from the cold air. If there was a consolation it was that the winds distracted me from the other dangers and encouraged us all to climb a little faster. It took four and half hours of solid climbing to finally step out of the Icefall.

By the time we reached the tents at Camp One the winds I thought would never end had in fact dropped and the sun was once again beaming overhead. I dropped my pack and opened up the top pouch, rummaging around to find a black and white Shemagh. It was identical to the head scarf made famous by Yasser Arafat, an attachment I chose to wrap around my head and face before tying off the ends to secure it. I might have looked like I was going to a fancy dress party but I was confident that my tongue and mouth would be sufficiently protected this time around.

The walk up to Camp Two was more arduous this time, carrying heavy packs. The only respite came when the three of us had a laugh thanks to the comment of an American who was walking in the opposite direction. When he saw my head scarf, he stopped and said, "Wow, you know when I came away to climb Mount Everest, I never thought that I would come across a terrorist!"

In all, with an hour's break at Camp One, we had been on our feet for eight hours to reach Camp Two. As I lay down in the tent to once again settle my heart rate, I felt satisfied that I'd managed to cover the distance in one day even if I was utterly exhausted. Surely sleep would come easily as blackness once more surrounded me. Wrong!

A splitting headache kept me awake most of the night, probably brought on by dehydration and the thinner air. Thankfully the next day was a rest day, which allowed most of us to catch up on some sleep to replenish our energy stores. Our only other task was to casually move up to end of the Western Cwm to gain an extra one hundred metres in altitude and study the route up the Lhotse Face.

After three consecutive nights at Camp Two it was a pleasure to begin the descent to thicker air, even though I found it intensely frustrating to be walking over the same ground again and again … particularly when we knew that in a few short days we would be slogging back up the same trail. At least we were getting quicker as our bodies acclimatised and we became more confident with the obstacles along the trail. When we started I wouldn't have believed it possible but somehow moving across the ladders had become second nature; no longer did we need our mates to hold the safety lines firm. However, on this particular decent we were reminded of the need to avoid complacency.

As Pommy and I headed over the last few mounds of the Icefall we came across a mob of ten people. They were pulling and pushing on a stretcher that had an unconscious Italian strapped down tight. The climber had fallen when crossing a ladder and slammed head first into one of the crevasse walls. Fortunately for him a team of Sherpas were available and quickly sent up to carry out the arduous and complex task of manoeuvring a stretcher through the Icefall. It brought home the cold, hard, stark reality of the dangers associated with climbing the biggest mountain in the world from the south side. If any of us had an accident above the Icefall it was going to be virtually impossible to launch a recovery operation. It was simply too man-power intensive to bring a laden stretcher through the Icefall.

Early the next morning a helicopter landed only two hundred metres from our tents. The Italian climber was air lifted to Kathmandu; one of the fortunate ones to have escaped broken but alive.

On 3 May Henry requested six of us to join him in the comms tent for a briefing on our final acclimatisation trip. He had been monitoring the weather and was happy for us to depart the following day for a trip that would see us spend two nights at Camp Two followed by an overnight trip to Camp Three. Just in case one of us got in trouble at Camp Three, Henry took the opportunity to introduce us to the oxygen system that we would use when going for the summit. The oxygen system he used was from a Russian company called Poisk. The system was pretty simple in that it consisted of a heavy duty oxygen bottle with a regulator screwed to the top and a mask that was connected to the regulator via a rubber hose and bladder. The oxygen flow was controlled by the regulator which could be adjusted in either ¼ or ½ litre per minute increments, ranging from 1 to 4 litres per minute. On a flow rate of 2 litres per minute a climber had approximately 6.5 hours worth of oxygen. The oxygen flowed from the bottle into a bladder which was then sucked into the mask by the user.

Henry had us practise until we were proficient in adjusting the regulator and connecting up a fresh bottle. He finished by telling us that we were to climb on a setting of two litres per minute, unless he told us to change to another setting. We would have one bottle to get us from Camp Three to Camp Four, and three bottles to get us from

Camp Four to the summit and back down again to Camp Four.

I was pumped. Although we wouldn't use the oxygen until the summit bid, the thought of being up so high on Everest was not so surreal any more. I felt a tingle of excitement believing the summit was within my reach. It wasn't until I stepped off from Camp Two a few days later that I began to feel anxious once again. I was about to climb to altitudes higher than the summit of Ama Dablam and couldn't help but wonder how my mind and body were going to react.

As I walked across the Western Cwm towards the Lhotse Face I looked up at the sheer wall. It stretched into the sky for two kilometres. I searched hard to see if I could find the tents at Camp Three. They were not visible with the naked eye even though I knew they had been pitched approximately two thirds of the way up. The scale of everything was almost beyond comprehension.

Kahuna was still down at Base Camp, opting to pair up with Tim who had returned to Base Camp after a successful recovery further down the valley, which left Pommy and I to team up in our bid to tackle the Lhotse Face. I clipped on to the fixed line with a jumar and began up the 45-60 degree incline. It was hard going to slam the crampons into the side of the slope with every step; in fact after only twenty slow steps I was forced to stop for a few minutes to regain my breath. Climbers above us unknowingly kicked off chunks of ice that came spearing towards us. I could hear Pommy yelling out expletives as he tried to avoid balls of ice the size of a cricket ball. We had no choice but to continue on up the ice wall that shone blue whenever the sun peeped out from behind the clouds. Strong winds had battered the face most afternoons, polishing the ice and cleaning the face of all snow.

Pauses were kept to a minimum due to the immense strain put on ankle and calf muscles from the steep incline. Every fifty metres or so there were natural ledges, no more than a square metre in size that allowed us to stand upright for a brief respite, albeit in cramped conditions as others had the same idea. After a few hours I felt compelled to glance back to see where we had come. Perhaps it wasn't the smartest move but curiosity got the better of me. In looking down it was blatantly obvious that if I was to fall at that point, without being connected to the rope, I would slide down an ice slope as hard as concrete for hundreds of metres. With bumps and small cliffs along the way a falling climber would be smashed to pieces by the time they reached the bottom.

As we began to climb into the area where tents had been pitched, evidence of the severe storms of days gone by could be seen. Fluttering in the wind, partially buried, were the remains of old tents. Strips of cloth, coloured green, yellow, red and orange flapped against the slope. This year's tents were pitched alongside the colourful remains, etched into the side of the face on ledges that had been dug out with a snow shovel. A safety rope came off the main fixed line, leading all the way to the door of the tent. It was a welcome relief when I spotted the ICE 8000 tents as the afternoon weather was slowly coming up the Western Cwm below us. A thick white cloud built itself into a crescendo below as winds prepared to pelt the slope we were climbing once more. Remaining both prudent and vigilant I decided to stay connected to the safety line until I was safely and securely planted inside the tent.

It was another milestone for me. I'd reached 7200 metres; 400 metres higher than I'd ever been before. At that altitude, even when resting, my breath was laboured. This would be the highest point that we would go without the use of supplementary oxygen. Unsurprisingly I hardly slept a wink, laying awake wondering if my body would begin to suffer from the high altitude. I didn't vomit but did have a sick feeling in my stomach for the whole night and was unable to eat anything in the morning. Despite this, however, I felt happy with my overall condition. A climber in a nearby tent was not so fortunate; the poor bloke had been vomiting all night long.

A cloudless sky the next day brought little warmth to the freezing winds that swirled against the upper reaches of the Lhotse Face. Fatigue from a sleepless night and the cold encouraged Pommy and I to pack up and head off the face without delay. We felt no desire to stop for a rest until we reached the more liveable conditions at Camp Two.

As though it was an oasis in the desert, or at the very least a five star hotel in downtown Melbourne, when Pommy and I arrived back at Camp Two the first thing we did was sit down and eat a fry up of eggs, bacon, baked beans and spam. We had hardly eaten at all over the last twenty-four hours as the thin air had completely obliterated our appetites. We were both exhausted but equally elated, even though we were both painfully aware of how debilitating the summit bid was going to be.

SEVENTEEN
INSIDE THE DEATH ZONE

Not long after arriving back at Base Camp Henry pulled Pommy and I aside to brief us on his plan. He had been studying the various weather forecasts and concluded that there was a favourable "weather window" coming up in the next week or so. It was excellent news, fitting in perfectly with our acclimatisation schedule. We had five days in which to move back down the valley, bask in the thicker air, and get away from the camp environment. I packed up and bailed out quicker than anyone, probably because I had a greater incentive than the rest of the expedition members. Nud was somewhere on the trail.

The last time I'd spoken to Nud she was about to depart Kathmandu to make her way back up to Base Camp. Unless she had been held up she should have arrived in Periche on the day I left Base Camp. With that in mind I recklessly ditched the idea of walking slowly to conserve energy and walked flat out to reach Gorak Shep. It was a ghost town. The normally packed tea houses were barren and lifeless as the trekking season was over pending the arrival of the monsoon season. Although that sounded like bad news there was an upside to the changing weather;

the seasonal change brought with it a temporary lull in the jet stream winds that smashed into the upper sections of Everest for the remainder of the year, allowing us to physically stand on the summit (and not be blown off the side by the jet stream).

I skipped down the trail, hardly bothered by the physical exertion, even though it was cold and clouds filled the valley reducing visibility to twenty metres. For the first time in over a month I felt moisture in the air. The thick fog forced me to put on a raincoat as dew built up on my clothing. Although the temperatures were not as acute as what I'd become used to, the damp had an uncanny way of seeping into my bones. By the time I reached Periche common sense prevailed. I decided not to go any further, regardless of whether Nud was there or not. I was tired and wet, something I ardently knew I had to avoid if the temperature dropped further in the afternoon. I went straight to the tea house where we'd left Dad over a month before. Against the odds I couldn't help peering into the dining room window to see if Nud might be inside. Cold uninviting darkness glared back at me.

"Namaste … Is anyone home?" I called out hopefully.

"Namaste sir," a voice called back.

A young man in his mid-twenties came out from the kitchen and turned on a light in the dining room, helping to bring some life into the restaurant.

"Are you open?" I asked.

"Yes, sir. Please have a seat," he replied.

"Thank you. Have you had an Australian lady check in today with blonde hair?" I anxiously inquired.

"Yes, sir. She is over at the altitude research centre."

"Oh, okay," I replied. "I will wait for her here. Could I have a hot lemon please?"

Nursing my hot drink, feeling like a school boy about to go on his first date, I sat down in the dining room and watched and waited for Nud. Just as I finished the hot lemon drink, Nud appeared out of the fog. She walked straight for the entrance, making no attempt to peer in through the dining room window. I stood up and began walking towards her. As she entered through the door her face lit up with huge smile.

"Wow! I can't believe you've managed to make it all this way down the valley," she exclaimed.

We rushed towards each other and embraced. Even though the thick clothing we both wore made the hug feel physically distant, the reunion felt just great.

▲　▲　▲

For the next three days Nud and I hung out together and swapped stories from the previous weeks we'd had apart. From Nud's stories it sounded like Nepal was about to spiral out of control. The Maoists had entered Kathmandu and with the support of the people were enforcing the mother of all bandhs. She had spent many days locked inside our flat and was lucky to have battled her way through mobs of protestors to make it to the airport on the day she flew back to Lukla. It all sounded so far away from the world I had been living.

I used the opportunity of that brief respite from climbing to engage in a deliberate binge of eating and sleeping as much as possible. It was an almost inconceivable luxury to sleep on a foam mattress and to order food from a menu. With Nud alongside me as well, I felt fully energised after three days of relaxation. We both headed back to Base Camp together, stopping in Lobuche for one night to allow Nud to acclimatise.

Henry had confirmed that six of us would depart the next day for our one and only shot at the summit. Kahuna and Tim remained in the second group so that Tim had more time to settle his infected leg. Henry had allocated a Sherpa for each of us and said they would be ready to link up with us at Camp Four. As soon as I heard the news I went to the Sherpa's dining tent and introduced myself to Dorge (pronounced Door-je), the Sherpa that would assist me. He was shy and reserved in nature but looked young and fit, reinforcing my confidence.

It was minus ten degrees Celsius, pitch black, and time for me to get focused on the biggest challenge of my life. Everest was not visible as thick clouds fully blocked the near full moon that lurked somewhere above. For the final time, Pommy and I headed into the Icefall and made our way towards Camp Two. It only took us four hours to get out of the Icefall and another three to reach the camp. It was a good day. The sun was shining and we both felt strong and eager to get on with the rest of the climb, making a radio call to Base Camp to let Henry know we had arrived safely. He was happy with our progress and let me know that Nud had safely left Base Camp for Gorak Shep after a light breakfast.

The weather window was still looking favourable but Henry advised we would be better positioned if we stayed an extra day at Camp Two, meaning we would make our attempt for the summit on the morning of the 18th May. Two days later, as we walked across the last stretch of the Western Cwm, I looked up at the Lhotse Face and began to realise that many others were also positioning themselves on the mountain to take advantage of the same window of opportunity. A black dotted line weaved its way up from the base of the climb; there must have been at least thirty other climbers heading towards Camp Three and that was only part of the story. With twenty-two expedition permits (comprised of an average of ten climbers and ten Sherpas each) issued for this route alone, it was inevitable that we would face congestion problems at some point. The stretch of the climb we were currently negotiating was relatively straight forward but higher up it would be detrimental to be caught behind the majority of the pack. I made a promise to make sure that Pommy and I were first to make the starting line.

The climb to Camp Three was no easier the second time around. I pushed hard, passing a number of other climbers to reach the tents by 2pm. Pommy and I were able to move quickly, encouraged by the thought of resting on flat ground when we arrived at our destination. When I opened the flap of our tent I was greeted with a rather unpleasant welcome. Since the last time we'd been at Camp Three, clear skies had allowed the bright sun to warm the air on the inside of the tent. The snow that lay underneath the tent had been melted from the warm air, meaning the tents were now pitched over a one metre deep hole. Ignoring the predicament I hopped inside and tried to stretch out but was forced into a U-shape with my head and legs upper most. Digging out another ledge on the side of the slope at that altitude would have expended energy I could ill afford to lose so there was no option but to grin and bear it. The night ahead was miserable.

Annoyed and frustrated, I hardly slept a wink, which was the last thing I needed considering I would be up for the next 48-72 hours. Aside from the uncomfortable position, I spent the night dealing with anxiety, shortness of breath, and a thumping headache. Henry had advised us that 8am was a good time to leave Camp Three, giving us enough time for the sun to temper the sub-zero temperatures. Eight o'clock am could not arrive soon enough, not only to bid farewell to my 'hole in the ground' cradle but also because the pressure was on to reach the safety of Camp Four as quickly as possible in case the afternoon winds came in early.

Earlier that morning I'd screwed the regulator on to the oxygen bottle, set it to a flow rate of one litre per minute, and stowed it away in my pack. After clipping on my crampons I opened up the top flap of my pack and connected the hose to the regulator. Pommy bent over and picked up the mask which was attached to the other end of the hose, so I could swing my pack over my shoulders. He gave me the mask and I slid it over my head. It felt a little claustrophobic, which caused me to breathe in hard. Before I had a chance to adjust the straps on the mask, Pommy began the traverse across the face to the main fixed line that ran up and down the mountain. My climbing companion had a renewed sense of urgency spurred on by the fact that the window had opened up and the serious climbing was about to begin. Pulling back on the mask straps, I took off after Pommy, not wanting him to get away from me.

The fixed line continued up the Lhotse Face for another one hundred metres before gradually hooking to the left and traversing on a forty-five degree angle to the left extremity of the massive ice wall. As we neared the point where the rope began to veer left, an orange gortex bag lay resting on a small undulation. Inside was the body of a climber from the Czech Republic who had fallen just a few days earlier when climbing below the summit of Lhotse. He had neglected to hook onto a safety line and hence tumbled down the face for five hundred metres before finally coming to rest fifty metres above Camp Three. He had been climbing with just one other person who was unable to down-climb before night fall nor alert others for help as the only radio between the two of them was in the hands of the guy who fell. I'd heard that climbers at Camp

Three came out of their tents in the morning, looked up and saw the trail left by the fall. By the time they had reached the fallen climber he was only hours away from dying, unconscious and suffering from multiple fractures and internal bleeding. There wasn't anything that could be done. He was duly placed inside the orange goretex bag that would have previously been used to cover his sleeping back.

Quietly paying my respects I couldn't shake this glaringly stark reminder of the perils of this part of the climb. There was little chance that anyone would be able to provide physical assistance from this point on, should we run into trouble. It was hard enough to move around as it was, let alone with someone on your shoulders. I looked up at the ridge leading to the summit. It was less than one thousand metres away and I could clearly see the wind blowing plumes of snow off the side of the mountain. Somewhere up there lay many famous and seasoned climbers who had come before me and paid the ultimate price for their gallantry. Some had lost their lives in tragic circumstances beyond their control; others were put to rest as a result of their own decision making.

Pommy continued to set a cracking pace. Lower on the mountain he liked to stop on a regular basis for a quick chat and to catch his breath, but up at this altitude he kicked into high gear as we were finally at the business end of the climb. I tried my best to keep within earshot of him, which had been reduced to less than five metres because of the masks. The inability to communicate easily was yet another obstacle we had to acclimatise to in this, the final ascent in our attempt to reach the summit. At least Pommy and I had been fortunate enough to have been given a new generation of mask that Poisk had put out on the market in the last twelve months. They were made completely from hardened plastic, allowing for a greater seal around the lip of the mask and a more efficient set of valves; one to draw in the ambient air that was needed to supplement the oxygen and another to release the exhale. The older type was made of a stiff cloth material and had a single two-way valve made of metal that had to cater for both the inhale and exhale. Regardless of the mask used, the oxygen system only provided a supplement, unlike an underwater SCUBA diving system that provides one hundred percent of the needs. On the inside of my bright yellow Poisk mask I was huffing and puffing as hard as I had on any other part of the mountain. Even with the oxygen assistance it was a tough slog.

The diagonal traverse across to the left extremity of the Lhotse Face should have been easier than the previous line which had us assault directly up the wide open ice wall. What was I thinking? Easier? The amount of effort required didn't change. I was pumping hard, like a greyhound chasing a rabbit, my effort constant at a hundred and ten percent. Pommy was finally forced to stop when we reached the end of the traverse. Ahead was a choke point, where a few climbers had gathered, waiting their turn to scale the next obstacle; a multi-layered rock band that protruded out of the ice. This was the Yellow Band, a distinctly yellow limestone rock that was chunky and therefore not technically demanding. The initial step was about twelve metres in height and barren of ice and snow, which felt unusual compared to the Lhotse Face.

After getting over the Yellow Band I could for the first time see the beginnings of the famous South Col. This was the saddle that joined the south-eastern ridge of Everest and the north-west flanks of Lhotse. Rolling off the Col, towards the Western Cwm below, was a rock and ice spur, known as the Geneva Spur. From its beginnings at the South Col it gradually dissipated to the point where it turned into a sheer vertical cliff. We would continue heading diagonally up until we could safely traverse left to reach the upper sections of the Geneva Spur. Around a hundred or so metres before we were to begin the Geneva Spur traverse, Pommy decided he wanted to give his weary 40's something body a rest. Taking off his mask he yelled, "Hey, Squizza, do you feel like a quick break?"

I nodded. "Bloody oath," I managed to say in a muffled breath

Moving closer to Pommy I planted my feet firmly into the snow before sitting down on the uphill side of the fixed line and trail.

"Mate, we've been going at it for nearly five hours without a break," I gasped.

"Yeah, but have you noticed that we haven't passed anyone? That's because they aren't having any rests either," he replied.

"True. Just surprised that an old bastard like you can find the stamina to keep going," I quipped back.

"The Pommy's only just getting fired up, you Aussie git."

It felt good to have a laugh and get my breathing under control. I looked back down towards the Yellow Band where small groups of 2-4 climbers were slowly making their way towards us. Immediately behind us were a couple of Sherpas that had been slowly getting closer to us as the day went on and were now only thirty metres away.

"Hey, Pommy, have a look at these two," I said.

"Bloody hell, how the hell do they do it?" he exclaimed.

"And I think they are from our expedition as well."

The two of them were climbing without oxygen. They would start wearing their oxygen from Camp Four onwards. I watched in complete admiration, and a little amazement, as they approached our position not showing any signs of fatigue.

"Namaste," I yelled.

"Namaste, sir," one of them called back.

"You guys are looking good," I called.

"Yes sir, but clouds are coming," the voice came back.

I looked up towards the summit. Clouds were indeed swirling around the upper sections of the mountain. In the space of just a few minutes the initial swirls transformed into imposingly thick white clouds that blocked out the upper sections of Everest from our view. As we headed off after the Sherpas, we watched the clouds ominously multiply in size and begin their rapid descent towards the South Col. Within fifteen minutes the sun had been completely suffocated by the thick blanket of cloud that cast an eerie shadow over what was, at that moment, our entire world. The sudden and dramatic change in weather demonstrated the volatility of this part of the mountain.

I wanted to move quicker as it was obvious the weather was not going to improve, but this was not to be. As we began to traverse across the side of the Geneva Spur it was obvious that snowfall from the night before had blanketed the rocks with two feet of powder, making the rocky traverse difficult and unstable underfoot. To complicate the issue even more, a party of five was coming towards us from the opposite direction, demanding right of way. It was unclear initially what was going on but as the group got closer it soon became evident. One of the climbers was being rescued by the remainder of the team. The man was on his own two feet and able to move but he was not in control of his movements. Two Sherpas, one in front and one behind, were helping him with every footstep and holding up his body to keep him stable. The guy being rescued displayed all the classic symptoms of someone suffering from High Altitude Cerebral Edema, he looked as though he was blind drunk.

In the twenty minutes we waited perched on the side of the Geneva Spur, snow began to fall once more. The temperature rapidly dropped and visibility was reduced to thirty metres. With the onset of cold and fatigue, coupled with a reduction in the ability to communicate and see, I began to feel increasingly isolated. Even the constant noise of my masked heavy breathing no longer reminded me that I was in fact breathing, but rather it took on the sinister sound of Darth Vader's signature reverberation. I plodded on, with not much option to do otherwise, clipping from one safety line to the next. In the next hour we would reach the 'Death Zone'; a place where the human body rapidly deteriorated, shutting down completely after only a few days.

The rope stretched up over a steep rocky rise for four metres. Lower on the mountain this would have hardly have been a challenge, but at this altitude I stared at it for a full ten seconds to build up the strength of mind and body to attempt the manoeuvre in one shot. As Pommy crested the rise I began my awkward, weary climb. By the time I reached the top I was bent over with exhaustion, but this time there was relief. There was no other rope ahead of the one I'd just climbed; the trail ahead moved along a simple, gentle incline. I stepped off, overjoyed to be walking on ground that did not have an exposed drop of hundreds of metres on one side or the other.

After twenty minutes of walking up and around gentle undulations I saw the welcome sight of a yellow dome tent. A few steps later I started to see a variety of other tents in clusters of two or three. This was Camp Four on the South Col. According to the descriptions I'd been given, the Col was around three football ovals in size and littered with old oxygen cylinders. Sadly I was unable to witness this with my own eyes due to both the thick cloud cover and the snow that had buried all the expended oxygen bottles. I collected some snow and followed Pommy into the tent.

Unlike every other time we'd reached a camp, the tents in this instance were nothing more than a temporary refuge point. We entered just before three in the afternoon with the sole intention of holding ground until 9pm, at which time we would head off for the summit. As we went about our normal routine of melting ice, chewing on glucose tablets, and speaking with Henry at Base Camp, a storm began to brew. The walls of the tent started flapping furiously, causing a deafening noise that reminded me of the two nights I had spent with Andy on Ama Dablam. The difference was that on Ama Dablam we didn't have to climb at night.

EIGHTEEN
THE FINAL ASSAULT

Henry had assured us that the extreme winds at Camp Four were a common weather phenomena for this part of the mountain and so I confidently continued with my preparations for the summit bid. Opening up the top flap of my pack, I stored away a fresh bottle of oxygen, spare mittens, spare goggles, spare head torch, two litres of water, three energy bars, ice axe and a flag. I hung a video and digital camera around my neck and did up the outside of the fluffy down suit that covered me from head to toe. Wearing a down suit was akin to being in a tailor-made sleeping bag. It was bulky and awkward but essential for the temperatures that fall below -25 degrees Celsius at this altitude. Laying back and resting my mind for a few hours, I sucked in the remains of the oxygen cylinder that I had been using during the day.

At 8pm I began the final preparations, screwing the regulator on to the fresh cylinder in my pack and adjusting the setting for a flow rate of 2 litres per minute. I cracked open some instant heat sachets, and taped one each to the pulse on my wrists and ankles. These would help to heat the blood that was heading to my feet and hands. The next task was to check all of my clothing to ensure I hadn't forgotten anything: gloves, outer mittens, beanie, neck warmer, goggles, and balaclava. Although I was feeling sick in the stomach, I forced down another few sips of water and lay back for a few more minutes rest.

As I rolled back the end of my gloves to expose the face of my watch I realised it was 20:54. I couldn't wait any longer. It was time to leave the sanctuary of the tent and complete the final task before departure for the summit; reconnecting the crampons. The zip on the tent door was stiff from cold but yielded after a strong yank. Wind was gushing up underneath the vestibule flap bringing with it airborne snow flakes and grounded balls of ice. It was not encouraging. I shut my eyes and thought to myself, "Okay, this is going to be shit, but it is what has to be done, so get on with it."

I stretched out my legs so my boots were in the vestibule area, and reached forward for the crampons I had left outside the tent. They were nearly completely covered by hardened snow; the only way to clean them was to smash them several times against the end of my boots. The next task required the removal of my mittens. As the right one slithered off my hand I immediately felt the cold biting at my fingers which were protected only by a thin pair of fleece inner gloves. Frantically, I raised my right leg and slipped the crampon underneath the sole of my boot. It lined up perfectly first time. I immediately snapped closed the mechanical adjustment at the heel and as best I could tightened the strap that connected the heel and toe of the crampons. It had only taken thirty seconds in total but my fingers were already starting to feel numb and painful. In haste I tucked my right hand underneath my left arm pit for warmth. It soothed the numb feeling but was a stark reminder of the harsh conditions outside. The left crampon did not secure so easily. This time around I struggled to slide the strap through the buckle, which meant my fingers had been unprotected by the mittens for nearly two minutes and were aching with pain from the bitter cold by the time the crampon was secured. I removed the inner glove and placed my fingers directly on the heat sachet taped to my left wrist. This was the last opportunity I had to remove my gloves and tend to the numb feeling. The fierce winds would prevent this once I stepped outside.

Pausing to mentally check all of the preparations I had religiously followed over the last hour, I realised it was time to move. With the multiple layers of clothing restricting my movements, I awkwardly squeezed out of the tent door and under the vestibule flap. There I stood up and planted my crampons firmly into the snow below for traction. To my surprise, the cloud formation that had made the afternoon so ugly had completely disappeared and the sky was lit up with thousands of bright stars. Somehow their winking encouragement made me feel good about the climb ahead, even though the winds continued to blow at gale force. I lent down, picked up my pack, swung it over my shoulders and fixed the oxygen mask to my face.

I felt adrenaline rushing through my body. This was it. I moved my head from left to right, following the light of my head torch to look for Dorge. The rest of the team was mingling in front of me, putting on their packs and adjusting their oxygen masks. It was difficult to identify who was who as we looked like men about to walk on the moon, completely covered by thick puffy clothing and without any part of our faces showing. I should have thought of this in advance, and chastised myself angrily that I hadn't asked Dorge for the colour of his down suit when we had met in Base Camp. I did, however, manage to spot Pommy's distinctly red suit and walked towards him.

"Hey mate, you ready to go?" I yelled.

"What?" he yelled back, unable to hear over the howling wind.

I got closer to his ear and yelled again, "Are you ready to go?"

"Yeah mate! See you at the top!" he screamed.

With that he turned and started walking off behind one of the other bodies who had turned left, 90 degrees from the direction we had previously entered the South Col.

A short person in a blue down suit came up to me and yelled in my ear, "You Squiz?"

"Yes," I answered.

"Me Dorge," he replied.

"Great! Are you ready to go?" I asked.

"Yes, sir. Follow them," he yelled, pointing in the same direction taken by Pommy.

Excited and eager to get moving I headed off after the head torches that were slowly moving through the dark. Before long I came up behind the last person in the line of climbers from our expedition. There were twelve of us in total, six climbers and six Sherpas. Dorge and I were towards the back of the pack; I had no idea who was in the lead. Quietly I breathed a sigh of relief that I'd found Dorge or we could easily have found it difficult to chase down our group.

The ground we slowly tramped across was not very steep, leading me to believe I could increase the pace. For a moment I thought about overtaking but decided against it, remembering I'd gone out fast in the Melbourne Marathon and regretted it when struggling to complete the last ten kilometres.

The mask no longer felt awkward; I'd become accustomed to having it on my face and felt relaxed with the challenge ahead. The nerves of the last few days seemed to melt away now we were finally on the last leg and the incline was moderate compared to the Lhotse Face. We were still making our way off the South Col.

The first rope was a sure sign that the incline was about to increase. I bent over and picked it up but chose just to hold it, not seeing the point in clipping onto it if we were only moving up a gentle slope. After fifteen paces I changed my mind. We had reached the base of the Triangular Face, a wide slope with snow gullies that narrowed towards the top, hence the name. I'd missed out on seeing the face earlier in the day as the clouds had covered it from view by the time we reached the South Col. With limited vision provided by my head torch I could not see anything other than snow and those that surrounded me. It didn't matter too much though, as I knew we were on the right path and I was on track to finalise this adventure.

For two hours I stayed within five metres of the yellow down suit ahead of me. Even though I was climbing as part of a group that was larger than on any other part of the mountain, I felt more isolated than ever before. All verbal communication had ceased because of the winds and our constraining masks. My vision had been reduced to a few metres as that was the extent of the beam from my head torch. Adding to these difficulties was the debilitating cold. A forty-five second break was all I could take before chills began to work their way through my body.

I kept moving, breathing in hard to keep my body fuelled with oxygen. Suddenly the mask collapsed in on itself and I felt a suffocation sensation. I sucked in once more and had the same response. My lungs ached from the lack of oxygen. Instinctively, I reached up and ripped the mask off to get some fresh air. I was confused and unsure what had happened. Shining the head torch onto the front of the mask I saw a thick icicle hanging underneath the inlet valve. When I looked closer I could see that ice had built up within the valve, sealing it from the outside.

I looked back down the slope to get some advice from Dorge but he had dropped back by twenty metres. I put the valve in my mouth, hoping that the warmth would melt the ice. As soon as my mouth engulfed the valve I realised I had done the wrong thing. It was going to take a long time for me to thaw out the valve and my saliva was only going to add to the problem.

Angry with myself for not thinking through my actions before taking them, I was losing ground from the rest of our party who continued climbing without any knowledge that I was dealing with a problem. In frustration I continued to climb, no longer noticing the cold or heavy breathing; I was totally focused on the frozen mask. I put the valve back in my mouth but this time I gently clenched the outer ring with my teeth hoping to break the ice and free up the valve. For a moment I stopped moving to have a better inspection of the valve. It had worked. Some of the embedded ice clumps had broken away. More than relieved, I put the mask back on and breathed in hard. The valve was working once more. I was able to continue up the slope, but this time feeling particularly fragile and vulnerable.

I began to notice for the first time that my heavy breathing was causing a significant amount of saliva to build up in and around my mouth. This was most definitely the source of the blocked valve, but with my body screaming out for oxygen, I had no option other than to continue breathing heavily. I kept moving in silence, transfixed on the next inevitable blockage. I could feel the valve slowly block, then … it shut off once more.

I ripped off the mask.

"Son of a bitch!"

I stopped climbing.

I waited until Dorge reached my position.

"Dorge, my mask has frozen over!" I yelled.

Dorge took the mask and studied it. Without hesitation he raised his ice axe and tapped on the valve. Nothing happened.

He raised his ice axe once more and smashed down hard on the mask. Pieces of ice went flying off in the wind. He turned the mask and hit the other side of the valve. Again ice particles went flying, but this time a small piece of white plastic also parted from the valve.

My heart nearly stopped.

"Shit, the valve's broken!" I yelled.

"No problem, sir."

"Didn't you see that plastic bit go flying?"

"No problem, sir," he repeated, handing me the mask.

As I inspected the damage, other climbers clambered past us and continued on up the mountain. Following Henry's instructions, they left us to deal with our own issues, and continued on at their own pace. The valve didn't look completely destroyed, but I knew perfectly well that it was not designed to have pieces go missing. I felt profoundly frustrated by the complication, and desperately wanted to get moving again. Incredibly, although we had stopped for only five minutes I had not felt the cold as the mask drama had pumped me full of adrenaline, a perfect combatant for adversity.

Gazing upwards I saw the lights of the other climbers. The nearest was only twenty metres ahead, but the others appeared to be over a hundred metres further. I knew I could catch up with the last climber in less than ten minutes so, digging my feet into the slope with every step, I soldiered on. The snow was thinning out underfoot as the incline became too sheer to hold significant quantities of snowfall. Before long I gasped and stopped, completely out of breath.

When I reached an anchor in the rope, I would normally clip on to the next safety line, unclip from the previous rope, and continue climbing. Now I began using the change over point as an excuse to stay bent over and catch my breath. Even before I reached the anchors, I felt completely starved of oxygen and was forced to rest.

"Dorge, the mask is stuffed," I yelled.

"No problem, sir," he yelled back.

I signalled for him to pass me the radio, but we failed to reach Base Camp. Henry had mentioned that the radio reception would be weak or not possible at all between Camp Four and the Balcony. He was right. I psyched myself for a big effort, and we continued up the slope. With the others breaking away I had to keep moving if I was to rejoin them. After ten paces I was forced again to stop; my legs unable to make another step.

Only seven metres ahead was a rocky outcrop, with a rope veering round to the left. Determined to continue, I dug deep to find the energy to make it. It was intensely frustrating to be struggling with such a menial task. I stopped on top of the rocky platform and waited for Dorge to join me.

"I can't keep going like this," I told him desperately.

He checked the oxygen flow gauge on the hose. It looked to be in order.

"There is definitely something wrong with this mask," I insisted.

"No, sir, it's okay. Keep going to the Balcony."

I remembered Tim describing how they had turned around after reaching the Balcony during their 2005 summit attempt. There was another vague rocky outcrop ahead; it must be the Balcony. I knew I could make the distance.

Head torches from the other climbers spread out over our heads; it looked as if they were climbing a roof suspended above us. The mountain was becoming steeper and darker, adding to the optical illusion. I refocused on putting one foot in front of the other, channelling all of my energy towards my oxygen-starved legs. A little further … a little further…

When what I thought was the Balcony was within five metres I realised there was another snow gully beyond it. The rocky outcrop was not the Balcony after all. I stormed forward and sank down on the ledge on all fours. Resting my head against the snow, my stomach convulsed.

I ripped off the mask and vomited up two mouthfuls of water. In between gasps my body tried to vomit another three times, but nothing came up. My stomach was empty. The overwhelming feeling of weakness that follows a vomit passed through my body. I was spent and doubted my ability to go any further.

"Dorge, we have to swap masks or I'm finished."

"Sir, no problem, we go to the Balcony."

"I don't think you understand. I can't keep going like this. I want to try your mask and see if there is a difference," I requested, handing Dorge my mask.

Dorge took his pack off and started changing over the masks. I was still on my knees, so he could easily access my pack. It would have been easy to curl up and go to sleep.

As I began to spit out the acidic remains of bile, I felt some respite from my predicament. I noticed that the howling winds were beginning to lessen.

Dorge handed me his old cloth mask. I put it over my head and took a breath. It smelt so strongly of his breath I could taste the garlic from his dinner in my mouth. I didn't care. I just wanted to breathe freely.

After two minutes I felt that the situation was no longer deteriorating. I didn't care about catching the rest of the group, nor did I waste any energy trying to work out where the Balcony was. We were still somewhere below it, so we needed to go higher. The mask did not fit as snugly as the original one, but it was helping with my breathing and allowed me to get back into a routine.

Take 12-15 steps, stop for 20 seconds.

Move to the next anchor; clip on, clip off; take a few more breaths and then step off.

My stomach muscles ached from the relentless heavy breathing. The mountain was testing my spirit, and indeed the depth of my desire to stand on top. Until Camp Four, although I had been challenged, I had always felt within my threshold. At this point of the climb it was as though Everest was throwing everything left in her arsenal at me.

At five in the morning, eight hours after leaving Camp Four, Dorge and I stood on flat ground. In front of us was a big black hole. There were no more snow gullies to climb. To the left was a ridge. Lights in the distance from head torches dotted along the ridge like cat's eyes, indicating that it eventually curved to the right. We were finally at the Balcony, a flat area the size of a squash court.

As I sat and slumped against my pack, Dorge squatted beside me.

"Okay, sir?"

"Not good, but okay," I replied.

Dorge pulled out the radio and gave it to me.

"Base Camp, Base Camp, this is Squiz. Over."

The radio crackled: "Squiz, this is Henry. Where have you been? Over."

I immediately felt better. Henry's voice was reassuring, helping to take away some of the isolation.

"Henry, this is Squiz. I'm really stuffed. We've had some problems with the mask and I'm really feeling drained of energy. I'm finding it really difficult to move. Over."

"Squiz, this is Henry. Can you tell me where you are? Over."

"I think we are on the Balcony. Over."

"Okay, just wait a second. Over."

There was silence for a minute. My body began to shiver with cold. I needed to start moving again.

"Squiz, this is Henry. I have a plan for you. Over."

"Go ahead," I replied.

"Squiz, you are moving very slowly, you will have to go quicker if you want to make the summit. Get Dorge to crank your flow rate up to three litres per minute. It will help to increase your speed and warm you up. Some of the other guys are going really well, so I will have some extra oxygen left for you further up the mountain. How does that sound?" Henry asked.

"Okay, thanks. Can someone explain this to Dorge in Nepalese? He's not understanding my accent."

"Okay, put him on the radio and then get moving, Squiz. You need to gain some lost ground."

I handed the radio to Dorge who was attaching our regulators to fresh oxygen cylinders; mine being in my pack which was still over my shoulders. There was a quick exchange over the radio in Nepalese and then Dorge tapped me on the shoulder. He had fixed everything, and we were ready to go.

As we moved off along the ridge, a few head torches shone up at us from just below the Balcony. Another group was about to arrive at the 8,400 metre platform. It felt good to know that I wasn't the very last person on the mountain, I just hoped they hadn't left at midnight, the more common departure time from Camp Four, or I was really going slowly.

Walking with renewed drive I knew that the next section would feel easier with the additional assistance from the higher flow rate. It was also reassuring to have radio contact with Henry should I need it. The wind had dropped to a strong breeze and the bright stars above were beginning to fade. The sun was about to make a grand appearance. The gigantic silhouette of Everest's upper reaches slowly appeared into the ever-lightening sky. As the sun itself began to peer over the horizon it lit up the hundreds of white-capped mountain tops which surround Everest. Nestled between the peaks, thick cloud covered the deep valley floors. For the first time, I could see the summits of the three 8,000+ mountains that neighbour Everest: Makalu, Nuptse, and Lhotse.

A group of four passed us as we rested at the top of a rocky section. I was getting weaker and found myself stopping more and more frequently. The clear blue skies and additional warmth from the sun had done little more than inject a temporary boost to my performance. I was at my limit and my mind was in serious debate as to whether or not I should continue. I began to think of Nud, my parents, and two sisters whom I'd made a promise to: to return home safely regardless of the outcome. On the other hand, I'd also made a personal commitment to do everything in my power to make the summit, not just for myself, but for the 840 million people who went to bed every night with an empty stomach. I was doing it tough, but I wasn't doing it anywhere near as tough as those who searched every day for their next meal. I could endure more.

Reaffirming my refusal to surrender to exhaustion, dehydration, or muscle fatigue I noticed the various groups ahead of me were spread out along the trail, some climbing down towards our position. That was good news. The summit might not be too far away. Perhaps the rocks we had just scaled were part of the famous Hillary Step: the final rock climb before the summit.

As the oncoming traffic loomed closer, I noticed some of them were from our expedition. They did not deliver good news. The summit was still many hours away and I was currently climbing towards the South Summit: the false peak before the Hillary Step. After a two minute interlude I again found myself trudging along with Dorge in tow. To my right was a bird's eye view of the contentious lands of Tibet, the flat brown lands stretching for hundreds of kilometres to the horizon. In contrast, the landscape to the left was awash with white snow and jagged peaks. Ama Dablam, with its sharp and pointed summit, was far below and no longer looked impressive … from this angle it looked like a five storey building nestled between sky scrapers. I pulled out my camera and took a few quick snaps. I doubted it would get any better than this … I already felt like I was on top of the world.

The climb to the South Summit seemed never-ending. Without any rocks along the way or anything visible above the peak, perspective on the distance was almost impossible to determine. One thing was for sure though, with more groups overtaking us I was moving well below the average speed for this part of the mountain. My assessment was confirmed when Henry came on the radio, wanting to speak directly to me.

Digging my heels into the snow I sat back against the slope.

"Squiz, this is Henry. Come in. Over."

"Henry, this is Squiz. I'm here. Over."

"Squiz, I've just spoken with some of the other guys and they tell me you are still well below the South Summit. How are you feeling? Over."

"Henry, I'm still feeling like crap. I just can't seem to move without nearly huffing my guts up. Over."

"Squiz, this is Henry. It's nearly four hours since we last spoke. I needed you to make it at least to the South Summit in that time. I'm afraid you'll never make the summit and get back to Camp Four before the afternoon winds at the rate you're going. Over."

My heart sank.

"Henry, I'm actually not all that far from the South Summit. And I still feel as if I've got a bit of juice left in me. Over."

"Squiz, the bigger problem is your oxygen. Your oxygen bottle will soon be running low. I've left it until the last moment to contact you. You'll have to turn around now or you won't have enough oxygen to get back down. I've got a Sherpa coming off the Hillary Step at the moment who will catch up with you shortly and hand over the oxygen I organised for you earlier. You'll need it to get back down to Camp Four. Squiz, I know this is not what you want to hear, but I have no choice. Over."

I was devastated. Sitting only hours away from the summit, after six weeks of hard work and tens of thousands of dollars invested, I was being told to turn around. I wanted to argue against the decision, but knew that I had to listen to Henry; a decision that many climbers who failed to make it back alive had been unable to accept. Even though the weather was still fine and it was only 9am, it would be suicidal to continue without a greater supply of oxygen. Nonetheless I stubbornly refused to reply to Henry, hoping that I could find a way to broker a deal he would accept.

Wriggling out of my pack, I stood up and turned to face the backpack. I undid the top flap and began searching inside for the regulator. My eyes squinted hard as I stared closely at the oxygen level gauge. The red needle indicated that I still had over half a bottle of oxygen left. I was confused. How could that be? Fiddling with the oxygen flow knob I confirmed it was set on a flow rate of one litre per minute.

"For fuck's sake," I barked.

I'd been struggling for the last four hours with little more than a whisper of assistance from the supplementary oxygen. Dorge had accidentally turned down my flow rate instead of turning it up when we were at the Balcony. I felt like an amateur for allowing somebody else to do something that I should have done myself. I could only blame myself for being so dependant. But on the flipside the conservation of oxygen meant I did have the extra oxygen I needed. I got straight back on the radio.

"Henry, this is Squiz. I've just checked my oxygen gauge, and I've got over half a bottle left. My flow rate was not as high as it should have been. Over."

There was silence for an agonising twenty seconds.

"Squiz, this is Henry. That is good news. I will give you one more chance. I want you to set your oxygen to a flow rate of four litres per minute and then get on the move. If you are not on the summit in two hours, you have to turn around regardless of where you are. Over."

I was pumped! I'd been thrown a lifeline.

"No worries, Henry. I won't let you down. Over."

Adrenaline surged through my body re-energising my soul as I adjusted the oxygen flow rate and secured my pack. Success from this point on would depend entirely on my own actions and decisions. I looked over at Dorge, who had been listening in on the conversation, but had not been able to fully understand.

"Dorge, I'm going up now; very quickly," I said, motioning that I would be running.

"Okay, sir," he replied.

"I only have two hours. Then I start to come back."

I turned and began moving up towards the South Summit, renewed enthusiasm and determination lifting every step.

I took ten steps, then another ten, moving much quicker than any other time in the last twenty-four hours. I was still breathing heavily but the difference in speed was remarkable. The wall of snow in front of me suddenly looked smaller and less daunting. I felt bigger, stronger, and faster. I knew I could do it. I turned back and saw Dorge lagging behind with the yellow mask. We made eye contact and I indicated that I was heading off. He nodded, understanding that we would be separating.

Within ten minutes I crested the South Summit. In front of me was the final challenge: the famous Hillary Step. To get there I had to climb down a small four metre ice wall and move across a wafer thin ridge for eighty metres. Before beginning the ridge traverse I met the Sherpa who had been asked by Henry to hand over the extra oxygen. He rammed it into a pile of snow beside the trail, and wished me luck on getting to the summit. Other bottles lay along the trail, either empty or also waiting for climbers to return. It would have been safer to take the bottle with me, but the extra weight would hold me back. I left it. A calculated risk? An uncalculated one? I wasn't sure, but I was sure of one thing – at that point nothing was going to stop me. I took a snapshot in my mind of the location and pushed on.

Traversing across the ridge to the Hillary Step was renowned for being horribly exposed. To the left was a one thousand metre drop into Nepal, while the Kangshung face, a three thousand metre vertical slope, fell sharply away on the right. The strong winds that smashed in from the left created a wave-like cornice hanging over the side of the eastward looking face of Kangshung. However, fortunately, the trail was set a few metres down from the crest of the cornice, on the Nepal side, which helped block out the sheer drop into Tibet. As I crossed I kept fervently focused on the trail ahead, eventually noticing a climber at the base of the Hillary Step. He and his partner had been the last pair to overtake me. I was regaining lost ground; it felt good to be moving at a decent pace once more.

By the time I reached the base of the world's highest rock climb, the climber ahead had completed the first pitch and unclipped from the first rope. The crag was quite disjointed in that, after seven metres, the route swung around a boulder and ledge before heading up the remaining five metres. Hanging down from the ledge were around twenty ropes of different colours. Most were frayed and bleached from the sun, revealing their age. I pulled down tight on a bright green rope, which looked to be the newest of the bunch, and examined the climb ahead. Initially the first pitch appeared daunting, as it was vertical, but upon looking closer I noticed a series of small steps protruding from the rock and ice.

The additional oxygen flow was giving me a buzz so I opted to clip on a carabiner rather than use a jumar. Reaching up with both arms I grabbed a handful of the old ropes to stabilise my body as I stepped up from one step to the next. At the top of the first pitch I rested to catch my breath, only briefly looking back in the direction I had come. The three kilometre drop was not something I chose to stare at for any length of time.

The next pitch was chunkier and less steep than the previous, allowing for better foot placement. I superstitiously decided to use the same strategy and same coloured rope as the first pitch. When I neared the top of this pitch the wind picked up, bringing with it another sense of isolation. It was surreal to be finally scaling the upper reaches of the highest mountain in the world. It felt as though I had been working towards this moment for more than a lifetime and completion was tantalisingly close.

After the second pitch the route zigzagged through a narrow rocky strip that provided the bridge to the gentle ridge walk to the summit. The most difficult aspect of the rocky traverse were the dozen or so old ropes that remained treacherously tangled on the trail, often anchored to rocks at knee height. It looked like a spider's web, strategically woven to catch unsuspecting climbers. Foot placement was critical.

I moved off from the Hillary Step and the rope web which was like coming off a bumpy four-wheel drive track onto a smooth tarmac road. In front of me was the highway leading to a small pimple-like mound. The small rise was only one hundred metres away and quite obviously the summit as two dozen bodies wearing a multitude of colourful puffy down suits were loitering around, savouring their special moment. Shivers ran down my spine; not from the cold, but from the realisation that I was going to make it.

NINETEEN
FIGHTING HUNGER ON EVEREST

Tormentingly close to the top, the frustration of having to stop at intervals and let the body recover was more exasperating than at any point before. The wind was blowing hard from the left, picking up snowflakes and small ice balls along the way, before propelling them into the skies above the Kangshung face like frosted grenades. I was finally walking alongside the white plume that could be seen bellowing off Everest's summit from as far away as the valleys below Namche Bazaar.

I overtook the pair who had scaled the Hillary Step ahead of me, and paused to take a few deep breaths just thirty metres out from the roof of the world. Thirty metres … twenty-nine … twenty-eight …

With just 15 metres to go I stopped. As I regained my breathing I looked up and began studying the crowd ahead. A brief impromptu party ensued with the small group of climbers already assembled on the summit. They comprised of those who had followed the same route as myself, as well as those who had climbed from the Tibet side. This momentary gathering was the only time we spent together as the summiteers of 2006. Sitting quietly to the left of the group was a man in a red down suit. He raised his camera and took a shot as I made my way over to him. It was Pommy.

As I took the last few steps to reach flat ground I had a smile from ear to ear, albeit covered by the mask. I was ecstatic to see Pommy and finally reach our turn around point. It wasn't time for champagne yet but it felt damn good.

"Heeeey, Pommy, we made it!" I yelled euphorically.

I leant over and embraced him, but he hardly had the energy to reciprocate.

"Are you alright?" I asked, becoming a little concerned.

He shook his head. "I'm really stuffed. I need to get going soon. What took you so long, by the way?"

"Aagh, don't ask. I ran into all sorts of problems. That bloody yellow mask has caused all sorts of dramas. Poor old Dorge is struggling up the mountain with it at the moment."

"I know the feeling. I didn't do it too easily on the way up either."

I took my outer mittens off and looked at my watch. It was 10:05am. I'd arrived with plenty of time to spare.

"Hey, I need to call Henry to let him know I've made it. Can I borrow your radio?"

"It's broken," Pommy answered.

"Does Henry know that you are here?"

"Nope, we lost comms after the South Summit."

"Okay, I need to get some photos and then we'll get out of here. Dorge has our radio, so we can use that."

The winds had dropped and the sun was keeping the temperature just below freezing so I quickly removed my mask and detached the two cameras that hung around my neck. I handed them to Pommy's Sherpa and dived into my pack to find the flag. After a quick explanation on the use of the camera, I unravelled the United Nations World Food Programme flag and held it proudly on top of the world. It was the 18th of May 2006, three days before the WFP's Walk the World Campaign kicked off. On the back side of the WFP flag I had stitched the Fight Hunger logo that was specifically designed for those participating in the Walk the World promotion. Flipping the flag around for another few photos I puffed with pride at the perfect timing. I had three days left to get my photos and the story to the event organisers who were gearing up for the global awareness walk on the 21st May. It was time to get off the mountain.

TWENTY
DRAMAS ON THE WAY DOWN

At 10:45am Pommy, his Sherpa and I came across Dorge. He had just scaled the Hillary Step and was about to make his way across the final ridge walk to the summit.

"Hey Dorge, well done mate," I yelled.

"Namaste, sir," he replied.

"Mate … you've done an outstanding job. I can't believe how far you've managed to come. Do you want to continue to the summit?" I asked, pointing back from where we had come.

He looked ahead and saw the cluster of colourful down suits mingling on the crest of Everest and took a few seconds to mull over his decision.

"No, sir. I go down now."

"Okay, no worries. Could I borrow the radio? We still haven't called Henry to tell him we made it."

"Yes, sir. You want radio?"

"Yes please."

Henry was thrilled, as well as relieved, to hear the good news. He reminded us of the importance of getting back to Camp Four as quickly as possible, not that I needed reminding. Fortunately, as we peered over the upper sections of the Hillary Step, it became evident that the notorious choke point was free of climbers. That was one less stress to worry about.

The four of us climbed down the Hillary Step and moved across the exposed ridge to a little ledge just below the South Summit. The oxygen bottle that had been left for me previously was still sitting upright in the snow. I changed over oxygen bottles and sat back to have a drink of water. I had not taken in any fluids, nor eaten, for over fourteen hours. I tried to eat an energy bar but could only stomach two bites. I gave one of my other bars to Dorge who was patiently waiting for me once again.

"Holy Shit," Pommy suddenly screamed.

I looked up and saw Pommy flapping around with his mask.

"What the hell is going on?" he exclaimed.

Pommy's oxygen reservoir bag was quickly blowing up like a balloon. In less than thirty seconds it grew to the size of a basketball and the outer cloth sack split down the side to reveal the inner rubber bladder. It was all happening too quickly for our slow and weathered brains to compute.

Pop!

The bladder burst under the pressure and nothing more than a few strands of rubber were left flapping in the wind.

Pommy's Sherpa had moved across to provide assistance as soon as he saw the bladder expanding but was unable to do anything to prevent the eventual damage. We guessed a blockage must have occurred between the mask and the reservoir bag, although at that point investigating the cause of the problem was somewhat pointless. Pommy's Sherpa ripped the mask and what was left of the bladder from the tube that led to the oxygen bottle. He handed over his old cloth mask to Pommy before setting himself up so as he could suck directly from his cylinder using the tube from Pommys mask like a straw.

As I watched the support being given to Pommy I reflected on the amazing efforts of the Sherpas. Henry had left us to do the bulk of the climbing on our own but the Sherpas still played a pivotal role in getting us to the summit. For them it was not about reaching the top or making a big fuss about their achievements to the outside world, rather it was a job, a job that had them constantly making sacrifices for their customers. They were truly the unsung heroes of all Everest conquests. The Sherpas forged ahead of us on the lower sections, fixing the lines ahead and setting up tents in advance of our arrival. They came with us on the summit bid, moving at our pace and helping to solve all of our problems. And most of all they ensured we were safely delivered back off the mountain, when we were all so vulnerable.

Lured into believing my dramas were all behind, Pommy's were only just beginning. Unfortunately for him the issues unfolded slowly and without any warning. Coming off from the summit he struggled with fatigue, a broken mask and then freezing temperatures that were brought on by an afternoon storm. By the time he reached Camp Four poor Pommy was completely spent, and when the time came to turn lights out we'd both run out of oxygen leading to an additionally cold and uncomfortable night.

Pommy decided to keep his boots on over night, so as to utilise the extra thick insulation they provided. He also opted to unzip his sleeping bag and use it as a blanket rather than a bag. It seemed like a logical thing to do at the time as the down suits we wore provided our first layer of down and therefore acted as our primary measure against the cold. Overnight his fatigued body fell into a deep sleep for just a few short hours, unable to detect that the boots he wore were quickly freezing solid. Moisture had gathered in his socks during the climb, which froze once he stopped moving, effectively placing his feet in ice blocks.

Desperate to get out of The Death Zone we rose at 4:30am the next morning, our bodies crying out for thicker oxygen, food, water and a decent sleep. Moving off for Camp Three when the winds abated at 8am, Pommy grumbled on a few occasions about his feet but I didn't think much of it as we were all dealing with physical soreness of some sort.

At Camp Three we rested for a couple of hours in the midday sun. The team from Lhotse arrived soon after us, looking dishevelled and beaten. Apparently they had been unable to reach their summit due to poor weather and thick snow underfoot. Rob was among them, which was comforting as his relentless energy and enthusiasm helped to lift our weary souls. We began discussing the problems that Pommy and I had experienced with the yellow masks and learned that Dorge had followed the standard operating procedure when my mask had become frozen over. The old cloth masks could be smashed and beaten as the valve was protected by a metal ring and the components were made of more durable rubber rather than hardened plastic. Dorge, although a junior Sherpa whom I later found out had not himself reached the summit before, could not be blamed for smashing the valve. After explaining what had happened to Pommy's reservoir bag we all concluded that the new yellow masks were to be written off as unreliable and too flimsy.

Just as we were about to head off for Camp Two, Henry requested to speak with me on the radio.

"Henry, this is Squiz. Over."

"So, I see you've gone public!" his tense voice crackled over the radio.

"Umm … what do you mean by that? Over." I replied, sensing that something was not quite right.

"Don't be so condescending. I think it is time you got off the mountain and explained yourself."

I instantly felt a sick sensation in my stomach.

"Aggh, Henry … I'll reach Base Camp early tomorrow morning; can we have a chat then?"

He didn't reply.

I looked at Rob with wide eyes of utter confused dismay. He suggested that I call one of the other climbers in Base Camp from the second team on the satellite phone. It was a good idea because they were able to tell me exactly what the problem was. When back at Camp Four I had phoned Kathmandu and given a description of my climb to the summit for inclusion on the Walk the World blog. In the description I had been quoted as saying that 'during the climb I experienced problems with my oxygen system.' I hadn't realised the damage that such a general comment could have had on Henry at that particular moment in time. Unbeknown to me, he had been charged with manslaughter and would be attending court in a few months time. A twenty-two year old lad from the UK had died on Everest in the late 90's and his wealthy father was looking to vent his anger in the court room. Henry had been accused of providing a faulty oxygen system to the expedition leader of the deceased climber, which made my comments potentially incriminating evidence for the prosecutors.

I felt awful. Instead of savouring the elation and euphoria from being on the summit, I was stricken with guilt and anger. I immediately rang Kathmandu and asked for the comment to be retracted. It was like putting a band aid on a broken leg; the damage was done.

By the time I reached Camp Two my brain was tired of going back over the events that had led me to make the comment. It was particularly frustrating as I had deliberately used a general comment instead of pointing blame or mentioning the specifics of the equipment failure, but from Henry's perspective it didn't matter. It was the worst comment that could have been made. Pommy's feet were the only things that could distract me from the apprehension that was building up.

At Camp Two my climbing companion removed his boots and slowly peeled off his socks. The skin from the ball of his left foot clung to the inside of his sock. His toes were completely blistered and nearly doubled in size. I was amazed that he had been able to walk at all. A normal person would not have been unable to tolerate the pain, let alone walk without squealing. In that moment he proved that he was one hell of a tough bloke.

Rob organised for Pommy to have his feet placed in warm water. It helped to ease some of the pain and stimulate blood flow to the damaged toes but it was obvious that the next day's walk to Base Camp was going to be terribly painful for him. Being a real trooper, Pommy agreed I should head off early in the morning to sort things out with Henry, assuring me he'd manage without me.

Before going to bed I sent a text message to the satellite phone in the Gorak Shep tea house that was accommodating Nud. It read:

Message for Ms Ingrid Burt – All is well, don't come into Base Camp, I will meet you in Gorak Shep tomorrow evening. Love Squiz

After another pitiful night's sleep I woke and began trudging down the slopes, moving past a couple of lonely tents at Camp One and into the Icefall. Not long after entering the Icefall I came across Kahuna and

261

Tim who were making their way up to Camp Two in preparation for a summit bid in a few days time. They both looked fresh having spent the last week recuperating at lower altitudes. None of us wanted to linger in the Icefall and so our meeting was fairly brief but sufficient to pass on a little relief. Apparently Henry had calmed down after his initial outburst, the news of which enabled me to carry on with a little more optimism.

At 10am I sat down at the entrance to the Icefall and took off my crampons for the last time. A huge sense of liberation swept my body as the knowledge that I was out of the danger zone took hold. Finally I was able to walk the three hundred metres to our Base Camp tents pondering about the reception I was about to receive. I knew it wasn't going to involve a bottle of champagne.

Thirty metres out from the comms tent I paused, able to hear Henry talking on the radio. I waited for him to finish his conversation.

"Good morning, Henry. It's Squiz," I yelled.

The tent door unzipped and Henry appeared.

"Hi Squiz."

"Henry, I'm not sure if you would like to talk about things or if you would prefer me to just pack up and head off. I am happy either way."

"Of course you don't have to leave today Squiz, unless that is what you want to do. So I suppose if you stick around then we might as well have a chat," he said evenly.

"I'm actually planning to pack up and make a move this afternoon. I'm really keen to catch up with Nud. She's waiting for me in Gorak Shep as you know."

"Okay. I'll let the boys know that you will only be here for lunch."

"Thanks."

I moved across to my tent, wondering what our chat might be like, and began pulling out all of my clothing and kit. Without any weight on my shoulders and a warm sun shining down on my back I began to realise how tired I was. I could have easily flopped into the tent and slept for the whole day but stubbornly refused to give in to my body's yearning.

Twenty minutes later Henry came over and sat on a nearby rock. We spoke for two hours, in a very open and honest manner. It was soothing to be able to inform him of all the details he had missed because of our brief radio transmissions, and enlightening to hear Henry's side of the story. He explained a few things that revealed the ugly side of the high altitude climbing industry. Many of his competitors were supporting the manslaughter case against him as they wanted to see Henry out of business. It was nothing short of 'politics' on the mountain. They wanted to collapse Henry's exclusive arrangement with Poisk so as to prevent him from being able to dictate the price of oxygen on the mountain.

At the end of our discussion I realised there was a lot more going on behind the scenes than I could have ever imagined. We shook hands and Henry congratulated me for reaching the top. I thanked him for making it possible and apologised for my comments on the blog. At least the air was clear. All I could do for Henry from that point was hope for a good outcome.

It took me until 2:30pm to pack up, eat lunch and start heading down the trail. As I went out past the remains of the helicopter that had crashed a few years before, I looked back across at the Icefall for the last time. It was an emotional moment filled with thoughts of pleasure and pain tumbling across one another in a tangled spaghetti of interwoven memories. This was goodbye.

Scurrying across the undulating rocky glacier, jumping over the small streams that earlier in the trip were frozen solid, my heart was pounding with excitement. As soon as I arrived at Gorak Shep I walked quickly towards the first tea house, looking intently to see if I could spot Nud. She had already spotted me and came bounding out from the sun room with a huge smile on her face. We hugged each other tight as Nud congratulated me for making it to the top.

"So why couldn't I come into Base Camp to meet you?" she eventually asked.

"Hmm, good question. Let's go inside and sit down; this could take a while."

TWENTY ONE
LIFE CONTINUES

Pommy and the rest of the team arrived back in Base Camp during the course of the afternoon. It did not become apparent until after they exited the slopes that four of the six climbers had suffered serious injuries. Pommy and two others had severe frostbite and another had twisted an ankle. Henry organised for a helicopter and the four were evacuated to Kathmandu two days later.

Three out of the four climbers that were part of Henry's second team made it to the summit. Kahuna and Tim stood on the top together and returned safely to Base Camp a few days later. It was a remarkable effort for Tim as it was later established that he was in fact nursing a fractured femur.

Hundreds of climbers made it to the summit during the 2006 climbing season, making it one of the most successful years to date. Difficult weather normally fights back those who are not exceptionally tough and determined to battle it out in The Death Zone. With exceptionally favourable weather during the 2006 season there was a price to pay for having unusually large numbers high on the mountain. Many climbers, particularly on the Tibet side, were unable to get themselves back. They simply suffered from "summit fever" and failed to understand when their body was telling them that it was time to turn around. The media had a feeding frenzy when accusations were made that some climbers were left behind alive to fend for themselves. By the end of the season twelve people in total had died on the mountain. The mightiest peak in the world continues to add to her ever increasing toll.

On the 21st of May the Fight Hunger Campaign saw 700,000 people walk across the world. Every time zone had at least one group walk a short distance to raise awareness of the ongoing global hunger situation. In Kathmandu my colleagues walked through the streets with three thousand children and an elephant, all adorned in Fight Hunger gear. I was still stomping back to Lukla at the time but managed to send my photos through to be included in the global media broadcasts. The Everest climb played a fundamental role in the 2006 Fight Hunger Campaign.

Pommy returned to England and endured the very painful ordeal of recovering from frostbite. He ended up losing the two big toes from each of his feet. The frost bite damage has not deterred or perturbed the tough Pommy, however. He continues to head back to the Himalayas in search of thin air, completely addicted to the Himalayas' tempting snare.

Henry returned to England and faced his manslaughter charges. After a long, and what must have been stressful period of time, the case against Henry was thrown out of court. The judge ruling that "… In my judgement there is not one scrap of worthwhile evidence that when on this day a large party, including Michael (the deceased), ascended to the summit, any of them was then using faulty oxygen equipment. Nor is there any evidence that on the descent Michael's oxygen equipment became defective … the notion that Michael's oxygen cylinder was in any way faulty and that this was a material contributing factor to his death, let alone that it caused it, is based upon pure, and wholly impermissible, speculation."

Henry continues to run successful trips on Everest and other Himalayan mountains.

In November, 2006, WFP posted me to Sri Lanka. Bidding a memory-filled farewell to Nepal, Nud and I departed to set up home in the capital city of Colombo; where I began to tackle the issues arising from the protracted conflict between the Sri Lankan Government and the Liberation Tigers of Tamil Eelam. In January 2007 I found the right moment to ask the love of my life and soul mate, to marry me. Nud accepted. We returned to Australia to get married a year later, overjoyed that Goz flew in from Timor Leste to be my best man at the wedding. Goz continues to work for the people of Timor Leste through the charity of Love, Life and Hope.

Nud and I reside today on a small hobby farm on the outskirts of Melbourne with our two young sons; Oscar and Digby. In between short term security jobs in war zones I provide keynote speeches and team bonding activities (www.marksquirrell.com) to help motivate, inspire and enhance the performance of corporate clients. The experiences outlined in this book form the basis of the insights and have helped to shape a number of the performance enhancing activities.

Of course, there continues to be hunger, corruption, disease and desperation in the world, but I hope my meagre contribution to raise awareness and leave the world a slightly better place will have a ripple effect both on those I have touched personally and on you as you think about what you will do tomorrow.

As the famed writer and philosopher, Ralph Waldo Emerson, said:

To laugh often and much;
To win the respect of intelligent people and the affection of children;
To earn the appreciation of honest critics and endure the betrayal of false friends;
To appreciate beauty;
To find the best in others;
To leave the world a bit better, whether by a healthy child, a garden patch, or a redeemed social condition;
To know even one life has breathed easier because you have lived...
This is to have succeeded.

ABOUT THE AUTHOR

Mark Squirrell, more commonly known as Squiz, was born in Melbourne, Australia, where he grew up on a 40 acre hobby farm on the outskirts of the city. Whilst studying a Bachelor of Business at university, Squiz joined the Australian Army Reserve and was quickly identified for Officer Training. Squiz excelled in the competitive and difficult environment and was promoted to Lieutenant in March 1992.

The recruitment industry in Melbourne provided the natural career progression upon graduation from university. However, after a few short years, Squiz's passion for physical challenges and outdoor activities drove him to focus his attentions on pursuing acceptance into the Australian Special Forces. In 1996 Squiz passed the arduous and unforgiving Commando Officer Selection course and was awarded the coveted "Green Beret" soon thereafter.

Four years later Squiz found himself in the heart of the East Timor crisis but without a weapon or uniform. He had gone to assist the people of East Timor as a 'civilian' with an Aid Agency. It was to be the beginning of a journey that would take him across the globe and to the highest point on earth.

Squiz returned to Australia in December 2007 where he now lives with his wife and two sons on an adjacent hobby farm to the one he grew up on. He continues to consult on a casual basis to the United Nations and has established a Corporate Performance consultancy (www.marksquirrell.com).

ACKNOWLEDGEMENTS

To the countless people along the journey, thanks for making it such an enjoyable and insightful trip. Sincerest thanks go to my colleagues and friends that are now spread across the globe, it has been a 'thumpin' pleasure to meet you and I look forward to the next time we catch up.

Heartfelt thanks go to those who have made the making of this book possible – whether directly assisting with its editing and structure or indirectly through support and advice. In addition to this a special thanks must go to a number of individuals who have patiently and generously contributed their expertise to help shape the book. These being: Melanie Wood, Ken Croft, Rodney Cocks, Luke Gosling (Goz), Nathan Mullins, Margaret Brophy, Andrea McNamara, Bryan Rush, The Brolga Team and my ever faithful guide in life, Dad.

Mum, Dad and my two sisters, Carolyn and Absy, thanks for the great childhood and ongoing love.

Writing this book has been a lengthy, and at times, frustrating undertaking. I could not have completed this task without the unwavering love and support from my wife and best friend; Nud. You are a true champion.

Be Published

Publishing through a successful Australian publisher. Brolga provides:
- Editorial appraisal
- Cover design
- Typesetting
- Printing
- Author promotion
- National book trade distribution, including sales, marketing and distribution through Macmillan Australia.

For details and inquiries, contact:
Brolga Publishing Pty Ltd
PO Box 12544
A'Beckett St VIC 8006

bepublished@brolgapublishing.com.au
markzocchi@brolgapublishing.com.au
ABN: 46 063 962 443